T0355502

MONGREL NATION

Ashley Dawson

MONGREL NATION

Diasporic Culture and the
Making of Postcolonial Britain

THE UNIVERSITY OF MICHIGAN PRESS

Ann Arbor

Published in the United States of America by
The University of Michigan Press
Printed and bound by CPI Group (UK) Ltd, Croydon, CR0 4YY

2010   2009   2008   2007   4   3   2   1

A CIP catalog record for this book is available from the British Library.

Library of Congress Cataloging-in-Publication Data

Dawson, Ashley, 1965–
    Mongrel nation : diasporic culture and the making of postcolonial
Britain / Ashley Dawson.
       p.   cm.
    Includes bibliographical references and index.
    ISBN-13: 978-0-472-09991-7 (cloth : acid-free paper)
    ISBN-13: 978-0-472-06991-0 (pbk. : acid-free paper)

    1. English literature—Minority authors—History and criticism.
2. English literature—20th century—History and criticism.
3. Commonwealth literature (English)—History and criticism.
4. Postcolonialism in literature.   5. Immigrants in literature.
6. Minorities in literature.   7. Literature and society—Great
Britain—History—20th century.   8. Postcolonialism—Great Britain.
9. Pluralism (Social sciences)—Great Britain.   10. Ethnic groups—
Great Britain—History—20th century.   I. Title.

PR120.M55D39   2007
820.9'3552—dc22   2006036421

    ISBN13 978-0-472-02505-3 (electronic)

Thus from a mixture of all kinds began,
That Het'rogeneous Thing, *An Englishman:*
In eager Rapes, and furious Lust begot,
Betwixt a Painted *Britton* and a *Scot:*
Whose gend'ring Offspring quickly learned to bow,
And yoke their Heifers to the *Roman* Plough:
From whence a Mongrel Half-Bred Race there came,
With neither Name nor Nation, Speech or Fame.
In whose hot Veins new Mixtures quickly ran,
Infus'd betwixt a *Saxon* and a *Dane.*
While their Rank Daughters, to their Parents just,
Receiv'd all Nations with Promiscuous Lust.
This Nauseous Brood directly did contain
The well-extracted blood of *Englishmen.*

Acknowledgments

THIS PROJECT HAS BEEN VERY LONG IN THE GESTATION, and, consequently, bears with it an immense number of debts. If I have neglected anyone in this long list of thanks, I beg your forgiveness.

First of all, I would like to thank Rob Nixon, who encouraged me to think of myself as a public intellectual by example and through his consistent emphasis on the craft of writing. For this shaping impact and for the continuing help given since I finished my studies, I am and will always remain deeply grateful.

In addition, I must offer thanks to Jean Franco and Anne McClintock who, along with Edward Said, offered great inspiration to me during my graduate work. I will always be indebted to them for their powerful example as engaged intellectuals and teachers.

Members of Columbia University's Postcolonial Collective made the difficult life of a graduate student bearable. In particular, I want to acknowledge the impact of the many late-night conversations I had with Nikhil Pal Singh during these formative years.

While researching this manuscript I benefited from discussions with many members of Britain's black and Asian communities. I very much appreciate the willingness of so many to discuss their work and lives with me during the research phase of this project. In particular, I would like to thank Paul Gilroy, Gita Saghal, A. Sivanandan, and Nira Yuval-Davis for speaking to me and, more broadly, for the inspiration they provided me as activists, thinkers, and writers.

I owe a great deal to my colleagues in the Department of English at the University of Iowa, where I was lucky enough to land my first tenure-track job. They provided a model of collegial warmth and conviviality during the stressful early years of my career. I was particularly fortunate to be associated with wonderful mentors such as Dee Morris, Brooks Landon, Philip Lutgendorf, Jael Silliman, and Paul Greenough during these years. I am also indebted to Iowa for various grants— including two Old Gold Summer Fellowships, the Miller Trust Fund Travel Grant, and a Dean's Summer Travel Grant—that afforded me travel funding as well as time to research and work on this manuscript.

CUNY, my current home institution, has also generously aided me with relief from teaching through the PSC-CUNY Grant. My thanks to Janet Dudley Ng for her unstinting support as a friend and mentor during my early years at CUNY. More broadly, the militant struggle of colleagues within my home department as well as within my union in general for public higher education has been a tremendous inspiration while I was working on this manuscript.

I would also like to thank the two anonymous reviewers at the University of Michigan Press for their insightful suggestions on an early draft of this manuscript. I am of course to blame for any errors and/or dodgy historical and textual interpretations.

Thanks to extended family members John Dawson, Bernie Smallman, and Jim and Jane Pettit for putting me up in their homes in London during various stages of my research. And to Ann and Nigel Dawson, whose immense and unstinting love during the long years that I worked on this project can never be adequately repaid.

Finally, my deepest thanks go to Patrizia Palumbo and Sofia Palumbo-Dawson for their support and forbearance during this project. This project has grown up with you, Sofia, and yet you and your mother have seldom chided me for the time this twin of yours has taken away from you both. Thank you both for sticking by me to the end.

Contents

Colonization in Reverse An Introduction *1*

1 **"In the Big City the Sex Life Gone Wild"**
Migration, Gender, and Identity in Sam Selvon's
The Lonely Londoners *27*

2 **Black Power in a Transnational Frame**
Radical Populism and the Caribbean Artists Movement *49*

3 **Behind the Mask**
Carnival Politics and British Identity in
Linton Kwesi Johnson's Dub Poetry *73*

4 **Beyond Imperial Feminism**
Buchi Emecheta's London Novels and Black British
  Women's Emancipation *95*

5 **Heritage Politics of the Soul**
Immigration and Identity in Salman Rushdie's
The Satanic Verses *121*

6 **Genetics, Biotechnology, and the Future of
"Race" in Zadie Smith's *White Teeth*** *149*

Conclusion: "Step Back from the Blow Back"
Asian Hip-Hop and Post-9/11 Britain *175*

Notes *189*
Index *221*

Colonization in Reverse

An Introduction

THE ICONIC IMAGE OF POST-1945 MIGRATION TO BRITAIN UNWINDS on a grainy old Pathé newsreel. Standing on the wooden deck of a battered troop carrier named the *Empire Windrush* as it docks at Tilbury on 21 June 1948, the calypso singer Lord Kitchener offers up a lyrical performance of a song composed specially for the occasion. Lord Kitchener's "London Is the Place for Me" conveys the immense optimism felt by this initial group of migrants to the colonial metropolis:

> London is the place for me
> London, this lovely city
> You can go to France or America
> India, Asia, or Australia
> But you must come back to London City
>
> Well believe me, I am speaking broad-mindedly
> I am glad to know my mother country
> I've been travelling to countries years ago
> But this is the place I wanted to know
> London, that's the place for me
>
> To live in London you're really comfortable
> Because the English people are very much sociable

They take you here and they take you there
And they make you feel like a millionaire
So London, that's the place for me[1]

Lord Kitchener boarded the *Empire Windrush* with his fellow singer
Lord Beginner at Kingston docks, Jamaica, departing for Britain appropriately enough on Empire Day, the twenty-fourth of May. Four hundred and ninety other predominantly male passengers from various
islands in the Caribbean accompanied the calypsonians. "London Is the
Place for Me," which Lord Kitchener composed during the voyage
across the Atlantic, is the fantasy of a colonial subject who imagines
himself returning to the welcoming bosom of his mother country. In
retrospect, the song seems painfully naive. But, of course, there is a history behind this precarious innocence. Schoolchildren in Britain's
many tropical colonies had been fed a diet of British literature for a half-
century or so by the time Lord Kitchener set sail for Britain.[2] According
to colonial ideology, Britain originated democracy, the rule of law, and
the ethics of good sportsmanship.[3] How could she fail to provide an
adequate welcome to her colonial sons and daughters? Sung in Standard
English rather than the Trinidadian creole that typified most calypso
songs, "London Is the Place for Me" dramatizes the crushing weight of
Britain's colonial educational apparatus, which taught colonial subjects
that they should be proud members of such a great and beneficent
empire. Lord Kitchener's own bombastic sobriquet itself appears to tes-
tify to the tenacious hold of this imperial mythology on members of the
colonial working classes.

     Yet the buoyant optimism of the song also illustrates the powerful
feeling of agency inspired by this voyage to the metropolis. The
Caribbean men and women on board the *Empire Windrush* had, after
all, booked passage from the colonial periphery to London, the center of
the world at the time. In fact, a significant number of the boat's passengers had already been to Britain, helping to defend the motherland from
the Nazi onslaught during the Second World War.[4] Walking down the
gangplank at Tilbury, many of these migrants from the Caribbean felt
that they were coming to collect the reward for their faithfulness as
British subjects.[5] Others, intent on helping to rebuild the devastated
motherland, saw the voyage to Britain as a continuation of their
wartime sacrifice.[6] Some, Lord Kitchener apparently among them, sim-

ply sought the affluent and cosmopolitan life represented by the London of their dreams.

Would the British cities inhabited by these Caribbean migrants and those who arrived later from Asia and Africa correspond to the glamorous image conjured up in Lord Kitchener's calypso? In a poem published early in the postwar period, Jamaican poet Louise Bennett poses precisely this question. As the host of a BBC radio weekly focusing on Anglophone Caribbean culture during the late 1940s and early 1950s, Bennett was particularly well placed to address the issue of migration from the colonies. Acting as a cultural broker, Bennett documented life in the Caribbean for a British audience, recording the experiences of migrants who arrived in the metropolis filled with the high hopes instilled by the colonial educational system. Her poem "Colonization in Reverse," written in a playful Creole vernacular voice that evokes the lively oral culture of her island's peasantry and working class, reflects a sense of excitement and ambition similar to that found in Lord Kitchener's work.[7] As its title suggests, however, Bennett's poem is also permeated by a witheringly ironic attitude toward the imperial legacy that connects Caribbean colonial subjects to the British motherland. Migration to the metropolis is not simply a footloose escape from the parochialism of the islands for Bennett. Her poem implicitly suggests that this migration is also a willful and aggressive act, one that springs from the bloodstained history of colonialism and slavery in the Caribbean:

Wat a joyful news, Miss Mattie,
I feel like me heart gwine burs'
Jamaica people colonizin
Englan in reverse.

By de hundred, by de t'ousan
From country and from town,
By de ship-load, by de plane-load
Jamaica is Englan boun.

Dem a-pour out o' Jamaica,
Everybody future plan
Is fe get a big-time job
An settle in de mother lan.

Wat a islan! What a people!
Man an woman, old an young
Jusa pack dem bag an baggage
An tun history upside dung![8]

Miss Lou, the opinionated and cantankerous persona whom Bennett employed in many of her dramatic monologues, is clearly given to comically hyperbolic accounts of contemporary events. Although her zealous description of the postwar exodus from Jamaica may magnify the truth in order to impress her friend Miss Mattie, it nonetheless is shot through with stinging insights concerning the historical conditions that occasioned this migration. It is patently clear to Miss Lou, for instance, that the relation between Britain and Jamaica is far from the benign one conjured up by the cliché image of the motherland. Instead, that relation is grounded in exploitative and at times violent colonial power. To migrate to the motherland is, then, to issue a radical challenge to this history of subjugation. The passengers on the *Empire Windrush*, Miss Lou says, turn history upside down.[9]

Like Lord Kitchener, Miss Lou acknowledges that Jamaicans are packing their bags for economic reasons, participating in the cycles of poverty-driven migration that the people of the Caribbean endured after the abolition of slavery and the economic decline of the sugar plantations. But the passage to Britain was not simply another arduous trek in search of a decent wage, with all the pain of ruptured family relations and cultural alienation that such a history implies. Rather, "Colonization in Reverse" describes a mass migration that overturned the spatial and cultural apartheid cementing colonial rule. For despite the powerful fiction of British subjecthood, which suggested that all the members of the empire were equal in the eyes of the reigning king or queen, imperial power was based on a firm distinction between colonial metropolis and colonized periphery. Subjecthood and citizenship were distinct and uneven categories.

There was a tight economic logic to this unequal imperial dispensation.[10] Resource extraction took place in the colonial periphery: slaves from Africa, sugar from the Caribbean, cotton from India. Conversely, manufacturing and the accumulation of capital took place primarily in the metropolis.[11] Both poles in this uneven relationship were essential components of the system, but they had to be kept distinct. If the colonies began to manufacture and sell finished commodities outside the sphere of imperial preference, for instance, they would have a powerful lever with which to pry themselves out of a subordinating colonial relationship. By the 1930s, the campaign of India's Congress Party for precisely such economic and political autonomy, known as *swaraj,* had gained critical momentum. In addition, waves of strikes and radical union agitation spread across the Caribbean and Africa as the worldwide economic depression hit home during the late 1930s, in many cases unleashing movements for political independence.[12] In all of these cases, popular struggle focused not simply on national autonomy, but on overcoming the underdevelopment that colonial power patently imposed on the periphery. Driven by this history of uneven development, the migration of colonial subjects to Britain brought the economic subordination integral to the colonial system home to the metropolis, sparking correspondingly intense political struggles.[13]

There was a potent cultural logic to this brutal arrangement as well. Postwar Britain inherited a tradition of imperial arrogance. For instance, during negotiations that led to the Atlantic Charter, Churchill sought to diminish any suggestion that proclamations concerning the Allies' fight for democracy in World War II might apply equally to the colonies.[14] Although there was certainly an element of cold political and economic calculation in Churchill's hypocritical stance, cultural attitudes concerning the inferiority of colonial subjects played an equally important role. The colonies were not sufficiently mature for self-rule, British leaders such as Churchill believed. Implicit in this tutelary position was a long history of racist state power and ideology. During the middle to late Victorian era, the zenith of British power, European imperialists legitimated their subjugation of other parts of the globe using a variety of pseudoscientific biological theories that ascribed natural dominance to northern Europeans. Racial theorists such as John Knox drew on social Darwinist doctrines to argue for the supremacy of the European racial "type," which was conceived as absolutely distinct from other human populations.[15] This spurious appropriation of Darwinian theory assumed a linear, teleological model of temporal evolution and imposed this model on the space of the globe. The metropolis was seen as the summit of a refigured Great Chain of Being, with the colonies representing an evolutionary prehistory of modern humanity.[16] A natural corollary of this spatiotemporal grid was a concern with the possible degeneration of Europeans when they encountered the less evolved peoples of the colonial periphery.[17] Crystallizing in eugenics, late imperial concern with the purity of European bloodlines led to the proliferation of campaigns for improved birthrates and selective steril- ization under the aegis of the racial state. After 1945, state-mandated management of sexuality in the quest to prevent the proliferation of mongrel breeds was transferred from the colonies to postimperial Britain.[18]

These ideologies of difference and innate superiority were far harder to dismantle than the political-economic system of imperial preference. Long after Britain lost its colonies, it retained its insular sense of cultural superiority. Indeed, the more potency they lost on the global stage after the eclipse of imperialism, the harder some Britons clung to the illusory status symbol that covered their bodies—their white skin—and the immutable cultural difference that it seemed to sig- nify. Of course, this reified model of national identity had no historical foundation. As long ago as 1700, Daniel Defoe described the English as a "Mongrel Half-Bred Race."[19] Ethnic and national boundaries and the legal definitions that police them are mutable, and are always subject to dispute and negotiation.[20] The exclusionary and insular character of British national self-definition is in fact evidence of the unstable, mixed-up identity of Britons. Stability, after all, is only sought in situa- tions of significant flux.[21] The migration of colonial subjects to the British metropolis forced this mongrel nation to reckon with its long history of imperialism and racism.[22]

It is far from clear that Britain has reconciled itself to this legacy. Admittedly, the British government has acknowledged racial inequality and persecution through legislation such as the Race Relations Act and has engaged in remarkably candid examinations of institutional racism in recent years such as the MacPherson Report. Nevertheless, over the last half-century British political leaders have repeatedly resorted to the scapegoating of so-called ethnic minority groups for the nation's social problems.[23] Indeed, what Stuart Hall called "popular authoritarianism" has become a fundamental characteristic of British political and cultural life. Writing in the context of the manifold crises of the late 1970s, Hall and his colleagues at Birmingham's Center for Contemporary Cultural Studies argued that British leaders were dismantling social democracy and the redistributive role of the state. Both dominant parties legiti- mated this transformation through an ideology of law and order that singled out Britain's nonwhite population as the cause of the nation's economic and social ills and that subjected them to punitive forms of policing that, in turn, catalyzed uprisings which tended to confirm white stereotypes about black lawlessness.[24] While this popular authoritarianism may have been particularly evident during the crisis conditions of the 1970s, Britain's black and Asian populations were ostracized and targeted for repressive policing and immigration legislation from the onset of mass migration. They remain so today, as the behavior of New Labour after 9/11, which I discuss in my conclusion, has made clear. From the Notting Hill riots of the late 1950s to the murder of Stephen Lawrence forty years later, Britain has a long tradition of both institutional and popular racism that legitimates harsh treatment of those who are not perceived as "native." Such enduringly exclusionary discourses of national identity and the popular authoritarian ideologies they help legitimate are an integral element not simply of domestic policies such as refugee and asylum laws, but also of Britain's enduringly imperial stance in the world, as the nation's role in the "War on Terror" suggests.

Mongrel Nation documents the history of resistance by African, Asian, Caribbean, and white Britons to such insular representations of national identity.[25] As was true of anticolonial culture in general, such resistance was never exclusively reactive. Instead, antiracist struggles galvanized the cultural resources of oppressed peoples, creating dynamic new aesthetic and political constellations whose transforming thrust exceeded the struggle immediately at hand.[26] In postcolonial Britain, resistance to exclusionary nationalism led immigrants and their children to invoke the heritage of internationalism that developed during anticolonial struggles in Africa, Asia, and the Caribbean. Diasporic communities in Britain denaturalized the confining boundaries of the nation-state by marshaling these internationalist traditions. In addition, by enacting fresh ways of being British, members of the postcolonial diaspora helped to reconfigure social categories such as race, gender, and sexuality that cemented conventional definitions of national identity.[27] Although many white Britons found the novel cultural practices of postcolonial migrants profoundly threatening, the newness introduced to Britain by members of the Asian and African diaspora also offered important routes of escape for many from stultifying local traditions. Investigating the legacy of Britain's imperial past, *Mongrel Nation* provides a historical account of the novel identities created in the factories, dance halls, streets, and other contact zones of postcolonial Britain.[28]

The Political Economy of Racism in
Twentieth-Century Britain

So-called ethnic minorities currently constitute less than 6 percent of Britain's total population.[29] Approximately 30 percent of this number is of African descent, 61 percent are of Asian descent, and 9 percent classify themselves as of mixed-race background. Of course, these groups are disproportionately concentrated in urban areas, where they often constitute the majority population of any particular borough, making the designation "ethnic minority" particularly misleading. In addition, a significant percentage of Britain's African, Asian, and Caribbean population was born in Britain.[30] Unlike the United States, which actively encouraged skilled immigrants from around the world to settle within its borders after 1965, Britain ended primary immigration from its former colonies in 1971. As a result of this policy, more people have left Britain during the last fifty years than have immigrated into the country during the same period. What then explains the moral panic over inundation by foreigners that vexes postimperial Britain?

The increasingly restrictive immigration laws of the postcolonial era have long been interpreted as a response to popular racism.[31] Typically, the racial bigotry of substantial numbers of ordinary Britons is seen as having placed pressure on the state to deal with civil discord. Leading members of both liberal and conservative parties, it is argued, responded to white racism such as the 1958 Notting Hill riots by enacting increasingly restrictive immigration legislation. During the period after 1948, such legislation gradually led to the transformation of British subjecthood from a universal category based on the extensive geography of the empire *(ius soli)* to an exclusionary identity based on notions of racial purity *(ius sanguinis)*.[32] However, this reading of Britain's postcolonial racial politics ignores the driving force of the state and the elite groups that dominate it in codifying forms of racial difference and in catalyzing racist reactions to the presence of postcolonial subjects in Britain. Indeed, state racism preceded popular antipathy to the presence of nonwhite immigrants in Britain by at least a century.[33] Postcolonial racism in Britain has been seen by critics who ignore this lineage of state racism as a product of the inherent xenophobia of individual Britons, a phenomenon that is completely divorced from state policies and their underlying economic motives.[34] British society is consequently viewed as an undifferentiated aggregate, a description that derives from stereotypical discourses on national character. Against this ascription of mass pathology, *Mongrel Nation* insists on the embedding of cultural phenomena such as racism in a political-economic framework.[35] Processes of racialization in Britain were clearly initiated by the state after 1948 through particular government policies. Although policymakers often clashed over the measures the government should adopt, their decisions were always informed by the economic imperatives and crises produced by Britain's declining imperial power. By tracking the novel articulations between culture, the state, and capital that arose as Britain lost its imperial hegemony following 1948, *Mongrel Nation* captures the relational nature of the interlocking cultural, political, and economic processes at play across contemporary geographic spaces.

The British state and the elite who dominated and directed it reacted to their imperial subjects' claims to freedom of movement and equal opportunity after 1945 with hostility bred from the attitudes of racial supremacy fostered by centuries of imperial power. The policies they instituted after the arrival of the *Empire Windrush* played a pivotal role in disseminating exclusionary definitions of national belonging and are hence directly culpable for the rise of racism and fascism in postimperial Britain.[36] For example, when the *Empire Windrush* docked in Tilbury, Clement Attlee, the prime minister, described the nonwhite imperial subjects who disembarked as engaging in an "incursion" into Britain and made minimal provision for their successful resettlement in the metropolis.[37] Another member of the Cabinet suggested transporting those aboard the *Empire Windrush* to East Africa, where they might be of economic utility without sullying the blood of Britain's white population. Yet Attlee and his Cabinet ultimately made no attempt to ban the entry of colonial subjects. This ambivalence on the part of the policymaking elite was a product of the economic and political contradictions in which Britain found itself following the war. Of course, Britain had just won a war against fascist powers whose doctrines of racial supremacy formed an explicit and essential part of their national ideology; in such a context, the British government could ill afford to adopt overtly racist policies. In addition, deeply in debt and with a shattered infrastructure, Britain needed the captive markets and opportunities for capital accumulation afforded by imperial preferences and the sterling area in order to rebuild its economy and shore up its eroding status as a world power.[38] Yet settler-populated dominions such as Canada and Australia were growing increasingly restive with the forms of political and economic subordination required by the commonwealth system. In addition, India's long struggle for independence finally bore fruit in 1947. Faced with such threats to the empire, Attlee's government passed a Nationality Act in 1948 that established the universality of British subjecthood, offering a powerful symbolic reaffirmation of the imperial system. By proclaiming formal equality throughout the empire, the 1948 Nationality Act sought to defuse anticolonial nationalist movements and to placate the declared anti-imperialist position of the United States, the preeminent capitalist power after the war.[39] However, this measure conformed to the system of global apartheid that had characterized British imperialism: imperial subjects were to be formally equal but geographically separate. As a consequence, the government moved to fill the postwar labor shortage by recruiting European—in other words, white—workers rather than citizens from the colonies.[40] When colonial subjects like those aboard the *Empire Windrush* began to exercise the rights the Nationality Act guaranteed to them by migrating independently to the motherland, the forms of racial hierarchy and subordination that underpinned the empire and the government's labor recruitment scheme quickly surfaced. The government's proclaimed inclusive legal model of national belonging, it became clear, fundamentally contradicted the exclusionary definitions of national identity developed during Britain's colonial expansion and imperial rule.

Despite the small number of immigrants arriving from the colonies during the early postwar years, the increasingly apparent hostility of both Labour and Tory governments to their presence in Britain had a significant impact on the conditions under which they lived.[41] For instance, despite the apparent clash of interests between employers seeking workers and the government, which, as the 1949 *Report of the Royal Commission on Population* made clear, feared racial hybridity, official hostility toward nonwhite immigration had an economic functionality. By eroding the political and social rights of migrants, government policies made them more vulnerable to superexploitation. As it had to a more limited extent during the interwar era, British capital attempted to employ workers from abroad to further accumulation following 1945. Migrant labor in general is attractive to employers because the state has to bear little of the cost of their social reproduction.[42] With the full employment that accompanied the economic boom of the 1950s and early 1960s in Britain giving employers relatively small leverage on workers, migrants from the colonies played the vital role of replacing white workers who refused to take up physically demanding and socially undesirable forms of manual labor.[43] Despite their impressive qualifications on average, British employers and the state slotted these nonwhite immigrants exclusively into unskilled positions. This policy could only be legitimated on racist grounds: nonwhites were perceived as simply unfit for skilled tasks, despite their formal qualifications. By failing to challenge such employment policies, the British government implicitly gave its imprimatur to strategies of subordination derived directly from colonial policy. In addition, as it did in European countries such as France and Germany that encouraged labor migration from their colonies or poorer neighbors, migration to Britain played the vital role of restraining wage increases during the postwar period.[44] By tacitly aiding employers in their search for a more "flexible" and hence more easily exploitable workforce, the state helped undermine the power of organized labor and advanced a strategy of accumulation based on the fragmentation of the working class along racial lines.

Notwithstanding the utility of migrant labor in the postwar era, the policymaking elite evinced significant resistance to the presence of colonial and postcolonial subjects in Britain. Although the commitment to maintaining imperial power initially prevented the state from moving officially to restrict nonwhite immigration, various administrative measures were adopted that were intended to discourage would-be migrants. Colonial officials, for example, were encouraged to make passports far more difficult to come by at points of embarkation. Such measures did little to offset the economic pressures that encouraged emigration, and, as migrants continued to arrive in the metropolis, British policymakers became actively involved in legislating a transparently racial model of national identity that represented some British subjects as more authentically British than others. In March 1954, a small number of Tory members of Parliament began a debate by alleging that "immigrants" were abusing the welfare state and that "virile young men" from the colonies posed a threat to law and order.[45] Two years later the Tory government established a working party on immigration whose final report was not published since it failed to find substantial economic grounds to restrict immigration. However, when racist riots erupted in 1958 in Nottingham and in London's Notting Hill neighborhood, the government found the excuse it needed to introduce legislation restricting immigration. Although the rioters were universally condemned by the press and by members of the government as

hooligans, Prime Minister Macmillan argued that their violence neces-
sitated the introduction of legislation that would maintain public order
by restricting immigration from the Caribbean and South Asia. The
sheer presence of nonwhite citizens was thus seen as a natural and
inevitable catalyst of white discontent, making black Britons responsible for the disorder produced by racist whites. By portraying the
Caribbean residents of British cities as the catalysts of racial conflict, the
government conveniently brushed over its own role in fostering the
social conditions that helped generate conflicts such as the Notting Hill
riots. Cuts in spending for social services such as housing provision and
education during the post-*Windrush* era helped ensure competition
between Commonwealth migrants and the most marginalized sections
of the white working class. State policies thereby fostered conflicts that
exacerbated tensions deriving from the postwar strategy of capital accumulation, which often pitted white and black workers against one
another.[46] As it had in the colonies, this strategy of divide-and-conquer
produced predictable forms of conflict along the reified racial lines that
the state itself had played the primary role in fostering.

Just over a decade after establishing the liberal Nationality Act of
1948, the British government effectively if not formally repealed the
right of imperial subjects to reside in Britain. The Commonwealth
Immigrants Act of 1962 subjected immigrants from the colonies to
numerical controls based on their skills and job prospects, notwithstanding their formal citizenship as British subjects. No corresponding
effort was made to control migration from Ireland and other European
nations. This act thus codified the forms of racist discourse that had circulated informally among members of both Labour and Tory governments since the arrival of the *Empire Windrush*.[47] Ironically, the act precipitated a vast increase in the number of migrants, who sought to gain
entrance to the promised motherland before the gates were slammed
shut. Further measures to heighten the juridical insularity of British
nationality followed in short order. Despite having condemned the 1962
act as racist, the Labour Party shepherded its own restrictive legislation
through Parliament only six years later.

The xenophobic discourse that characterized demagogues such as
Enoch Powell, whose notorious speech of 1968 predicted "rivers of
blood" unless black Britons were rounded up and deported, was the
logical outcome of this competition between the mainstream political
parties to pass racially exclusionary immigration legislation. During the

mid-1970s, for instance, the explicitly racist and fascist National Front achieved significant electoral impact by calling for the repatriation of all black British citizens, whether or not they had been born in the country. In 1981, Margaret Thatcher effectively inverted this relationship between the radical racist fringe and the mainstream by drafting a new Nationality Act that formally rescinded the provisions of the 1948 act. British national identity, long based on exclusionary informal parameters, at last became a matter of blood belonging.[48] While explicit talk of repatriation died down following Thatcher's politically astute co-option of the fascist vote, exclusionary definitions of national identity had been codified that sanctioned myriad forms of racist denigration, harassment, and inequality.

The Nationality Act of 1981 also bore the clear stamp of eugenically tinged fears concerning the purity of British bloodlines. Since representations of the nation as a patriarchal family codified in the act of 1948 were no longer tenable because of their blatant gender discrimination, the new act substituted an imagined community of gender equality that was predicated on clearly defined racial boundaries.[49] As Louise Bennett suggests in "Colonization in Reverse," black women were a particularly virulent problem to both these versions of community. As potential reproducers of difference within the homogeneously conceived body politic, black women as well as people who engaged in sexual relations across cultural and racial lines threatened to transgress the assiduously maintained boundaries that circumscribed the pure community of Britishness. If, as Ranu Samantrai puts it, "nationality is lived in the modality of gender," definitions of belonging were articulated during the post-*Windrush* era in a manner that underlines the intersections between gendered and racialized definitions of national belonging.[50]

It was around the question of gendered representations of racial difference, then, that the historic compromise that extended full citizenship—in the political, economic, and civil senses of the term—to all residents of Britain during the post-1945 period was most clearly unraveled.[51] Unable to resolve the contradictions in conditions of capitalist production and reproduction, neoconservatives adopted a strategy of racial scapegoating to cement their political hegemony. As the state came to penetrate social life to an unparalleled degree after 1945, so it became ever more split between the conflicting imperatives to satisfy the economic conditions for capital accumulation, on the one hand, and, on the other hand, to secure the social conditions for self-legitimization. With the internationalization of significant sectors of British capital after the 1960s, few incentives remained to stimulate the creation of a national strategy for capital restructuring.[52] Given the internationalization of capital after 1970 and the uneven impact of Britain's decline, the tendency of what Bob Jessop calls a two-nations project was to expand privileges for those perceived as good citizens in areas such as transport and housing where private property entrenched privilege. At the same time, the "bad citizens," who suffered the brunt of widening differentials within the wage-earning classes and the shift of public wealth to private hands through neoliberal privatization, were increasingly stigmatized.[53] Of course, black and Asian Britons suffered disproportionately from the blighting economic and social impact of post-Fordism.

The role of racial scapegoating in postcolonial Britain highlights the links between cultural phenomena such as "race" and broader political-economic currents. By unraveling such links, black British activists and critics sought to debunk exclusionary definitions of British identity. The antiessentialist aspects of this critique have helped stimulate significant interest in black British cultural studies. Too frequently, however, such interest has focused exclusively on the cultural plane, ignoring the political economy of racial subordination that was an important element in the militant antiracism developed by African, Asian, Caribbean, and white Britons in response to the scapegoating policies of the postimperial era.[54] *Mongrel Nation* recuperates the radical critique of racial capitalism developed by black British activists and theorists. This recuperation makes possible a political economy of culture and resistance that spans the shift from Fordism to post-Fordism in Britain after 1945. In addition, as its title suggests, *Mongrel Nation* emphasizes the enduring saliency of the nation-state as the primary scale at which transnational flows of capital, culture, commodities, and people are regulated. Through its emphasis on the consistency of postimperial British racial politics and economics, *Mongrel Nation* helps challenge the elisions that have characterized recent theories of diaspora and globalization.

READING RESISTANCE FROM BELOW

Louise Bennett's "Colonization in Reverse" satirizes the essentialism and ahistoricism of the British racial imaginary and, in doing so, offers a remarkably prescient overview of the specific forms of xenophobia that developed in Britain during the half-century after the arrival of the *Empire Windrush*. To start with, Miss Lou, Bennett's humorous speaker, delivers a swift and cheeky jab to the common charge that migrants from the Caribbean were stealing white people's patrimony in one way or another:

> Oonoo [You] see how life is funny,
> Oonoo see de tunabout,
> Jamaica live fe box bread
> Outa English people mout'.

> For wen dem catch a [arrive in] Englan,
> An start play dem different role,
> Some will settle down to work
> An some will settle fe de dole [public assistance].

> Jane say de dole is not too bad
> Because dey payin' she
> Two pounds a week fe seek a job
> Dat suit her dignity.

> Me say Jane will never find work
> At the rate how she dah-look,
> For all day she stay pon Aunt Fan couch
> An read love-story book.

> Wat a devilment a Englan!
> Dem face war an brave de worse,
> But I'm wonderin' how dem gwine stan'
> Colonizin' in reverse.

If Caribbean people become parasites on the British welfare state, Miss Lou argues implicitly, they are simply engaging in an inversion of the long colonial history of expropriation and exploitation. In the metropolis, former colonial subjects can refuse work that does not suit their dignity, a luxury that was obviously seldom a possibility for the vast majority of the colonized. The British public, masters of the art of taking bread out of other people's mouths according to Bennett, now protest hypocritically about competition from former colonial subjects. Bennett may seem to homogenize the English here. Perhaps she should have spoken only of the ruling class. However, even the British working class came to constitute a labor elite during the imperial period, with all the relative entitlements in comparison with the working classes of the colonies that this entailed. The empire thus helped to create a culture of consolidation that united working and upper classes within Britain.[55] After 1945, this imperial legacy was invoked to portray colonial and postcolonial immigrants as aliens whose presence threatened fundamental British traditions. Miss Lou's caustic exclamations over the difficulty the British have in adjusting to migration from the colonies satirizes precisely the kind of rhetoric deployed by ideologues of both mainstream and fringe political parties after 1945.

The racist stereotypes conjured up by Miss Lou do not, however, relate simply to economic issues. For while she sits at home collecting public assistance, Jane is reading romance novels. This suggests that she is not simply an unproductive subject, but is also endowed with an active emotional and sexual imagination. Through the figure of Jane, "Colonization in Reverse" conjures up the phobic image of black women's reproductive capacity. The lingering, eugenically tinged construction of national identity in postwar Britain ensured that black maternity would be represented as irreconcilable with national belonging.[56] During the postwar period, the state's focus on the reproduction of a pure body politic in fact shifted from the empire to Britain itself. As immigrants began arriving from the colonies, concerns about the constitution of the British people were increasingly aired. In 1949, for instance, the Royal Commission on Population declared in its report:

> British traditions, manners, and ideas in the world have to be borne in mind. Immigration is thus not a desirable means of keeping the population at a replacement level as it would have in effect reduced the proportion of home-bred stock in the population.[57]

Britain's recent defeat of fascist powers like Germany and Italy—both of which had placed a strong emphasis on control of women's sexuality—made it difficult for policymakers to advance openly eugenicist policies. However, cultural assumptions concerning the overlap of "race" and nation did have pronounced effects. The specter of racial degeneration was a driving force behind state immigration policies in the second half of the twentieth century. These policies, in turn, had a strong influence on popular consciousness in Britain, catalyzing increasingly harsh forms of racial prejudice, inequality, and, ultimately, violence as the nation sank deeper into a postimperial funk. Using the disarmingly satirical voice of Miss Lou, Louis Bennett's "Colonization in Reverse" charts the course that an increasingly exclusionary construction of British identity would take during the next half century.

As Bennett suggests, migration to Britain was the initial, foundational challenge to the imperial system that had heretofore structured the world of the colonized.[58] In laying claim to the rights of passage from the periphery to the metropolis, colonized and postcolonial subjects sought to dismantle the political, economic, and epistemological hierarchies on which imperialism rested.[59] Migrants from the Commonwealth forced former colonial nations to confront the decentering experiences undergone by colonized peoples for centuries.[60] This spatial mobility was not, however, the only act of resistance engaged in by migrants to Britain. Myriad other forms of insubordination necessarily followed in the wake of this seizure of control over geographical movement, as Britain's racist imperial culture was imported back home. Not all of these acts were political in the usual sense of the term. In fact, in order to register the acts of quotidian resistance engaged in by former colonial subjects in Britain, traditional definitions of political action need to be expanded radically. At least three generations of black and Asian Britons have now encountered and fought back against various forms of institutional and popular racism. Some of them have certainly resorted to parliamentary agitation, organized social movements, and demonstrations in the streets of Britain's cities. But the resources that enabled these communities to overcome racism have never been limited to such institutional, state-oriented sites.[61]

"Colonization in Reverse" again proves prescient in this regard, subtly suggesting some of the other cultural resources Britain's black and Asian communities have had at their disposal. Miss Lou's young friend Jane engages in the kind of everyday acts of sabotage that were important weapons in the arsenal of the racially oppressed in Britain.[62] She loafs. She refuses to look for a job that doesn't satisfy her. She brazenly exploits Britain's relatively generous welfare state. This ability to thrive while living without a wage became more rather than less important to second-generation black and Asian women and men as Britain's postcolonial crisis spiraled out of political control after the 1960s.[63] Other significant forms of opposition that *Mongrel Nation* discusses include subcultural sartorial styles, illicit sexuality, performative traditions such as carnival, calypso, reggae, dub poetry, bhangra, rock music, and street riots.[64] The subversive content in these traditions is not always immediately apparent. As James Scott argues, forms of resistance among subordinate individuals and groups are not always legible by those in positions of power, and therefore constitute "hidden transcripts" that intersect with the sphere of formal politics only on occasion.[65] Since history tends to be written either by or at the behest of socially dominant groups, Scott turns to these hidden transcripts in order to recuperate and record the experiences of subordinate people whose lives would not otherwise be accessible.[66]

When intellectuals such as Louise Bennett migrated to Britain, they brought radical anticolonial traditions of cultural recuperation and expression along with them. British culture thereby came to be infused with practices of internationalism that prominent British radicals of the era overlooked, to their great detriment. Moreover, the work of writers such as Bennett provides examples of precisely the kind of counterhegemonic blend of aesthetics and politics that cultural studies scholars have helped excavate in recent years. Louise Bennett's "Colonization in Reverse," for example, does not simply document acts of sly sabotage engaged in by recent immigrants. In addition, the poem itself is an act of resistance. Bennett's use of the Creole vernacular is part of a nationalism from the bottom up that has consistently animated diasporic writers and artists in Britain over the last fifty years.

Mongrel Nation's analysis of the making of postcolonial Britain begins with discussion of Sam Selvon, one of the most important writers of the post-1945 Caribbean Renaissance to settle in London during the 1950s. Unlike contemporaries of his such as V. S. Naipaul and George Lamming, both of whom lived in London in this period but wrote predominantly about life in the Caribbean, Selvon depicted conditions for his countrymen and women *in Britain* in his groundbreaking novel *The Lonely Londoners*. Following in the footsteps of earlier cultural nationalists such as Trinidad's Beacon Group, Selvon used vernacular Caribbean speech patterns and scabrous popular cultural forms such as calypso, documenting the struggles of the first generation of migrants to Britain rather than looking back with nostalgia or anger to life in the tropics. The veiled eugenicist concerns over the purity of British blood that figured in public policy of the era are mirrored, I argue, in Selvon's accounts of the sexual exploits of predominantly male migrants in the metropolis. If his work offers a poignant depiction of the isolation and alienation black Britons faced during the early years of settlement, Selvon's poetic novel also limns the resources of resistance transmitted through transnational expressive culture, resources that empowered postcolonial settlers in Britain as they demanded access to the pubs, the streets, the airwaves, and other important public spaces of the nation.[67]

Once postcolonial subjects from the Caribbean, Africa, and Asia settled in Britain, distinctions between migrants from different areas of the former empire tended to melt away in the furnace of racial subordination. The significant disparities between people arriving in Britain from independent island cultures such as Trinidad and Jamaica became less important, for instance, as people from the Caribbean had to band together against white lynch mobs such as those who roamed the streets during the Notting Hill riots of 1958. Similarly, their considerable cultural differences did not prevent people from the Caribbean, Africa, and Asia from uniting in the face of exclusionary definitions of national identity that reduced all nonwhites in Britain to the status of illegitimate "aliens." Intent on blocking such divide-and-rule strategies, activists among the immigrant communities in Britain adopted the unifying label *black* in order to strengthen the bonds of solidarity among those subjected to racism in the metropolis. As the contributors to *The Empire Strikes Back* pointed out, it made little difference whether immigrants to Britain were called "blacks, browns, darkies, nig-nogs, or Pakis."[68] The goal of such derogatory racial labels was the same: to represent nonwhites as outsiders, an invading force of dangerous aliens who threatened British identities that were conceived as pure and perpetual. Collective action, postwar immigrants to Britain quickly learned, was the only viable means of combating such forms of xenophobia given their minority status. The label *black* thus came to operate primarily as a political signifier, denoting experiences of racialization and resistance shared by the African, Asian, and Caribbean settlers of the postwar period.[69] Unlike in the United States, in other words, where *black* refers exclusively to people of African origin, in Britain the term functioned less as a category of shared biological identity than as a form of conscious affiliation based on political solidarity. This usage helped to highlight the arbitrariness of racial categories. The political practices of black Britons suggested that "race" was not based on primordial phenotypical or other forms of biological difference, but was instead a mutable social construction.[70] Behind seemingly commonsense racial categories lay

specific histories of contested domination and subordination. By reject-
ing essentialist models of racial difference, the political solidarity of
Asian, Caribbean, and African communities dismantled monolithic
representations of national identity. Antiracist struggle thereby came to
function as a contact zone, a cultural space in which cosmopolitan cultures interacted with one another to create new, radically composite
formations that enabled black Britons to militate against exclusionary
nationalist traditions in postcolonial Britain.[71]

Traditions of overtly internationalist cultural politics were most
evident in Britain during the 1960s and 1970s, when the Caribbean
Artists Movement and offshoot groups such as the Race Today collective were active. I discuss these groups and the cultural politics of internationalist antiracism in my second and third chapters. "Black Power in
a Transnational Frame" highlights the conversations that took place
between pivotal figures of the period such the Trinidad-born civil rights
activist Stokely Carmichael (aka Kwame Ture) and the poet Edward
Kamau Brathwaite. These personal and political exchanges took place
against the backdrop of the global antiracist struggle during the 1960s, a
context that has come to seem increasingly relevant with the revival of
traditions of internationalism and anti-imperialism over the last
decade. Activists such as Carmichael drew explicit parallels between
anticolonial freedom fighters in the Third World and antiracist militants in core nations such as Britain and the United States. Although
black Britons lacked mass-based formal national antiracist organizations such as the Student Nonviolent Coordinating Committee (SNCC)
of the United States, the proximity to colonial experience of first-gener-
ation immigrants to Britain meant that Black Power's anticolonial lexi-
con had great resonance on both sides of the Atlantic. Cultural politics
played a crucial role in activating this transnational imaginary. Indeed,
a crucial component of the era's radical internationalism was a political
and aesthetic populism grounded in the vernacular cultures of diasporic
groups in Britain. Thus, Stokely Carmichael helped articulate a transnational black activist imaginary grounded in a signifying homology
between the racialized ghettos of the developed world and the colonies
of the Third World. By contrast, for Caribbean Artists Movement
cofounder Edward Kamau Brathwaite, whose epic poetic cycle *Rights of
Passage* traces the black Atlantic migrations of the peoples of the African
diaspora, the key to the subterranean unity of peoples of African
descent is to be found in "nation language" and other popular expres-

sive forms that survived the Middle Passage. Drawing on their knowledge of diasporic history and culture, Carmichael and Brathwaite
helped flesh out the transnational antiracist imaginary invoked by radical young Black Power activists, models that have gained revived resonance in the work of contemporary theorists such as Paul Gilroy.

Invocations of anticolonial struggle in the metropolis took on
increasing saliency during the 1970s. Britain avoided the massive urban
upheavals that took place in the United States during these years as well
as government-orchestrated surveillance of and attacks on activists such
as the FBI's Counter Intelligence Program (COINTELPRO). Nonetheless, as the serried crises of Britain's welfare state unfolded, black and
Asian Britons' access to public space was radically curtailed through a
number of draconian state policies. Perhaps most pivotal was the
conflict between the British police force and black communities over
carnival celebrations during the mid-1970s. The work of dub poet Linton Kwesi Johnson, an active member of the Race Today collective and
one of the first artists to articulate a specifically second-generation black
British idiom, lies at the center of my discussion of the politics of
belonging in this period. Johnson and the Race Today collective were
actively involved in the revival of carnival as a celebration of diasporic
culture in these years. Blending insurrectionary celebrations of
antiracist culture in the Caribbean with popular license in the streets of
Britain's capital city, carnival was viewed by British authorities as a
menace to public order. They responded to carnival just as colonial
authorities had in Trinidad, attempting to suppress it by main force.
The battles that erupted around the annual carnival were symptomatic
of broader policies of harsh policing that were imposed on black communities during these years. Linton Kwesi Johnson's mobilization of
dub music and reggae poetry to document and intervene in these struggles extended the tradition of vernacular cultural activism of previous
generations while offering a novel voice that appealed to young, second-
generation black Britons. As I document in this chapter, LKJ's celebration of the Caribbean carnival tradition also inspired young Asian and
white activists, allowing them to jump the scale of the nation-state and
offer searing critiques of the contradictions of countries such as Britain
that proclaimed their liberalism while clinging tightly to imperial traditions.[72]

Despite their obvious merits for antiracist organizing, Black
Power–derived models of internationalist solidarity were challenged by

the emergence of new voices within black British communities during
this period. By the late 1970s and 1980s, groups like the Organization of
Women of Asian and African Descent (OWAAD) disputed the patriarchal characteristics of black nationalism while asserting their loyalty to
the broader antiracist struggle.[73] At the same time, a series of provoca-
tive films by independent black media collectives such as Sankofa highlighted the importance of sexuality and sexual orientation.[74] In "New
Ethnicities," Stuart Hall provides a theoretical overview of these shifts,
arguing that traditional, homogenizing definitions of blackness were
being destabilized by other cultural affiliations to class, gender, sexuality, and ethnicity.[75] Yet despite the decentering of the label *black British,*
Hall held that the term should not be jettisoned. Racism's tenacious
grip on public life in Britain underlined for Hall the enduring necessity
of collective solidarity, notwithstanding an increasing sensitivity toward
cultural differences. The findings of the MacPherson report concerning
the breadth of institutional racism in British society have confirmed the
necessity of unity among Britain's racialized groups during the new millennium.[76]

Hall's acknowledgment of new ethnicities is, of course, a product of
the increasing strength of struggles by women and gay people for equality in Britain. Although these movements began to impact black and
Asian communities during the 1970s, gender and sexuality have been
important issues within ethnic minority communities since the inception of mass immigration after 1948. Louise Bennett's "Colonization in
Reverse," with its satirical invocation of colonial eugenicist discourse,
underlines the interarticulation of diverse axes of identity, including
gender and race, in postcolonial Britain. The reproductive capacity of
black women like Bennett's character Jane was, as the poet implicitly
predicted, a target of both formal and informal regulation by British
authorities after 1948.[77] Similarly, stereotypical and phobic representations of black male sexuality often sparked various forms of white terror
in postcolonial Britain. Processes of racialization cannot therefore be
understood without also examining the role of gender and sexuality in
constituting competing forms of black British identity and resistance.

Buchi Emecheta's London trilogy anticipates many of the themes
developed by radical black and Asian feminist groups such as OWAAD.
By injecting perspectives and concerns derived from her Nigerian heritage into the parochial world of nascent British feminism during the
1970s, Emecheta was one of the first voices in what would grow to be a

chorus interrogating Western feminism, pushing for a decolonized theory and practice of transnational sisterhood. One of the first black women novelists to be published after 1945, Emecheta documents her experiences as a Nigerian immigrant to Britain isolated both by an oppressive marriage and by popular and state racism in Britain. Emecheta's brutally frank depiction of her by turns parasitic and domineering husband offered a direct challenge to unitary models of black subjectivity by challenging their primary ground of articulation: the family. Indeed, by exposing the patriarchal character of certain African traditions, Emecheta disrupted facile Afrocentric philosophies of the era. As I demonstrate in chapter 4, however, Emecheta also drew strength from her Nigerian roots, and thereby offered an implicit rebuke to the largely unchallenged universalistic tenets of the socialist feminism that dominated in Britain during these years. In addition, Emecheta used her documentary fiction to criticize the position of dependency foisted on poor white and black British women by the postwar welfare state. If she rebelled against the family-based oppression of her marriage, Emecheta is just as critical of the infantilizing ministrations of the welfare state. In place of both these institutions, her novels call not simply for a more inclusive model of British national identity, but for new forms of social citizenship grounded in radical democratic practices among working-class women of all colors. Drawing strength from the traditions of women's solidarity she experiences while living "in the ditch," Emecheta finds an experiential basis for the kind of transnational feminist solidarity that theorists such as Hazel Carby subsequently analyzed.

Despite the saliency of these issues for black and Asian Britons, historians and cultural studies analysts have devoted relatively little attention to the relations between race, gender, and sexuality during the postcolonial era.[78] This should perhaps not be so surprising given the fact that it is in the areas of gender and sexuality that the most intense struggles *within* black working-class cultures have taken place in Britain.[79] Faced with persistent institutional and popular racism in Britain, community leaders have often been tempted to play down class and gender differences in order to close ranks and don the mantle of community representatives.[80] While such cultural nationalism may help consolidate resistance to oppression, it tends to be underpinned by a reactionary politics of authenticity. For instance, women are frequently represented under such circumstances as pivotal symbols of autonomous cultural identity and tradition, placing enormous pressure on them to conform to the dictates of conservative traditions.[81] Strong resistance has emerged from within black British communities to this arrogation of authority and suppression of internal difference by leaders who are often male and middle class. These struggles challenge the tendency among both critics and policymakers to embrace monolithic definitions of community.[82] By tracking clashes over gender and sexuality, *Mongrel Nation* offers a history of black and Asian cultures in Britain in all their vital and sometimes contradictory complexity, looking at where ordinary people are rather than where it might seem politically desirable for them to be.[83]

If Emecheta's feminism provoked criticism for undermining black unity in the face of British racism, Salman Rushdie's novel *The Satanic Verses* definitively disrupted any lingering illusions about simplistic black-white binaries. Significant segments of the Asian community had been chafing against the *black British* label for some time before the firestorm over Rushdie's novel erupted, arguing that it elided the specificity of their experience.[84] As prominent a theorist as Paul Gilroy, for example, discusses resistant cultural traditions in relation to a geographical framework—the black Atlantic—that renders the colonial experience of Asians invisible.[85] By 1989, when the crisis over Salman Rushdie's novel *The Satanic Verses* tore the British public sphere apart, the Asian community had itself begun to fragment along religious lines that echoed the communal fractures on the subcontinent all too closely. British Muslims felt that other Asians had done little to support their efforts to challenge what they perceived as insulting and stereotyping representations of Islam, and began to identify themselves through their religious affiliation rather than their geographical origin. This internal cultural segmentation not only made it less likely that African, Asian, and Caribbean communities in Britain would adopt a common political identity by the 1990s, but also brought the politics of South Asian communal boundary policing home to the postcolonial metropolis.[86] If earlier generations of activists were animated by links to anticolonial nationalist movements around the world, by the late 1980s the exhaustion and corruption of such movements and their displacement by the insurgent force of religious fundamentalism became evident within Britain itself. In my chapter on *The Satanic Verses*, I discuss the novel's depiction of the policing of women's sexuality within these communal conflicts in South Asia and, increasingly, in Britain. While Rushdie is certainly no paragon of feminism, his novel does spotlight the homology between control of the Word and control of women that underpins fundamentalist religious movements of all denominations. As Rushdie's work makes clear, transnational movements such as political Islam are shaped significantly by their local articulations. Consequently, this chapter explores the interarticulation of struggles over communal identity and honor with policies advanced by the British state in the name of multiculturalism and immigration control during the 1980s. If Rushdie's attempt to dismantle both nascent Islamist movements and the racist British state helped catalyze a lamentably Manichaean culture war, his project of developing critical voices *within* the main religious traditions has been taken up by courageous British-based groups like Women Against Fundamentalism.

As we have seen, British authorities and opinion-makers have a long tradition of downplaying racial conflict and inequalities while simultaneously pursuing policies that foster such divisive forces. This remains true in the postracial, multicultural Britain trumpeted by Tony Blair's New Labour Party. In my sixth chapter, I discuss the lingering career of racial difference in Britain through the unlikely lens of Zadie Smith's *White Teeth*. Although this novel was justly celebrated for its vivacious depiction of the hybrid cultural world of second- and third-generation, mixed-race British youths, Smith's novel focuses on the novel forms of biopower that are the flip side of these sunny forms of cosmopolitanism. Fittingly, Smith's portrait of colliding multiracial dynastic families over the last half-century is preoccupied with the history and contemporary return of eugenics. *White Teeth* offers a witheringly satirical take on the overweening ambitions of contemporary genetic engineering as well as the often-dogmatic beliefs of those who would challenge new forces of biodeterminism. Smith's work thus highlights the extent to which issues of racial difference continue to structure British identity in this supposedly "postracial" age.

Since the publication of Smith's debut novel, Tony Blair has led Britain into a "war on terror" that has seen the revival of many of the imperial age's hoary rhetorical chestnuts. Yet Britain's renewed imperial zeal has not simply surfaced out of the blue. Apologists for "humanitarian intervention" abroad and the clampdown on civil liberties within Britain have drawn on racialized discourses of national identity that did not simply disappear when Britain lost its colonies. As *Mongrel Nation* demonstrates, representations of insular and exclusionary

British identity helped legitimate popular authoritarian ideologies and practices throughout the period after 1945. Essentialist accounts of Britishness have been at the bottom of practices as diverse as the informal "color bar," racialized immigration policies, and draconian policing practices. Despite the gradual implementation of antiracist, multicultural state policy, Britain has retained structures of racial inequality and the popular authoritarian ideologies that legitimated them throughout the last half-century. Recent celebrations of Britain's hybridity tend to highlight the cultural impact of black and Asian Britons while ignoring the enduring obstacles they face. Indeed, the effect of racial discourses is evident in the reified notion of a "clash of civilizations" to which current leaders have recourse in order to legitimate their policies of imperial invasion and occupation.[87]

Today, however, there is no neat distinction between the empire and the "mother country." The rhetorical convolutions of Tony Blair's opposition between "good" British Muslims and the "bad" Muslims of Al Qaeda are an indication of the difficulty of legitimating imperial policies that results from the mongrelization of Britain. Such facile discourses of assimilation to a homogeneous British national identity have become increasingly untenable as the inequalities and consequent conflicts of neoliberal globalization have come home to roost in Britain. Just as the popular authoritarianism of Britain's postcolonial period was consistently criticized, opposed, and, at times, successfully dismantled by antiracist activists over the last half-century, so contemporary opposition to the Anglo-American invasion of Iraq draws on reservoirs of anticolonial internationalism illuminated by *Mongrel Nation.*

"In the Big City the Sex Life Gone Wild"

Migration, Gender, and Identity in Sam Selvon's
The Lonely Londoners

On a Friday evening in late August 1958, a Swedish woman named Majbritt Morrison fell into an argument with her Jamaican husband Raymond as they left the Latimer Road underground station in London's Notting Dale neighborhood.[1] People congregated as the Morrisons' dispute grew more heated. The conflict was suddenly transformed when a man in the crowd began shouting racial slurs at Raymond Morrison, apparently believing that it was his duty to protect a white woman from a threatening-looking black man. Majbritt Morrison stopped arguing with her husband and began defending him from this attack, leading some members of the crowd to turn on her, calling her a "nigger lover." A group of the Morrisons' West Indian friends arrived as the shouting escalated and a fight broke out. Although no serious injuries resulted from this scuffle, it was the initial spark in the first major racial conflagration of postimperial Britain.

The night after the Morrisons' fight, crowds spilled out of local pubs in Notting Hill, brimming with beer and antiblack feeling. Spotting Majbritt Morrison on her way home down the high street, a crowd chased her to her house, volleying taunts of "black man's trollop!" and throwing milk bottles. When Morrison stood her ground outside her house and refused police orders to go inside, she—rather than the members of the marauding crowd—was arrested. The mob made off down the road, smashing windows in a side street and preparing to attack a house party organized by one of Britain's first sound-system operators, Count Suckle. The police, arriving just in time to stop this attack, dealt with the conflict by escorting Count Suckle and his friends out of the neighborhood. This apparently confirmed the impression of many in the crowd that their actions were helping purge West London of blacks. Mobs numbering in the hundreds roamed the streets of Notting Hill during the following nights, attacking any West Indians they could lay their hands on. Despite the eerie calm that reined over the rest of London during the rioting, groups of primarily young working-class men flooded into the streets of Notting Hill from surrounding parts of the city and began wreaking havoc. Although a few members of the white community defended their black neighbors, during the rioting the majority of the neighborhood's whites kept a complicit silence as lynch mobs roamed their streets. Neofascist organizers were quick to capitalize on this quiescence. Oswald Mosley's Union Movement circulated leaflets and held public rallies in the area. The perils of miscegenation featured prominently in the propaganda disseminated by such groups. For instance, National Labour Party leader John Steel was quoted as saying: "We will be a nation of half-castes. The result is that the nation will possess neither the rhythm of the coloured man, nor the scientific genius of the European. The only thing we will ever produce is riots, just as do the mixed races of the world."[2]

The Notting Hill riots, as this week of violent mayhem came to be known, were a watershed for Britain. They shattered the long-standing metropolitan illusion that racial conflict was un-British. It suddenly seemed that Britain was destined to face unrest on a scale not so different from that experienced by former settler colonies like the United States and South Africa during the late 1950s. Moreover, the riots established some of the fundamental themes of racial antipathy that would characterize postimperial Britain. The gender of immigrants (until 1955, 85% were male) was a pivotal issue in this regard. As the conflict over the Morrisons' interracial marriage and the propaganda disseminated by neofascist leaders demonstrates, anger over sexual relations between black men and white women was a crucial catalyst of the riots. Agitators such as John Steel played on fears that sex between Englishwomen and black male immigrants from the Caribbean would create a mongrel population in Britain. Notwithstanding their formal rights as British subjects, in other words, black migrants were viewed by the neofascists, by many members of the political establishment, and by much of the populace in general as a threat to racial purity and, consequently, to national identity.[3] White women such as Majbritt Morrison who consorted with black men were likely to be stripped of their racial identity.[4] As they had been in Britain's colonies, black masculinity and sexuality became the subject of lurid interest and concern during the initial decade of mass migration from the Commonwealth, with particular alarm concentrating on the charged erotic relations of black men and white women.[5] The profound anxiety created by the blurring of boundaries separating the metropole and the colonies that characterizes postimperial Britain is, in other words, displayed in particularly stark form in the arena of sexual relations.

Stereotypical images of black men's potent sexuality and concerns about white women's potential infidelity to the race-nation had a direct impact on state policy during this period. The war against Nazism and fascism, with their overtly biological constructions of racial hierarchy, had rendered explicit racist appeals illegitimate in post-1948 Britain. However, notions of sexual conduct helped blur the line between biological and cultural notions of difference. Parliamentary opponents of immigration from the Commonwealth nations could avoid overt racism by alluding to supposedly insuperable cultural differences between postcolonial subjects and native Britons.[6] Hoary stereotypes dating back to antiquity that represented non-Europeans as given over to sexual abandon so excessive that it bordered on the bestial permeated public discourse in surprisingly frank terms. Sexual mores were seen as a vital index of broader cultural differences, with critics objecting to the "completely promiscuous method of breeding" that "tropical peoples" imported into Britain.[7] Through this focus on the sexual, the "culture bar" was substituted for the color bar. In the process, the image of Britain as an embattled nuclear family replaced that of imperial Britannia as the mother of a geographically dispersed extended family of colonial peoples. Racist violence such as the Notting Hill riots was viewed by many mainstream commentators and legislators as the logical outcome of aversion to the foreign cultural practices of colonial subjects.[8] The deplorable racist attacks that took place during the riots could only be prevented, it was argued, through the diminution of Britain's black population. By 1962, when an immigration act that effectively transformed postcolonial migrants into second-class citizens was passed, such arguments had largely prevailed.

The evident continuities between colonial and postcolonial subordination in Britain ensured that heterosexual self-assertion was a crucial component of the immigrant experience for many West Indian men.[9] Moreover, Britain offered male migrants occasions to assert their self-worth in the arms of white women, opportunities for experiences of sexual and emotional intercourse that were far more severely policed on colonial terrain. As Frantz Fanon put it, "When my restless hands caress those white breasts, they grasp white civilization and dignity and make them mine."[10] This urge to self-realization through sexual entanglement was particularly strong for Anglophone Caribbean male migrants, who had been exposed to the powerful assimilatory pedagogy of the British colonial education system without encountering the full panoply of racial terror to which African-American men were regularly submitted.[11] For Fanon, however, this strategy of revenging oneself on the colonial apparatus through sexual conquest, predicated as it was on the desire to merge with or at least be validated by whiteness, is animated at bottom by dependency and deep self-alienation.[12] Like many recent critics of metropolitan racism, however, Fanon largely neglected to consider the impact such attitudes would have on women.[13]

To what extent is Fanon's gloomy portrait of mental colonization borne out by the experience of migrants to Britain? Published contemporaneously with Fanon's work and two years before the Notting Hill riots, Samuel Selvon's *The Lonely Londoners* depicts the first generation of overwhelmingly male immigrants from the Caribbean struggling to cope with the stereotypes and prejudices they encountered in Britain. Of late, Selvon's work has been celebrated for its account of West Indian resiliency within the urban metropolis. Recent critics have argued that British cultural hegemony was significantly unsettled and undermined through the postimperial encounter with migrants from the colonies.[14] Selvon's work is certainly noteworthy for the confidence with which it draws on the creolized forms of Caribbean vernacular culture, calypso foremost among them. Yet celebratory readings of Selvon's work in particular and of the impact of early waves of migration in general tend to underemphasize the forms of institutional racism and structural exclusion faced by migrants to Britain.[15] *The Lonely Londoners* depicts the impact not simply of racism in housing and the workplace but of racial fetishism in the sexual arena. Selvon thereby underlines the damaging effects of racism on immigrant cultures on both a material and a psychological plane. Moreover, Selvon's jocular accounts of the escapades of "the boys" in the face of such racism encouraged his overwhelmingly British readership to empathize and even identify with West Indian people such as those found in *The Lonely Londoners*. To stress the hybridizing impact of migration alone is therefore to miss the role of Selvon's novel as an intervention in an increasingly racist public sphere in Britain during the mid-1950s.

In contrast with the relentlessly misogynist writing of the so-called Angry Young Men, Selvon's depiction of the pathos of macho values among the black immigrant community prepares the ground for a critique of black men's complicity with structures of patriarchal subordination in Britain and its colonies.[16] As is true at present, popular culture was the most important site for the articulation of such attitudes.[17] After World War II, calypso music became one of the dominant forms of popular culture on a global scale, fostering pan-Caribbean exchanges, rejuvenating the recording industry in both the United States and Britain, and catalyzing the growth of Hi-Life music in colonial West Africa. This chapter therefore begins with a discussion of representations of black male identity in calypso music of the 1940s and 1950s. My discussion of the specific historical roots of the extravagant braggadocio of the period challenges pathologizing assumptions of a timeless black machismo. When calypso artists and their audiences traveled from the Caribbean to Britain, they brought their attitudes about gender power with them, values that Sam Selvon represents with great clarity and pathos in *The Lonely Londoners*. Selvon's work foreshadows many subsequent texts that deal with issues of masculinity, sexuality, and identity fragmentation, including George Lamming's *The Emigrants* and *The Pleasures of Exile*, Tayeb Salih's *Season of Migration to the North*, and Andrew Salkey's *The Adventures of Catullus Kelley*. Through its exploration of racial inequality and gender power, Selvon's *The Lonely Londoners* offers a powerful call for an egalitarian and postimperial Britain.

Calypso, Masculinity, and Power

Calypso music has its origins in the stick fighting that accompanied the canboulay festival in colonial Trinidad. Centering on the ritual burning of cane fields during the era of plantation slavery, canboulay also included fights between rival groups of slaves using long sticks or staves. These street skirmishes were propelled by secret African martial societies as well as by the plantation-based fraternities that succeeded them following the Middle Passage.[18] Indeed, the most frequently cited derivation for calypso is *kaiso,* which is in turn a corruption of an expression of approval similar to "bravo" in the West African Hausa language.[19] Stick fights were preceded by ritual boasts in which a griot-like figure called a chantwell taunted members of the opposing band with stories of his leader's physical prowess. The fights themselves were accompanied by kalindas, bitingly satirical songs sung by the chantwell and a chorus that belittled their opponents and promoted their own band. The by turns outrageously boastful and wittily barbed verses of the kalinda were traditionally composed extempore by the chantwell. This tradition of improvised bravado and satire remained a core of calypso music following emancipation in the mid–nineteenth century, becoming known in Creole as *picong,* from the French term *piquant* (stinging, insulting). The calypso is thus grounded in hyperbolic assertions of masculinity that were forged in the context of the systematic emasculation administered by the institutions of racial slavery.

After emancipation, calypso songs became an integral component of the carnival tradition, which consisted of a mas' band or group of revelers wearing masquerade costumes. These bands paraded through the streets accompanied by a chantwell and chorus singing the band's praises and mocking rival groups. British colonial authorities, who repeatedly sought to suppress the Creole institution of carnival during the second half of the nineteenth century, not surprisingly became the butt of the chantwells' satirical verses. Calypso songs increasingly addressed topical and potentially inflammatory subjects such as the difficulty of life for the denizens of the urban slums known as barrack yards. In 1883, for example, the colonial government passed a ban on drumming, an Afro-Creole practice on which kalinda depended, in an effort to abolish practices associated with carnival. Kalinda singers subverted this proscription, however, by substituting bamboo instruments that provided rhythmic accompaniment to the kalinda for traditional drumming practices. By the end of the nineteenth century, the calypso tradition had become a central venue for the expression of popular discontent with colonial subjugation, often using forms of satire and indirect insult to challenge British cultural and institutional power.

At the same time, calypso songs gained increasing autonomy from the carnival itself with the establishment of the tent, an informal arena set up so that a mas' band could practice its songs prior to the annual carnival parades. Just as pioneering figures of the Trinidadian literary scene such as Alfred Mendes and C. L. R. James began writing about the barrack yards, calypso singers expanded the topicality of their material by focusing in more detail on the everyday lives and vicissitudes of the poor.[20] Calypso singers, or calypsonians, were by this time singing mainly in English, reflecting the Anglicization of Trinidadian society in general, although the English spoken in the tents was a highly creolized form that included many elements of French and West Africa patois. One of the greatest of these calypsonians, Chieftain Douglas, was also responsible for the transformation of calypso from impromptu sessions held in mas' camp tents to formalized, programmed, and commercially sponsored events.[21] Competition among the calypsonians, deriving from the days of the chantwells, was institutionalized in 1939, when the first island-wide Calypso King competition was held. Although the British colonial population and the small black middle class remained aloof, French Creole intellectuals began supporting calypso, seeing it as a genuine expression of indigenous national identity.

The calypso aesthetic saturates *The Lonely Londoners*.[22] Selvon's debt to the genre is most evident in the novel's apparently loose-knit string of humorous anecdotes depicting the lives of flamboyant characters in London's Caribbean immigrant community.[23] To this appropriation of the structure of calypso ballads, Selvon adds adaptation of the pervasive use of melodrama, satire, and irony that characterized the calypso tradition. In addition, in *The Lonely Londoners* Selvon creates a narrator whose synthetic Creole dialect overcomes the dichotomy between popular and literary tradition that marked his first two, Trinidad-based novels.[24] Selvon's creolized narrative voice and adaptation of the calypso tradition served as a beacon to Caribbean intellectuals of the period, many of whom joined Selvon in exile in Britain during the 1950s.[25] If residence in the colonial metropolis magnified the legacy of cultural schizophrenia bequeathed by colonialism, Selvon's calypso aesthetic offered a paradigm for a populist cultural nationalism that resonated strongly with the intellectuals of his generation.[26] Selvon's appropriation of calypso allowed him to commandeer the British novel and transform it into a vehicle for the expression of postcolonial Caribbean identity.

While *The Lonely Londoners* pioneers the creolizing strategies with which members of the West Indian renaissance of the 1950s and 1960s reworked the English language and the metropolitan literary tradition, it also depicts the mutability of British identity. Selvon's protagonists inhabit the capital city, using the famous sites of the metropolis as conjure words to define their upward mobility.[27] Britain does not, however, offer the boundless opportunity that in many cases inspired the immigrants' departure from the Caribbean. Confronted with London's numbingly cold winters and the institutional racism of the color bar in housing and employment, Selvon's characters band together in the basement flat of his protagonist, Moses Aloetta, in order to swap tall tales of their misadventures in the metropolis. The social solidarity embodied by the men's storytelling circle is an important antidote to the isolation and frequent humiliation they experience in their everyday lives in Britain. Indeed, Selvon's characters overcome the petty loyalties to their natal islands in the Caribbean and to Africa in the name of a more cosmopolitan sense of diasporic unity forged through the picaresque tales they tell one another in Moses' basement. Although their rambunctious camaraderie cannot be equated with the kind of political organizing that unfolded following the Notting Hill riots, the social solidarity depicted in the novel establishes the bonds of trust and mutuality upon which such organizing would be built in the following two decades. This small community of men therefore constitutes a kind of seed or microcosm of the unity developed by black Britons in the face of racism.

Although *The Lonely Londoners* celebrates the resiliency of Moses and his comrades, the novel also lays out the flaws of a resistant cultural nationalism grounded in misogynistic, homophobic bonding between men.[28] Confronted by pervasive forms of racist stereotyping and discrimination, the community of male immigrants depicted in the novel all too often responds with forms of masculine self-aggrandizement that hinge on the debasement of women, both white and black, as well as on overt forms of homophobia. Like many other aspects of the novel that have been celebrated by critics, this reflex is grounded in the calypso aesthetic.[29] Indeed, there are strong parallels between the braggadocio of calypso songs of the era and the treatment of women in the novel by male characters. Selvon's depiction of masculine bonding, misogyny, and homophobia in *The Lonely Londoners* testifies to the potent influence of popular traditions such as calypso on the identity of immigrants to Britain.

Despite the gradual commercialization of calypso during the early twentieth century, calypso singers themselves lived precariously in

Trinidad. Although calypso music was beginning to be recorded, there was no system of copyright through which calypso artists could gain royalties for their songs. Lacking access to such revenues, calypsonians' primary regular source of income was the prize money available during the annual carnival competitions. However, since the carnival took place only once a year, calypsonians—an almost exclusively male group—often relied on female backers of the tent or mas' band for economic support during the rest of the year. They were consequently seen by much of the conservative Trinidadian middle class as ne'er-do-wells, despite their ability to articulate social grievances in scurrilously amusing terms. While they were only one component of a notably heterogeneous genre, the exaggerated sexual innuendo and rodomontade that had by this time become a standard part of the calypso repertoire reflected these contradictory material and social conditions. Economically dependent on calypso audiences in general as well as on their girlfriends, calypsonians relied on their verbal facility and boastful self-confidence to garner the popularity necessary to survive from one carnival season to the next. Since they tended to be an economic drain on the women who supported them, calypsonians could seldom depend on stable or long-term relationships, let alone on marriage, for economic and emotional support. The braggadocio of calypso music papered over the conditions of economic dependency and insecurity to which the calypsonians were consigned.

If calypsonians tended to cast themselves in inflated terms in reaction to the damaging psychological residues of plantation slavery and colonial underdevelopment, they offered no such boon to women in their songs. Self-inflating descriptions of masculine sexual superheroism were instead twinned in the calypso music of the first half of the century with stinging attacks on women. Calypsonians often sang of their insatiable sexual appetites, describing the many women they left prostrate in ecstasy, begging for more or groaning in agony in response to the powerful lovemaking they had experienced.[30] Women were consistently treated solely as sexual objects and denigrated with wittily cloaked put-downs and punning scatological catalogs of their supposed physical and hygienic deficiencies. If a woman sought to assert herself by abandoning her philandering boyfriend, she was subjected to harsh attacks and violent threats for her perceived infidelity. The calypso song thus became a way of disciplining women, who feared the opprobrium that would be brought upon them were they to become the subject of a

blisteringly satirical attack. Such assaults were seldom challenged by
society at large; as Trinidadian novelist and critic Merle Hodge notes,
"The calypsonian, the folk poet, is assured of heartfelt, howling
approval when he devotes his talent to the degradation of women."[31]
Where did this strong streak of misogyny come from? Of course, colonized and enslaved women were, with virtually no exceptions, severely
disadvantaged within their societies prior to the advent of colonial rule
and enslavement.[32] Colonial hierarchies impinged on, grew entangled
with, and were to a certain extent transformed by the forms of gender
power they encountered. Yet, while the misogyny evident in preinde-
pendence calypso lyrics may have reflected interlocking traditions of
male gender power, the phallic self-assertion of the calypsonians was a
painfully ironic reflection of their acceptance of white supremacist representations of their economic and social castration.[33] The extravagant
sexual machismo of the calypsonians can thus be seen as a form of compensatory disavowal. Once dominant notions of castration had been
accepted, male potency tended to be asserted through anxiety-ridden
and excessive demonstrations of mastery over black women.

Far from being simply heterosexist, however, Selvon's *The Lonely
Londoners* offers an explicit and prescient critique of these modes of
black male style and the cultural nationalism they embody. Selvon
engages in this critique by rendering the forms of objectification and
fetishization that attended black male immigrants' sexual relations with
white English women far more explicit than in calypso music of the
time. Sexual relations, often represented as a form of aggressive conquest, are nevertheless accompanied in the novel by a sense of ambivalence and defensiveness. In addition, *The Lonely Londoners* also stresses
the hollow character of the sexual adventurism of "the boys," suggesting
that their triumphs in the bedroom fail to create truly egalitarian and
postimperial relations among the novel's characters. Instead of dismantling colonial power relations, that is, the boys' conquests simply invert
those relations through the creation of gender hierarchy. Black male
self-assertion ends up mirroring the forms of violence that characterize
white supremacist patriarchy. To drive this critique home, Selvon's
novel documents instances of domestic violence within the black community and offers an example of a strong black woman who challenges
such forms of abuse.

The ballad of Cap, a dissolute Nigerian native who spends his nights
partying and his days sleeping, illustrates many of these themes. Cap is

an unrepentant freeloader, a man who hoodwinks a string of European women into supporting him using his personal charm and the women's stereotypical notions of black masculinity. Moses' grudging admiration for Cap stems from the fact that he is able to thrive without submitting himself to the disciplined workday of industrial capitalism. As a kind of sexual con man and trickster, he rejects the dehumanizing routine of manual labor, offering the spectacle of seemingly endless leisure to a man like Moses, who, despite working for nearly a decade in Britain, has little to show for his labors.[34] It is no coincidence that Cap's ballad is immediately preceded by Moses' visit with the recently arrived Galahad to the employment office. Like the vast majority of immigrants from the Caribbean, Galahad is a skilled worker, yet the employment office has nothing to offer him.[35] Instead, he is banished to an adjoining building to register for unemployment insurance. This place is a devastating reminder of the vulnerability of Caribbean men to the whims of British employers. Black workers were consistently downgraded and deskilled following their arrival in Britain. In addition, British labor unions were uniformly hostile toward black workers, despite the rhetoric of working-class solidarity articulated by national union leaders. Black workers tended to be accused of undermining the unions' closed shop policy and of helping employers break strikes by working as "black legs."[36] The sense of identity and stability guaranteed by a good job was consequently denied to many migrants.[37] As Moses comments when he and Galahad stand surveying the depressing spectacle in the National Assistance office, "When a man out of work he like a fish out of water gasping for breath" (45). Adding to this prejudice in the private and union sectors, the state itself often railroaded black workers into the least desirable jobs. As Galahad's application is processed, Moses reveals that his colonial origin will be noted in red ink on top of the form. This is to save time, Moses says, so employers who don't want black men working for them won't be bothered with job applicants from the Caribbean. This apparent lack of anger at the exclusion of blacks from all but the least desirable jobs is qualified by Moses' revelation that most of the job announcements were stripped from the walls after a Jamaican man tore up the office in a fit of rage (46). If working-class men's identity was often intimately tied to their pride in manual labor, employment conditions in Britain systematically undermined black men's sense of self-worth, leading to levels of despair and incandescent anger that *The Lonely Londoners* communicates despite its overriding comic tone.[38]

Cap's flagrant sexual opportunism thus needs to be seen within the context of the systematic humiliation meted out to migrants in the workplace and elsewhere.[39] His ability to survive without wages offers a striking challenge to racism in the workplace, not to mention the diverse other forms of prejudice previously anatomized by Moses. Yet Cap's life of apparent leisure is the product of strenuous, increasingly desperate hustling. A promising son of the educated Nigerian elite, Cap drops out of law school in London in order to devote all of his attention to the seduction of English women. After his father cuts him off, Cap lives a totally unstable, itinerant life, dodging from one hotel room to another using his ability to con people into believing that he is the reputable student he once was. Moses calls him "the wandering Nigerian." This nomadic life cuts Cap adrift from the network of black friends he initially made in London. As a result, he comes to depend increasingly on the women he seduces.

Why is Cap so consumed by sexual desire? As Moses describes his antics, Cap is driven not simply by physical need, much less by a hankering for genuine intimacy and mutuality. Instead, Cap achieves a symbolic victory over colonial racial subordination by making his girlfriends dependent on him. His Austrian girlfriend sells off most of her material possessions, for instance, in order to support Cap. She also puts up with his blatant, chronic infidelity. Cap has evidently decided that the arms of a white woman offer a far more immediate form of gratification than laborious and protracted legal studies. Yet this conquest of European femininity fails to confer any sense of self-worth on Cap.[40] Instead, Cap's sexual drive becomes increasingly compulsive as he wears out his sole suit of clothes, loses his friends, and leaves the life of bourgeois respectability he came to London to achieve further and further behind. When his Austrian girlfriend eventually tires of his parasitism and pushes him to get a job, for example, Cap pretends to have found work but actually goes off hustling other women when he's supposed to be at work (53).[41] He eventually dumps this Austrian for a French girl, whom he marries and then abandons since he has no place to take her on their wedding night. When his friend Daniel—whose address Cap has given the girl—finds Cap, he is paralyzed. Although Moses describes Cap as a kind of hapless, comic trickster figure, his compulsive sexual drive nevertheless indicates the dire need Cap feels to affirm his sense of manhood through predatory sexual relations.[42] Sitting in the café trying to hustle women, Cap suffers through a dissociation of sensibility that allows him to forget the new bride who waits for him at Daniel's apartment completely. Like Galahad, Cap's psyche becomes fragmented, his past split off from his present as he strives repeatedly and obsessively to find new sexual partners. Of course, the women he seduces are nothing more than objects in the service of his quest for fresh flesh, a status that the novel underlines through its frequent references to women as "things" and as "cat." Yet in seeking validation through European women, Cap ironically places himself in a position of dependency. Each new sexual conquest holds out a promise of affirmation that is necessarily withdrawn continually since such validation is premised on Cap's self-alienation in the first place. Cap's compulsive hustling may free him from the deadening routines of the workday and may represent a superficial conquest of white femininity, but, as Moses' account makes clear, it does not constitute a triumph over racialized dependency, still less a rejection of gender hierarchy.

Cap is hardly alone in his search for sexual gratification. Admittedly, none of Selvon's characters ever articulate a conception of sexual relations as a form of revenge on a par with Eldridge Cleaver's theory of the political use of rape. Nonetheless, for virtually all the characters, the seduction of European women offers an implicit reclamation of their masculinity, belittled in so many other ways in Britain. Indeed, the majority of the ballads that compose the novel detail the misadventures of Moses and his friends as they search for the "bags of white pussy" they imagine the metropolis offers. Yet by choosing sex as one of their primary means of self-assertion, the characters conform to stereotypical representations imposed on colonized men by Europeans across the centuries. As many theorists of colonial discourse have emphasized, in the "porno-tropics" of empire, black men were represented with dramatically exaggerated phalluses that reduced black masculinity to the level of the genital.[43] Such representations were marked by deep ambivalence and splitting. On the one hand, the supposed phallic power of black men produced dramatic levels of anxiety that were often at the root of campaigns of white terror such as lynching. The specter of miscegenation, stemming in colonial contexts from fears over the loss of control of property and labor, produced anxiety-filled, vituperative discourses concerning the mutual attraction of black men and white women. On the other hand, the reduction of black men to sexual fetishes placed them in the passive position of the sex object.[44] Colonial and racist discourses, in other words, rendered black men as both hypermasculine and feminine at one and the same time. According to Fanon's nuanced historical materialist analysis of the dependency complex, the chronic ambivalence of these dominant discourses left black men in constant combat with their own self-images.

These ambivalent discourses concerning black masculinity had a dramatic impact on race relations during the early years of migration to Britain, as the sexual escapades of Selvon's characters underline. Recounting his sexual adventures in London, for instance, Moses remarks:

> In the big city the sex life gone wild you would meet women who beg you to go with them one night a Jamaican with a woman in Chelsea in a smart flat with all sorts of surrealistic painting on the walls and contemporary furniture in the G-plan the poor fellar bewildered and asking questions to improve himself because the set-up look like the World of Art but the number not interested in passing on any knowledge she only interested in one thing and in the heat of emotion she call the Jamaican a black bastard though she didn't mean it as an insult but as a compliment under the circumstances but the Jamaican fellar get vex and he stop and say why the hell you call me a black bastard and he thump the woman and went away. (109)

The Jamaican man described by Moses confronts objectification at the hands of a wealthy British woman. As Moses notes, the white woman's avant-garde artistic inclinations ironically make her particularly prone to indulge in fetishizing fantasies concerning black masculinity.[45] Despite her passing enthusiasm for her lover, this woman is thoroughly complicit with subordinating discourses of racial difference.[46] Indeed, as Moses' narrative suggests, there is little chance that the Jamaican will be able to parlay his treatment as a sexual fetish into class mobility or even the acquisition of cultural knowledge. Instead, he is reduced to the level of the genital in an exchange that is, ultimately, emasculating. This objectification elicits a particularly violent reaction not simply because it participates in the racism so evident in other quarters of British society. In addition, the Jamaican finds himself placed in precisely the position that so many of Selvon's migrants attempt to vacate. By reducing women through slang terms such as *cat* and *thing* to their sexual organs, Moses and company treat them not just as objects of exchange between competing, racialized patriarchies but as split-off, butchered aspects of themselves. Women become the receptacles of disavowed aspects of the men's femininity in forms of gender power intimately tied to racial hierarchy.[47] When women such as the wealthy artist described above treat Moses and his friends purely as sex objects, they undo this disavowal, forcing the men to confront their emasculated status in the most immediate terms. Expanding on this theme, *The Lonely Londoners* also depicts encounters between Cap and a transvestite (56) and between Moses and a gay man (107–8). Despite being treated in comic terms, both these encounters threaten to unman Moses and Cap by interrupting the position of masculine dominance that they struggle to establish in London. There are certainly significant differences between Moses, Cap, and the other characters, with Cap demonstrating the limit case for the instrumental treatment of women. However, when Moses and his friends perceive themselves as passive and feminized sexual objects as a result of racial fetishism, their response is typically articulated through strong compensatory assertions of their masculinity.

ALTERNATIVE DISCOURSES OF GENDER AND RACE

The late 1950s and early 1960s were an era of rampant male insecurity in Britain. The established Left dealt with its historical setbacks through the flagrant misogyny evident in works such as John Osborne's play *Look Back in Anger.* The behavior of characters such as Cap is not so extraordinary when juxtaposed with works such as Alan Sillitoe's *Saturday Night and Sunday Morning,* with its philandering young protagonist. Although this kind of behavior was celebrated in calypso songs composed in Britain such as Lord Kitchener's hit "Nora," this was not the only model of male behavior available. Traveling with Lord Kitchener to Britain aboard the *Empire Windrush,* Lord Beginner also recorded songs inspired by the taboo topic of interracial relations. Lord Beginner, a member of the so-called Old Guard, often took international events as a subject of his songs, as his song "Mix Up Matrimony" demonstrates:

> Racial segregation gone to hell,
> They happenin' nowadays I can tell
> Mixed marriage seems to have a stronger tide than the pure one

For I don't know why
The races are blendin' harmoniously
White and coloured people are binding neutrally
It doesn't take no class to see how it come to pass
Coloured Britons are risin' fast

(Chorus)
The organs are always playing
And the preachers are saying:
"Please cooperate and amalgamate"
Oh some are seeing well and the others catchin' hell
"Please cooperate and amalgamate"

The great part that Seretse Khama played
We appreciate the move that he made
The Bangamwato tribe he always thinking of
He lost his throne for the girl that he love
For he knew that a good wife today is hard to find
So he find one so he had to treat her kind
So if you're in your prime run to the preacher any time
For your love it is not a crime.[48]

Lord Beginner's song demonstrates the resonance of events in Africa for members of the diaspora resident in Britain, even after the departure of important anticolonial nationalists such as Jomo Kenyatta, Kwame Nkrumah, and C. L. R. James.[49] In 1948, the heir to the Bamangwato throne in Botswana, Seretse Khama, married a white Englishwoman named Ruth Williams while completing his studies in London.[50] Khama's unorthodox marriage threatened his succession to the throne and generated an international diplomatic crisis. Khama's uncle and guardian, Tshekedi, declared the marriage a breach of Bamangwato custom and, along with other influential elders who feared the tainting of bloodlines and potential erosion of territorial sovereignty, threatened to disinherit Seretse. When the Bamangwato nevertheless granted Seretse the chieftaincy in 1949, Tshekedi led a group of dissenters into voluntary exile. The British government, anxious not to alienate South Africa's recently elected apartheid regime, from whom it wished to purchase uranium for the manufacture of nuclear weapons, sided with Tshekedi and banished Seretse and his wife. The diplomatic storm that erupted over Seretse's marriage nearly brought down the British government at the time, but was ultimately resolved in the name of personal love instead of ethnically pure succession.

"Mix Up Marriage" suggests that Seretse's ultimate triumph resonated powerfully with some members of the diasporic community in Britain. Defying not only the customs of his own people but also the forms of racial segregation being installed in South Africa at the time, Seretse offered a model of individual devotion rising above the inflexible and exclusionary dictates of blood, belonging, and bureaucracy. This is not to say that the issue of dependency was not a factor in Seretse's marriage, but rather that Lord Beginner chooses to emphasize Seretse's courage and devotion to his wife rather than the Manichaean vision of racialized sexual relations presented by other calypsonians in Britain. Indeed, "Mix Up Matrimony" extrapolates from the Khama affair to cast mixed-race relationships as a form of antiracist activism. Yet, although Lord Beginner's song stresses the liberty to choose a romantic partner exemplified by Seretse Khama and experienced to a certain extent by black men in Britain during the early and middle 1950s, the song cannot fully escape the issue of gendered power relations. If, in the utopian rhetoric of the song, "white and coloured people are binding neutrally," such relations constitute a form of upward mobility for black men in Britain, who consequently "are risin' fast." This reference to what Fanon called "lactification" inevitably raises concerns about the injunction to "cooperate and amalgamate." Is this a form of racial suicide? Does the song, with its belief in the racial goodwill of the established church, not reflect the naive faith of colonials in the "mother country?" While these concerns are subordinated to the song's message of free choice and refusal of ethnic essentialism, questions of assimilation and identity nevertheless lie not very deep below the surface of Lord Beginner's song.

Unlike Lord Beginner's work, Selvon's *The Lonely Londoners* contains not one example of an interracial couple able to overcome the barriers introduced by the combination of gender power and racial hierarchy. For Selvon, discourses of difference apparently seemed insuperable during the 1950s. Even Galahad, whose name connotes sexual purity, describes his encounter with a white girlfriend using the violent, dominating metaphor of a "battle royal" (93). The equation of domination and sexuality is most evident, however, not in relation to white women such as Galahad's girlfriend but in relation to black women. If white women offer an ambivalently regarded avenue to assimilation or revenge on British society for its racial discrimination, black women's sexuality is openly perceived as a threat in Selvon's text. Not only can black women potentially cuckold their partners, but their sexual agency can also rupture the binary oppositions that are integral to racial antagonism and the exclusionary dynamics of ethnic solidarity.[51] Although very few black women are represented in Selvon's novel, when they do appear, their sexuality is a pivotal issue and is closely policed. The novel thus demonstrates the extent to which incipient black male nationalism reproduces the violent gestures of white supremacist patriarchy.

The ballad of Lewis is crucial in this regard. Rather than simply acting as narrator for this ballad, Moses takes an active hand by persuading his gullible friend Lewis that women in London habitually engage in adulterous trysts while their husbands are at work (68). Lewis responds by going home and beating up his wife, Agnes. Each time Moses equates the cosmopolitan life of the metropolis with women's sexual infidelity, Lewis resorts to unprovoked domestic violence. When Lewis eventually asks Moses whether he's doing the right thing, Moses replies that he never claimed that Agnes was herself engaging in this kind of behavior. "Women in this country are not like Jamaica, you know," Moses announces, "they have rights over here, and they always shouting for something" (69). Moses thus seems to spur Lewis to gratuitous violence solely in order to gull his friend, perhaps teaching him not to be so trusting, and consequently passive and effeminate, in the future. Yet this ugly incident of masculine assertion allows Selvon to demonstrate women's solidarity in the face of domestic violence. Tolroy's aunt, Tanty, who appears to be completely naive during the Waterloo Station scene at the beginning of the novel, intervenes repeatedly on behalf of Agnes, offering her shelter after she's been attacked by Lewis, encouraging her to leave him after his unwarranted beatings, and ultimately advising her to bring him up on charges of assault. As far as she is concerned, Tanty says, legal action is the only measure that will make Lewis stop his abusive behavior (72). Tanty's advise to Agnes is particularly significant since black women in Britain have often been told to keep quiet about their personal affairs and accept domestic violence in the name of family and community unity in a racist milieu. By using the British legal system against such abuse, Tanty suggests that challenging patriarchal violence, rather than undermining solidarity, is an integral aspect of defending the black community.[52]

CONCLUSION

The Notting Hill riots of 1958 offer a now nearly forgotten flash point that illuminates the birth of modern British racism. During the ten years that preceded the riots, colonial discourses of racial difference had been redeployed and fine-tuned in the metropolis, establishing the foundation for manifestations of British racism to this day.[53] In his account of the riots in *Absolute Beginners,* Colin MacInnes creates a fictional editorial that typifies this redeployment of racist discourse. Although the editorial, written by a toffee-nosed journalist who snubs the working-class narrator earlier in the novel, begins with complaints against black immigrants who scrounge off National Assistance, it clinches its case through an argument that highlights the centrality of sexuality to racial discourse:

> Then there was the question of women (Old Amberly certainly went to town on this woman question!) To begin with, he said, mixed marriages—as responsible coloured persons would be the very first to agree themselves—were most undesirable. They led to a mongrel race, inferior physically and mentally, and rejected by both of the unadulterated communities. . . . The well-known propensity and predilection of coloured males for securing intimate relations with white women—unfortunately, by now, a generally observed phenomenon in countries where the opportunities existed—led to serious friction between the immigrants and the men of stock so coveted, whose natural—and, he would add—sound and proper instinct, was to protect their women-folk from this contamination, even if this led to violence which, in normal circumstances, all would find most regrettable. But this was not all: it was time for plain speaking, and this had to be said. The record of the courts had shown—let alone the personal observations of any attentive and anxious observer—that living off the immoral earnings of white prostitutes, had now become all too prevalent among the immigrant community.[54]

Written in response to rioting in Nottingham, Amberly Drove's editorial is clearly part of a groundswell of racism that led one week later to the Notting Hill riots in London. The key ingredient of such racial discourses was the representation of black men as an internal threat whose sexual liaisons with white women promised to make Britain a mongrelized nation. Black men were not simply reduced to the realm of the physical but were explicitly associated with contamination. By suggesting that black men are not simply responsible for miscegenation but also for the pimping out of white women, Drove's editorial adapts paradigmatically colonial discourses concerning racial purity to a urban, working-class, metropolitan context. Two years prior to the Notting Hill riots, the Suez Crisis had signaled the definitive deflation of Britain's pretense to postwar imperial stature by the new global hegemon, the United States. When the riots tore apart the working-class zones of West London, the colonial chickens finally came home to roost in Britain.

The riots had a galvanizing impact on Britain's black community. The vague sense of futility and despondency with which Selvon closes *The Lonely Londoners* was transformed by crowds of marauding white youths. During the riots, informal neighborhood groups such as the clutch of men who gather to "coast lime" in Moses' basement were galvanized to form self-defense organizations. The turning point in the riots occurred when a group of West Indian men and women, organized by Frances Ezzrecco, Michael de Freitas, and Frank Critchlow, burst out of a building under siege wielding improvised weapons such as knives and Molotov cocktails and chased off the marauding white crowd. This counterattack, which took place on the fourth day of rioting, finally pushed the police to take a more active role in suppressing the lynch mobs that had previously roamed the neighborhood virtually unmolested.[55]

In addition to challenging the tacit acquiescence of the police, the successful self-defense effort led by Ezzrecco, de Freitas, and Critchlow underlined the need for new forms of autonomous organizing within the black community. In his account of the riots, George Lamming states: "The West Indian, until then, had an implicit faith in the Law, and some ancient certainty that the police would be on his side. Where the Law was concerned, the West Indian was colour blind. . . . I recall a feeling of utter stupefaction; for I had argued in America—a year before—that it was difficult to draw parallels in spite of prejudice, for Georgia or Alabama just could not happen anywhere in England."[56] The naive trust in the justice of British law that the Caribbean community harbored was shattered by the riots of 1958. This led to a renaissance of political organizing after the hiatus following the departure of anticolonial activists such as C. L. R. James and George Padmore after World War II. Frances Ezzrecco and Michael de Freitas formed the Coloured People's Progressive Association and went on to be two of the most important exponents of black nationalism in Britain during the 1960s. Claudia Jones, the Caribbean-born radical who arrived in Britain after being deported from the United States for her activities on behalf of the Communist Party, used the recently founded monthly *West Indian Gazette* as a mouthpiece for these organizations. Faced with the failure of Britain's liberal establishment to condemn and defend them from racism, black communities began questioning their allegiance to the "mother country." Their faith in British justice sorely tried by the conduct of the police, magistrates, and government during the Notting Hill riots, black activists and intellectuals turned away from the project of assimilation and began the search for forms of commonality that came to be known as Black Power.[57] Self-defense and pride in black culture were thus intimately connected. The Notting Hill carnival, founded by Claudia Jones in the months following the riots of 1958, exemplifies this blend of autonomous cultural and political organizing.

The Lonely Londoners is an important document of immigrant life in Britain prior to the galvanizing events of 1958. Selvon's novel contains an exhaustive catalog of the forms of discrimination endured by Caribbean migrants as they sought housing and employment in Britain. Perhaps more significantly, however, *The Lonely Londoners* also documents the impact of racist discourse on migrants' attitudes toward the "mother country." Arriving in Britain filled with illusions about gaining access to metropolitan capital and culture, migrants quickly found that discourses of colonial difference had not disappeared, as the rhetoric of British "fair play" suggested they would. This process of disillusionment was nowhere more apparent than in the charged arena of sexual relations. *The Lonely Londoners* suggests that success in the metropolis was signified for many of the predominantly male migrants during the first decade of mass immigration from the Caribbean to Britain by sexual conquest. Drawing brilliantly on the calypso tradition, Selvon's novel sets out a series of ballads that depict the picaresque adventures of "the boys" as they attempt to conquer white womanhood. Although the novel does not offer a substantial account of working-class white women's subjectivity, it does document the travails of their black male lovers. For the men Selvon depicts, sexual conquest was the paradigmatic way of asserting their masculinity in the face of the myriad forms of humiliation and alienation meted out by racist discourses and institutions in Britain. Moreover, accounts of their sexual adventures with white women were an important vehicle for male bonding. Moses' narrative is, in fact, an extended example of the kinds of calypso-influenced ballads exchanged among "the boys," who meet in his basement and attempt to stave off the chill of London's weather and social conditions through amusing stories.

Like many calypso singers, most of Selvon's male characters approach sexual relations as a form of anticolonial struggle. Cap, Galahad, and Moses thus see white women as symbolic embodiments of dominant European culture. By gaining mastery over white women, Selvon's characters strive to overcome the forms of racist denigration they experience in everyday life in the metropolis. These conquests are necessarily marked by ambivalence and anxiety. By choosing the terrain of sexuality on which to assert themselves, the characters of *The Lonely Londoners* often fall victim to the very objectifying and emasculating discourses that they seek to invert. In addition, all too often their sexual adventures reproduce hegemonic patriarchal masculinity. The implications of this ultimately misogynistic strategy become most clear when the binary relations of black men and white women are interrupted through the presence of black women. Although Selvon's novel is a profoundly androcentric text, it does gesture toward the destructive impact of patriarchal violence within the black community. As a result, while documenting forms of alienation that characterize the period before the advent of Black Power, *The Lonely Londoners* also suggests the importance of challenging hegemonic gender roles within the nascent autonomous black public sphere.

Black Power in a Transnational Frame

Radical Populism and the Caribbean Artists Movement

AFTER TAKING THE STAGE AT THE ROUND HOUSE IN NORTH LONDON, Stokely Carmichael (aka Kwame Ture) asked the audience to rise and remain silent for a moment in memory of John Coltrane, who had died the previous day.[1] Into the silence created by this commemoration of the great jazz musician and "cultural warrior," Carmichael proceeded to pour words more combustible than gasoline. The "Congress on the Dialectics of Liberation" whose stage he occupied had, according to the Trinidad-born leader of the Student Nonviolent Coordinating Committee (SNCC), little relevance either for black struggle in the United States or for the oppressed masses around the world with which the movement identified. How could a conference organized around the notion of *individual* alienation, Carmichael asked, shed any light on the circumstances of black people, who are exploited and despised *as a class*?[2] Convened in July 1967 by a group of radical psychiatrists that included R. D. Laing, the "Congress on the Dialectics of Liberation" aimed to link "the internalized violence said to be characteristic of psychotic mental illness with the mentality which fuelled the US war in Vietnam."[3] The congress, in other words, was intended to extend the New Left's exploration of the cultural components of hegemony in late capitalism, and featured, among others, Frankfurt School luminary Herbert Marcuse discoursing on the manufacturing of ersatz needs in the consumer society.[4] By reducing oppression to a purely psychological level, however, the congress organizers unwittingly directed attention away from the institutional character of racial inequality and imperialism. Carmichael, one of the only black people invited to attend the congress, offered a blunt reminder of the parochial character of the British Left at a time when, with the Vietnam War heating up and the U.S. ghettos on fire, questions of international solidarity should have been paramount.[5]

For the members of Britain's black community in attendance at the congress, Carmichael's words were electrifying. Barbadian-born poet and historian Edward Kamau Brathwaite later wrote that the speech was one of the most important moments of the decade. For Brathwaite, Carmichael's words "magnetized a whole set of splintered feelings that had for a long time been seeking a node."[6] Carmichael's speech, that is, transformed the isolation experienced by intellectuals such as Brathwaite by limning the material and cultural connections between members of the black diaspora and the colonized peoples of the Third World. According to Brathwaite, Carmichael "enunciated a way of seeing the Black West Indian that seemed to many to make sense of the entire history of slavery and colonial suppression, of the African diaspora in the New World."[7] Like previous Pan-Africanist activists, Stokely Carmichael offered his audience a transnational perspective that transformed them from an isolated and outnumbered national minority to an integral part of a militant global majority. For Brathwaite, this unifying perspective meant not only that "a Black international was possible," but also that "links of sympathy . . . were set up between laboring immigrant, artist/intellectual, and student."[8] Black Power thus overcame the alienation of displaced West Indian writers such as Brathwaite by simultaneously reviving a heritage of transnational solidarity and by grounding intellectuals in the rich cultural traditions of communities throughout the black diaspora.[9]

The resonance of Stokely Carmichael's black nationalism suggests that a transatlantic *convergence* of diasporic politics and culture took place during the late 1960s.[10] Elective affinities that developed between diasporic communities during this period, however, were significantly different from the idealist return to African roots that characterized previous waves of Pan-African mobilization.[11] While these affinities were elicited by a common experience of racial slavery and capitalism that linked the continents abutting the black Atlantic, there were specific historical and material conditions that stimulated black nationalism's transatlantic resonance during this period. The Black Power movement has commonly been represented as arising in the United States during the late 1960s with a revolt against the implicit self-abnegation that oriented the integrationist leadership of the civil rights movement.[12] Militant leaders such as Carmichael and, most famously, Malcolm X, refused to surrender their own cultural traditions in order to gain admission to the stratified class society of the U.S. mainstream. Instead, they insisted on their prerogative to power on their own terms. This demand was truly threatening, for it promised to transform U.S. culture on a fundamental level, as the integrationist tenets of the civil rights movement never had.

In Britain, by contrast, there was no significant national civil rights movement by the late 1960s.[13] In addition, while Britain lacked the tradition of pervasive racial terror that characterized the United States, during the course of imperial expansion it had developed a potent pedagogical apparatus in the colonies that emphasized the benefits of cultural assimilation for the colonized.[14] When members of the Commonwealth nations migrated to Britain, however, they quickly found that the notions of British fair play they'd absorbed from the colonial education apparatus were pure fiction. In addition to experiencing institutional racism in housing, employment, and education, black immigrants also witnessed the passage of a series of patently racist immigration laws in the course of the 1960s that dramatically undermined the mythical notion of universal British subjecthood. In one watershed decade, Britain thus moved from putatively accepting postcolonial immigrants with open arms to codifying explicitly biased laws designed to exclude all nonwhite British citizens from residence in the "motherland."

Shorn of their illusions by dint of bitter experience in the postimperial metropolis, black Britons were primed for Stokely Carmichael's militant insistence on self-definition and transnational black solidarity. Yet Carmichael's message of black autonomy was contradicted, to a certain extent, by the "telescope effect," which led many black Britons to look to the antiracist movement in the United States as a vanguard.[15] The role of the U.S. struggle as a model is made particularly apparent by the strong impact of visits to Britain by American leaders such as Dr.

Martin Luther King Jr., Malcolm X, and Carmichael, each of whom stimulated significant institutional and ideological transformation in the movement for racial equality in Britain. If, as Carmichael emphasized, cultural autonomy was key to political self-reliance, surely this ideal should militate against dependence on other black nationalisms as much as it applied to mimicry of white culture. In fact, the cultural traditions of black Britons differed significantly from those of African-Americans, despite the common matrix of racial oppression out of which cultures of solidarity sprang in the Black Power era. As a result, the political culture of Black Power was articulated along parallel but significantly different lines in Britain and the United States.[16] To put it another way, while important transatlantic convergences took place under the aegis of Black Power during the late 1960s and early 1970s, these forms of solidarity were not simply examples of cultural and political mimicry, but rather instances of what Edward Kamau Brathwaite at the time called *inter/culturation*—"unplanned, unstructured but osmotic relations" that transformed the putatively authentic and autonomous signs of transnational black cultural solidarity based on local needs and cultures.[17]

Stokely Carmichael's visit to Britain provides a clear example of such local appropriation of Black Power discourse. Although the absence of a significant British civil rights movement helped generate radical, nonintegrationist sentiment at the grass roots, the specific character of Britain's "colonization in reverse" after 1948 shaped the character of this militancy, as Carmichael was to find out. Before delivering his speech at the congress, Carmichael was introduced to Michael Abdul Malik, a fellow Trinidadian and founder of the Racial Adjustment Action Society (RAAS), Britain's first Black Power organization. Abdul Malik, popularly known as Michael X since becoming a confidant of Malcolm X during the latter's visit to Britain in 1965, was, like his mentor, an ex-hustler and consequently knew the British ghettos intimately.[18] As Michael X escorted him around impoverished black communities, Carmichael was surprised to find that British Asians were just as galvanized by the Black Power movement as members of the African diaspora. Increasingly subject to violent attacks by members of the neofascist National Front, second-generation Asian youths, Michael X explained, were highly receptive to the Black Power message of self-defense. The recent visit of Muhammad Ali, who had heroically refused to enlist for service in Vietnam, had made a particularly strong impression on Pakistani youths, according to Carmichael: "Here comes the heavyweight champion of all the world, Black, sassy, and lo and behold, a Muslim, like them, and royally kicking white butt all over the place."[19]

Britain's Black Power movement, then, although seemingly riding the coattails of developments in the United States, had a far more cross-cultural character at the grass roots than did its American counterpart. As Michael X explained to Stokely Carmichael, British racism was at no pains to distinguish between different immigrant groups, and, consequently, antiracism was developing along lines of multicultural solidarity rather than reactive ethnic specificity, as it tended to do in the United States.[20] In addition, since Britain's immigrant population was separated by no more than one generation from the experience of colonial domination, the anticolonial rhetoric that was such an integral aspect of Black Power's model of convergence had particular relevance in Britain. Indeed, struggles for independence, federation, and Black Power in the West Indies and elsewhere had an impact on the black community in Britain analogous to that of the Vietnam War in the United States. Of course, Britain's nonwhite population was numerically much smaller than that of the United States, and the convulsions caused in the body politic by antiracist mobilization were correspondingly less intense.[21] Yet, despite its limitations, the Black Power movement in Britain offers a particularly powerful instance of diasporic internationalism as a result of the black community's relatively direct connections to antiracist and anticolonial movements in the United States, the Caribbean, Africa, and Asia.

Stokely Carmichael tapped these specifically black British reservoirs of anti-imperial sentiment during his blistering speech at the "Congress on the Dialectics of Liberation." Drawing on his youth in Trinidad, Carmichael recounted his experience of being forced to recite Rudyard Kipling's "The White Man's Burden" in school. His main memory of this experience, Carmichael explained to his audience, was wishing that the white man would simply leave him the hell alone.[22] If, as this anecdote suggests, the struggle for cultural integrity was a primary component of the Black Power movement, the lineaments of that autonomous culture were shaped by the particular processes of interculturation that took place in specific nodes of the black Atlantic. In the Caribbean, power relations were determined not so much by the Manichaean conflict between white and black (as they were in the United States) as by what Brathwaite called the *creole continuum* generated by a far more multiracial society, in which racial mixing was the norm rather than the exception.[23] Black nationalism in the Caribbean consequently pivoted less on notions of racial authenticity than on the tense relations between a metropolitan-identified neocolonial elite and the non-European culture of the subaltern masses.[24] This meant that the Pan-African theories that emerged from the Caribbean placed particular weight on recuperating the autonomous cultures of the region's popular classes rather than on simply opposing white hegemony.[25]

If Stokely Carmichael's "Dialectics of Liberation" speech, for which he was declared persona non grata by Britain's supposedly socialist Labour government, offered a galvanizing political perspective on the black diaspora, Edward Kamau Brathwaite's public reading of his epic poem *Rights of Passage* three months earlier had a similarly dramatic impact on an aesthetic plane.[26] Like Carmichael, Brathwaite articulated a vision of black suffering and struggle that linked three continents. Brathwaite innovated not simply in terms of his thematic focus on the black diaspora in the Caribbean, the United States, and Britain, but also by using the vernacular speech forms of the black masses that he called *nation language*. Black political internationalism thus not only shaped artistic expression but was given concrete form through aesthetic experimentation such as Brathwaite's. While his work therefore shares much with antecedent and contemporary movements such as negritude and Black Arts, *Rights of Passage* is distinguished by its emphasis on distinctively Caribbean processes of interculturation. Spawned by his extensive research into the history of creole culture in the Caribbean as well as his experience living on the three continents that surround the black Atlantic, Brathwaite's aesthetic of interculturation not only escaped the ethnic essentialism that often characterized aesthetic work affiliated with black nationalism during the late 1960s, but also resonated particularly strongly with the cross-cultural character of Black Power in Britain. Grounded in the stratified creole societies of the Caribbean, Brathwaite's aesthetic is particularly suggestive today, when the successes of antiracist and anticolonialist movements of the 1960s have led many to believe that we are "beyond race" even while racially based disparities are intensifying both between the North and the South and within the overdeveloped nations.[27]

CONVERGENCE AND AUTONOMY IN
BLACK POWER DISCOURSE

Five years before Stokely Carmichael addressed the "Dialectics of Liberation" conference, the political project of a federated West Indies collapsed. Set up by Britain in 1958 as a way of placating regional movements for independence, the West Indies Federation splintered in 1962 when the premier of Jamaica, Norman Manley, organized a referendum on secession. Passage of this referendum led to full independence for Jamaica; other relatively strong Caribbean nations such as Trinidad and Tobago followed quickly in Jamaica's wake. Although this declaration of independence from Britain was significant, the death of the federation was, as the black British *West Indian Gazette* opined at the time, a retrograde step in hopes for political solidarity against the colonial powers.[28] As nations in Africa and the Caribbean gained their independence in the 1960s, the long-standing dream of Pan-African unity foundered on the shoals of uneven economic development and fissiparous regional politics. What grounds, then, did Black Power leaders such as Stokely Carmichael have for invoking notions of transnational black solidarity? Didn't anticolonial nationalism around the world tend to undermine such claims to transnational unity? Was there any substance to the model of a convergence of interests between oppressed people in the metropolitan core and the peripheral colonized nations?[29]

In his speech at the "Dialectics of Liberation" Congress, Stokely Carmichael focused not so much on the political vagaries of Pan-Africanism in Africa and elsewhere, as on analysis of the institutional forces that structured the lives of blacks living in the urban zones of the United States and Britain. It was in the forms of political, economic, and cultural dependency and disenfranchisement that characterized the ghettos in developed nations that Carmichael found a correspondence with colonial conditions around the world:

> Now in the United States—and England isn't far behind—it is estimated that in another five to ten years, two-thirds of the twenty million Black people who inhabit the United States will be living in the ghettos in the heart of the cities. Joining us are going to be hundreds of thousands of Puerto Ricans, Mexican-Americans, and American Indians. The American city, in essence, is going to be

populated by peoples of the Third World, while the white middle classes will flee to the suburbs. Now the Black people do not control, nor do we own, the resources—we do not control the land, the houses, or the stores. These are all owned by whites who live outside the community. These are very real colonies, in the sense that they are capital and cheap labor exploited by those who live outside the cities.[30]

At a moment when many white liberals were bemoaning the eclipse of nonviolent leaders in the civil rights movement, Carmichael reminds his listeners of the structural violence that produced racially polarized cities throughout the United States during the twentieth century.[31] Like the apartheid system in South Africa, white supremacy in the United States and, he implies, the UK, effectively prevented the free movement of people of color in order to further the extraction of labor from this racialized industrial reserve army.[32] Carmichael makes this analogy with South African apartheid explicit in *Black Power,* published the same year as his address at the "Dialectics of Liberation."[33] South Africa is a particularly important point of comparison because, like other white settler colonies such as Australia and the United States, colonizer and colonized live in close geographical proximity. Of course, the correspondence between the United States and apartheid South Africa was not perfect. Carmichael admits that the decentralized, informal apartheid of the American system was significantly different from South Africa's formal policies of apartheid, but this fact, he argues, renders conditions in the United States even more alarming since it underlines the organic continuities in white supremacy across the different geographical and political spaces of America.

Carmichael's description of U.S. ghettos as internal colonies had a strong theoretical precedent, one that had, however, lain dormant for at least a generation as a result of the anti-Communist purges of the McCarthy era.[34] Carmichael's theory of convergence harked back to analyses of imperialism developed by the global Communist movement during the interwar decades. During the Sixth World Congress of the Comintern in 1928, for example, a resolution was passed asserting that African-Americans in the southern states of the United States and Africans in South Africa constituted oppressed nations rather than racial minorities or majorities without power. As oppressed nations, American and South African blacks possessed an inherent right to self-determination. The Comintern's position on black autonomy was the product of a series of debates earlier in the decade between Lenin and Indian Communist M. N. Roy.[35] For black revolutionaries such as George Padmore, the "black republic" scheme that resulted was a botched attempt to capture the remnants of the Garveyite movement in the United States.[36] Yet, despite the impracticalities of the "black republic" policy, in adopting Lenin's theses on black autonomy, the Comintern committed itself to supporting anticolonial and antiracist movements around the world during the late 1920s and 1930s. Perhaps equally importantly, it also lent the Communist Party's ideological validation to traditions of independent black revolutionary struggle *both* in developed nations such as the United States and throughout the colonial world. Blacks were seen as a vanguard whose struggles in the belly of the capitalist beast would awaken the rest of the proletariat and forge links with unfolding anticolonial struggles in Africa, Asia, and the Caribbean.[37] As C. L. R. James argued in an address on Black Power delivered in August 1967, it was this tradition of connection between independent black struggles around the world that Stokely Carmichael and predecessors such as Malcolm X had revived.[38]

James was particularly impressed to find that the Black Power struggles of the late 1960s adopted an inherently anticapitalist character. In *Black Power,* Carmichael argued that it is in the "objective relationship" between races rather than "rhetoric (such as constitutions *articulating* equal rights) or geography" that colonial relations could be discerned.[39] In pointing to the gap between the constitutional rhetoric of equal rights and entrenched material forms of racial inequality in the United States, Carmichael challenged an emerging normative narrative of the civil rights movement that emphasized a march toward racial progress.[40] In order to challenge the liberal outlook of some civil rights leaders, in other words, Carmichael adopted a historical materialist perspective that saw black oppression as a product of the inherently racial character of capitalism in the United States and elsewhere; as he put it during the "Dialectics of Liberation" conference, "A capitalist system automatically includes racism, whether by design or not."[41] The American ghetto for Carmichael thus highlighted the limits of the "fictitious universalism" of the liberal-democratic nation-state and of antisystemic movements that adopted this entity as their horizon of possibility.[42] While proclaiming itself a vehicle for universal equality, the liberal-democratic nation-state has been structured by and continues to perpetuate forms of racial differentiation. The framework of black consciousness should not, then, be the liberal constitutional order of the United States but rather structures of racial oppression and resistance that operate on the transnational plane of historical capitalism.

Far from being undermined by black unrest in urban areas, the concessions granted to integrationist civil rights leaders, according to Carmichael, were superficial and would not transform the institutional racism that was responsible for urban uprisings. These concessions to middle-class leaders were analogous, Carmichael argued, with the indirect rule policies deployed by Britain and other colonial powers in order to decapitate resistance to foreign rule through the creation of a stratum of pliable indigenous leaders.[43] Leaders who capitulated to such co-optation, Carmichael argued bluntly, betrayed the black masses, whose lives would not be transformed by the granting of hollow civil rights and economic perquisites to a privileged elite. Carmichael's approach to the urban unrest of the late 1960s sought, in other words, to emphasize the extent to which these uprisings reflected class divisions *within* black communities as much as broader anger with the lack of social transformation in the wake of civil rights agitation.

In addition, in his "Dialectics of Liberation" address, Carmichael suggested that historical precedent underlined the unwillingness of the ruling classes to engage in significant internal reform. Thus, when challenged by the labor movement earlier in the century, the United States and other capitalist powers sought to bribe the white working class using the surplus created by imperial pillage rather than investing surplus in domestic reforms: "United States capitalists never cut down on their domestic profits to share with the workers—instead, they expanded internationally, and threw the crumbs from their profits to the American working class, who lapped them up. The American working class enjoys the fruits of the labors of the Third World workers. The proletariat has become the Third World, and the bourgeoisie is white Western society."[44] By generating surplus capital and jingoistic rhetoric, imperial expansion had effectively blunted the radical thrust of the white working class.[45] The internal colonies of the United States performed a similar economic and ideological function of binding together a cross-class white supremacist coalition. Yet if the class compromise that headed off revolutionary politics in liberal-democratic capitalist nations was built on the backs of internal and external colonies, the post-1945 era had witnessed large-scale rebellion by the oppressed at both poles of this exploitative world system: the Third World and the ghettos of the advanced capitalist countries. The antiracist struggle in the United States was therefore integrally related to revolutionary anti-colonial struggles in the Third World.

For Carmichael, the ghettos were particularly strategic sites due to their proximity to the vital functions of the capitalist core:

> The struggle to free these internal colonies relates to the struggles of imperialism around the world. We realistically survey our numbers, and know that it is not possible for Black people to take over the whole of the United States militarily, and hold large areas of land; in a highly industrialized nation, the struggle is different. The heart of production, and the heart of commercial trade, is in the cities. We are in the cities. We can become, and are becoming, a disruptive force in the flow of services, goods, and capital. While we disrupt internally and aim for the eye of the octopus, we are hoping that our brothers are disrupting externally to sever the tentacles of the United States.[46]

Carmichael's assessment of the violent upheavals in cities such as Birmingham in 1963, New York in 1964, and Los Angeles in 1965 revived the Communist Party's "black republic" thesis, situating black efforts to assert self-control not in the so-called Black Belt region of the southern states as they had been during the 1930s but in the ghettos of urban America.[47] His analysis of the American ghetto as an internal colony anticipates the high-profile struggles of groups such as the Black Panthers to organize the black "lumpen-proletariat" and to establish traditions of autonomy among the urban black masses. The violent response of the state to such efforts, evident in the use of national guardsmen to quell urban riots and the COINTELPRO targeting of the Black Panthers, lent dramatic support to Carmichael's perception of a correspondence between external and internal colonies.[48]

In hindsight, Carmichael's hopes for this revolutionary alignment against the "octopus" of imperialism seem tragically utopian. First of all, he and other radical activists of the era seriously underestimated the full power of state repression that would be leveled against those seeking to strike the eye of this octopus. In addition, over the next decade, a significant political realignment took place in which what Stuart Hall called "popular authoritarianism" would come to form the core of a new, radically conservative hegemonic project in the United States and Britain.[49] As the axis of state power tipped increasingly toward explicit repression of dissenting elements of the population, so resources once devoted to securing consent would be progressively scaled back. Less than half a decade after Carmichael's speech, cities with substantial black populations like New York would pioneer neoliberal strategies such as the privileging of markets and the reorientation of government finance away from public services.[50] In Britain, a parallel process unfolded when the Thatcher regime cut off funding for radical local authorities such as the Greater London Council during the 1980s. Parallel with the dismantling of the Keynesian welfare state, the outsourcing of industrial production to offshore factories helped create a new international division of labor. These novel, intertwined strategies of capital accumulation and social regulation effectively obliterated the revolutionary energies and alignments hailed by Carmichael. Rather than occupying an empowering location in ghettos as he and others imagined they would, blacks in the United States and Britain were subjected over the following decades to further rounds of spatial apartheid whose most brutal realization is in America's prison-industrial complex.[51] The denizens of U.S. ghettos were rendered a form of surplus humanity, whose primary social utility lies in legitimating ever-intensifying levels of racially coded backlash. These tremendous setbacks have, however, further underlined the urgency of internationalist approaches to black liberation.

REPRESENTING THE CREOLE CONTINUUM

During the Black Power era, perhaps the crucial question for cultural activists of West Indian background in Britain was the issue of what Orlando Patterson called "an absence of ruins": the apparent lack of precolonial traditions that might legitimate viable independent political and cultural movements in the Caribbean.[52] Like Carmichael, in other words, cultural activists of the day were intent on elaborating international linkages that would help leverage otherwise isolated liberation movements. Patterson's perspective catalyzed heated debate among the members of the British-based Caribbean Artists Movement, many of whom saw his arguments as disempowering.[53] For a writer such as Edward Kamau Brathwaite, Patterson and previous writers such as

George Lamming and V. S. Naipaul had anatomized the fragmented, alienated condition of Caribbean modernity.[54] The task was to find ways to transcend and heal this condition.[55] This ambitious work of healing would, however, require a detailed investigation of the Creole societies of the Caribbean. In working out his theories of intercultura-tion, Brathwaite was also developing important models of collective identity and agency for contemporary black Britons.

If the project of Caribbean modernist writers was to make what Simon Gikandi terms a "forced entry" into history, Edward Kamau Brathwaite's work has been particularly informed by historical and ethnographic counterdiscourse.[56] Brathwaite's work demonstrates that historiography and anthropology could be appropriated and used against the very colonial discourses that they had traditionally helped legitimate. More specifically, anthropological discourse furnished a means to challenge the linear, progressive European account of Caribbean history by focusing on the disjunctive and multiple temporal frames that characterize postcolonial Caribbean culture. In other words, while anthropological discourse denied coevalness to the colonized Other, this very temporal alterity allowed writers such as Brathwaite to introduce dissident cultural voices that exploded the putatively unified time-space continuum of the nation.[57] Like Latin American writers such as Alejo Carpentier, José María Arguedas, and Miguel Angel Asturias, Brathwaite drew on ethnographic research to engage with and reanimate the indigenous and non-Western cultural practices suppressed in the course of colonial conquest and domination. In the case of traditions such as negritude, celebration of the indigenous Other's resilient traditions as an alternative to the corrupt and empty culture of Western modernity tended to perpetuate binary oppositions between the European Self and indigenous Other.[58] For a writer such as Brathwaite, however, this sort of primitivist embrace of alterity was impossible. In his historiographic work, Brathwaite was forced to con-front head-on the "absence of ruins" postulated by Orlando Patterson and other Caribbean writers such as V. S. Naipaul.

Brathwaite approached this problem of Caribbean modernity using a vocabulary drawn from the pioneering ethnographic research of scholars like Melville Herskovitz and Jean Price-Mars, who, Brathwaite argued, had exploded the "myth of the Negro (non) past."[59] For Brath-waite, the notion of the Middle Passage as a traumatic, total break was the product of a typically Eurocentric cultural perspective. Writing of the folk culture of Jamaican slaves, Brathwaite sought to explain the apparent lack of cultural tradition in the Caribbean through a discussion of the unique signifying practices of African religious culture:

> The significant feature of African religious culture was that it was (is) *immanent:* carried within the individual/community, not (as in Europe) existentially externalized in buildings, monuments, books. So that in a sense, African societies *did* appear to European observers to have "no culture," because there were no externally visible signs of a "civilization." That dance was African architecture, that history was not printed but recited, the contemporary Prospero could not understand. And yet it was the immanent nature of this culture that made its amazing and successful transfer from Africa to the New World/Caribbean, even under the extraordinary conditions of slavery[,] possible. The slave ship became a kind of psycho-physical space capsule, carrying intact the carriers of a kind of invisible/atomic culture.[60]

Brathwaite ingeniously suggests that it is the limited epistemological orientation of Eurocentric observers that explains theories of social death and mimicry such as those of Patterson and Naipaul.[61] Combined with the highly developed codes of cultural racism, this orientation killed off awareness of the living tradition of immanent culture that survived among the black masses in the Caribbean.[62] Like both James and Carmichael, in other words, Brathwaite is intent on attacking the cultural assimilation of colonial and postcolonial elites to Eurocentric values, suggesting that this internalization is an obstacle to the development of truly autochthonous cultural/political traditions. Yet while Brathwaite's analysis of what he dubs an African-derived "great tradition" is grounded in a model of colonially inflected class conflict within the Caribbean, he also acknowledges that European hegemony has forced this tradition underground for much of the region's history.[63] Submerged in order to survive, the immanent tradition has, according to Brathwaite, "suffered a slow but steady process of fragmentation and deformation."[64] Despite this fragmentation, this immanent tradition never completely disappears but rather wells up, Brathwaite suggests, like a subterranean spring during moments of particularly intense social conflict.

How can this "great tradition" survive the dominance of what

Brathwaite elsewhere calls "bastard metropolitanism" in the Caribbean? The answer lies in the fact that these two traditions cannot be seen as homogenous, monolithic opposites. In order to challenges ideas of the derivative character of Caribbean culture, Brathwaite developed a nuanced theory of creolization that undermines such Manichaean models of cultural difference. Central to Brathwaite's work is the repudiation of a totalizing synthesis of the composite traditions of the region.[65] For Brathwaite, creolization is characterized by two, intertwined processes: *ac/culturation,* or "the yoking (by force and example, deriving from power/prestige) of one culture to another," and *inter/culturation,* or the "unplanned, unstructured but osmotic relation proceeding from this yoke."[66] Brathwaite's model of creolization attempts to account for the hegemony of European cultural norms while also invoking the forms of reciprocal exchange between different ethnic groups that took place in the long history of modernity in the Caribbean. The result is not so much a model of cultural schizophrenia in which aesthetic and political movements oscillate between European and African traditions, as an "osmotic" process of cultural interpenetration in which each of these poles is itself transformed.[67] Emerging from his detailed analysis of Caribbean history, Brathwaite's model of creolization offered a pointed riposte to the nihilistic theories of Naipaul and Patterson. Thus, for Brathwaite, rather than simple mimicry, "Our real/apparent imitation involves at the same time a significant element of creativity, while our creativity involves a significant element of imitation."[68]

In addition to challenging notions of cultural mimicry, Brathwaite's osmotic model of creolization also had strong political implications. Although, as Frantz Fanon noted, binary forms of thought could be a galvanizing force for anticolonial nationalism, they were predicated on simplistic models of popular culture that offered little cognitive purchase on the heterogeneous composition of Caribbean cultures such as those of Jamaica and Trinidad.[69] For Brathwaite, *lateral creolization* between subaltern groups such as people of African and Asian ancestry was an important factor on such islands, one that became particularly prominent following decolonization.[70] While Brathwaite discusses traditions of creolization between ethnic groups such as the incorporation of people of African descent into the Asian Hosein festivities, he also points with great foresight to the intensification of ethnic conflict between such groups that characterizes the postcolonial scene in nations such as Guyana and Trinidad and Tobago. Brathwaite's analysis of creolization works against such exclusionary forms of ethnic identity by focusing on the osmotic character of cultural identities and on patterns of lateral as well as horizontal exchange.

Yet if the model of the creole continuum stresses mutability and fragility, Brathwaite seeks throughout his historical and poetic work to articulate the enduring character of the popular culture of the black diaspora. He therefore closes *Contradictory Omens* by arguing that the true cultural matrix of the Caribbean may be found not in the "bastard metropolitanism" of the elite but in the cultural traditions of the poor. Unlike many theorists of Black Power, however, Brathwaite's depiction of black popular culture is grounded in an understanding of the fluidity and dynamism of such cultural forms: "For the Caribbean, the basis of culture lies in the folk, by which we mean not in-culturated, static groups, giving little; but a people who, from the center of an oppressive system, have been able to survive, adapt, recreate. The unity is submarine."[71] Brathwaite's oceanic metaphor for black culture references the terrible suffering and loss of the Middle Passage. Yet if the Atlantic is literally the watery grave of myriad black lives, the ocean also offers a painful but potent reminder of the wonderfully mobile, adaptable character of black culture. Brathwaite returns frequently to this metaphor in his poetic corpus to render the dynamic connections that link the cultures of the black Atlantic.[72]

The Arrivants, the Caribbean's first epic poetic cycle, is a virtuoso evocation of the ties that bind the black diaspora across time and space.[73] Initially recited publicly in London on 3 March 1967 at the first of CAM's public readings, the opening section of the trilogy, *Rights of Passage,* traces an arc from loss and alienation to a revivifying reconnection to tradition and identity. The poem is divided into four sections, each of which is further subdivided into a number of long poems that together draw on a stunning variety of vernacular black cultural traditions and historical references. Beginning with a narrative re-creation of the westward migration of African peoples across the continent, *Rights of Passage* quickly picks up the theme of exile and the traumatic Middle Passage.[74] Written predominantly in Jamaica during the early to mid-1960s, the middle sections of Brathwaite's poem betray the impact of the generation of Caribbean writers who stressed black existential alienation. Yet while acknowledging and depicting these forms of cultural loss and crisis, Brathwaite offers a powerful riposte: the poem is itself a performative embodiment of precisely the historical and geographical webs of contact that the alienation thesis tended to negate.[75] Most significantly, *Rights of Passage,* as its title suggests, focuses on the tradition of migration that links diasporic communities in the Caribbean, the United States, and Britain. Through its verbal evocation of the historical and cultural convergences that weave together communities in urban nodes like Chicago, London, and Kingston, Brathwaite's epic conjures a black Atlantic imaginary into being in the teeth of historical suffering and loss.

The opening section of *Rights of Passage* focuses on the figure of Tom, an obvious reference to the integrationist Uncle Tom figures who were so reviled during the heyday of Black Power.[76] Yet Brathwaite's Tom is a complex character, one who embodies memories of African glory as well as the devastating loss and self-pity that followed the Middle Passage. Nonetheless, despite remembering the unification of the Ashanti peoples with pride, Tom is trapped in an empty present in which he has "created / nothing but these worthless / weeds" and who is only capable of uttering the paradigmatic words of utter servility: "Massa, yes / Boss, yes / Baas" (15). As well as offering an icon of subservience to white power that is represented as spanning centuries and continents, Tom also signifies the loss of intergenerational connection. "All God's Chillun" describes the mocking contempt with which Tom's children address him: crushed by poverty, his memories of Africa mean nothing to his sons. Educated in a white world and brimming with self-contempt, Tom's sons urge him to conform to racist stereotypes and play the "Black buttin' ram" of white racial fantasy that stretches from *Othello* to *Superfly* and beyond.[77] Tom's melancholy reaction to his sons' internalization of such caricatures emphasizes his feeling of utter powerlessness: "when release / from further journey? / Ease / up, Lord" (21).

Yet even in Tom's seeming admission of crushing defeat, Brathwaite embeds a form of affirmation. For central to the challenge sounded by *Rights of Passage* to the thesis of black "social death" is the poem's use of what Brathwaite termed *nation language,* the diverse forms of creolized English spoken throughout the black diaspora.[78] Brathwaite's epic poem was one of the first Caribbean works to break away from the use of Standard English and from the clockwork beat of iambic pentameter. In the place of these European forms, Brathwaite substitutes myriad diverse poetic forms, all of them interconnected, however, through their relation to black vernacular cultural forms.

While composing *Rights of Passage*, Brathwaite had been experimenting with poetic forms derived from the African American jazz tradition.[79] In his epic poem, Brathwaite expands his range of technical citation and adaptation, including, as previous references suggest, other African-American musical forms such as the blues and gospel. Thus, even while he invokes traditions of white appropriation of black culture in a poem such as "Folkways," Brathwaite reawakens the immanent cultural traditions of black America through virtuouso verbal performance: "I am a fuck- / in' negro, / man, hole / in my head / brains in / my belly" (30). Moreover, in addition to expanding his generic reach, Brathwaite also juxtaposes these African-American vernacular speech forms with examples of Caribbean nation language. The poem "Wings of a Dove," for instance, is written in a rhythm that mimics the heavy beats of reggae poetry and that adopts the Rastafarian lingo that radical Jamaican poets like Bongo Jerry and Linton Kwesi Johnson would use so effectively in the following decade. Grounded in Brathwaite's pathbreaking recuperation of nation language, the forms of creative diasporic stylistic appropriation and contamination of Standard English provide a concrete instance of creolization and give voice to the circuits of popular cultural exchange that link diasporic groups across geographic space.[80]

If these technical experiments instantiate the "subterranean unity" of the black diaspora, the theme of migration that permeates and structures *Rights of Passage* suggests further historical continuities. Black migration is, of course, a product of desperate attempts to escape the conditions of grinding poverty and exploitation meted out by structures of racial supremacy around the world. The resulting patterns of migration and urbanization link black populations in the Caribbean, the United States, Britain, and elsewhere. Brathwaite references these materials conditions as well as the significant social and artistic movements that emerged from black migrations around the world in poems such as "The Journeys" and "The Emigrants," the central poem in his epic's third section.[81] This latter poem embodies the kind of "magnetization" and unificatory vision that Brathwaite described Stokely Carmichael's speech effecting. The emigrants Brathwaite describes are driven by economic necessity into migrations that have little of the glamour associated with travel to exotic locations in a poem such as "The Journeys," with its sly references to Langston Hughes and the Harlem Renaissance. In contrast to the jazzed-up vision of the New Negro offered by the writers of the Harlem Renaissance, Brathwaite depicts a drab population with few aspirations and even fewer opportunities despite their ceaseless displacement. The poem's reference to these people as "Columbus coursing kaffirs" is laden with painful irony, since it implicitly suggests that diasporic migrants continue the colonial voyages of explorers such as Columbus while also referring to such migrants using the pejorative South African term for blacks. The implication is that dreams of wealth such as those Columbus harbored are illusions, particularly for a population whose movements continue to be controlled by structures of inequality equivalent to a form of global apartheid.

What would be the outcome of the aborted dreams of these migrants in search of their own Cathay? For Brathwaite, these restless journeys have created festering sores in the cities of the overdeveloped world. Brathwaite imagines urbanization creating a deprived mass poised to take radical action in the streets of cities around the world. Written in Rastafarian dialect, "Wings of the Dove" articulates the anger of the black masses against economic elites, no matter what their skin color, and looks forward to a fiery day of judgment in which the people will rise up and earthly injustice will be razed. Drawing on the dread rhythms of reggae, the voice of the Rastafarian prophet in this poem records the anger of the black masses living in ghettos such as Kingston's Trench Town. The warning Brathwaite issues is just as strong as that of activists such as Stokely Carmichael. Before the table of contents in *Black Power*, Carmichael and his cowriter, Charles Hamilton, offered a controversial prophecy that the conditions they were about to describe would lead to massive civil strife if the United States did not change course. In "Wings of the Dove," Brathwaite predicts a similar outcome, and thereby offers an indictment of the limited progress obtained during the era of civil rights and decolonization.

Yet to suggest that the fiery Rastafarian rhetoric of "Wings of the Dove" is Brathwaite's sole or even central response to the black condition would be to traduce the multivoiced quality of his epic. While he is anxious to record the righteous, revolutionary anger emerging from Rastafarianism and other militant Black Power groups, Brathwaite is equally intent on dramatizing the quotidian endurance that has helped members of the black diaspora survive four centuries of oppression. Thus, in "The Dust," Brathwaite captures the speech rhythms of poor women from the islands. The central narrative poem of *Rights of Passage*'s final section, "The Dust" centers on the exchange that takes place between a group of friends as they gather in a rural shop to make their purchases. Written in Caribbean nation language, the poem highlights the ancient herbal knowledge preserved by such women as well as the traditions of mutual aid through which the women keep their meager domestic economies afloat. Most importantly, however, "The Dust" highlights the women's attempts to survive in the face of often inexplicable and irresistible forces. The main speaker of the poem, Olive, attempts to explain a recent bout of illness on her island by recounting the tale of an eruption on a distant island of the archipelago that sends a cloud of volcanic ash into the atmosphere, blighting crops, swallowing up the sun's rays, and destroying the people's hope. Women such as Olive are the victims of what they see as the inscrutable gestures of a malevolent god. Although the other women remain skeptical about Olive's explanation for the "pestilence" that has afflicted them, Olive's narrative of woe demonstrates her ability to cope with everything, short, that is, of such apocalyptic natural events. Like the rest of this final section of the poem, "The Dust" offers a return to the Caribbean after the many journeys taken by the emigrants, signifying a reterritorialization for the exiled intellectual as well. Brathwaite grounds this return in popular cultural forms such as Olive and her friends' religious awareness. It is in such cultural resources that Brathwaite locates not only the inspiration for endurance in the face of adversity but also the creolized forms and practices that characterize Caribbean culture. In later books of *The Arrivants,* Brathwaite extends this analysis of black popular culture, turning to synchretic religious rituals of the Caribbean such as vodun, Santeria/*lucumi/shango/kele/etu, koromanti play/winti/kumfa,* nation dance, and *kumina,* as well as to the practices of more nominally Christian sects like Zion, Revival, Pukumina, Shouter, Shaker, and Spiritual Baptist. Within such quotidian sites, Brathwaite's epic cycle traces a genealogy of origins that leads from the Caribbean, across other nodes of the black diaspora in the United States and Britain, to Africa.[82] It is in *Rights of Passage,* however, that Brathwaite most powerfully articulates the migrations that link the black Atlantic. Brathwaite thereby offers a powerful aesthetic corollary to Black Power's most crucial argument: the convergence of urban black consciousness across a transnational space. Despite the extraordinary suffering and loss narrated in *Rights of Passage,* Brathwaite's epic poem creates a veritable chorus of voices whose collective utterances constitute a revived black diasporic imaginary.[83]

CONCLUSION

Despite many activists' feelings of being behind the curve, events in Britain during the 1960s foreshadowed the dystopian aspects of the civil rights movement. Unlike in the United States, where the civil rights movement seemed to be dismantling structures of juridical discrimination, in Britain both Tory and Labour governments repeatedly refused to pass antidiscrimination legislation in the 1960s. In addition, the Commonwealth Immigrants Act of 1962 effectively stripped blacks of their citizenship, torpedoing liberal hopes for integration such as those kindled in the United States during the civil rights era. Writing of the act in 1964, the Trinidad-born activist Claudia Jones argued that the implicit racial discrimination in the act effectively rendered nonwhite Commonwealth immigrants to Britain second-class citizens.[84] Rather than tending toward at least the illusion of racial reform, as the United States seemed to be under pressure from the civil rights movement, Britain was sliding toward neofascist policies of ethnic cleansing in the form of calls for the repatriation of black Britons by the late 1960s.[85] Claudia Jones's analysis of the Commonwealth Immigrants Act suggested that, far from being halting, incorporated into the liberal-democratic nation-state, blacks were essentially turned into scapegoats whose fear-inducing presence legitimated the dismantling of social democracy.[86]

Claudia Jones was well placed to assess this turn toward neofascism in Britain. A former head of the Young Communist League in New York and editor of the CPUSA's newspaper, the *Daily Worker*, Jones had lived through the worst years of the anti-Communist backlash in the United States during the Cold War. Her writings for radical organs following World War II stressed the link between European fascism and manifestations of white supremacy within the United States, making the argument that the U.S. claims to hegemony as a leader of the "free world" would only resonate with movements for decolonization if America succeeded in eradicating manifestations of domestic "Hitlerism" such as lynching.[87] For her efforts to eradicate racial terror, Jones was arrested and charged with seeking the violent overthrow of the U.S. government following the passage of the McCarran Act in 1948. During her hearing, however, Claudia Jones placed the U.S. government itself on trial, arguing, in a letter sent to the recently created United Nations, for an international investigation into the way in which

immigrants were being treated under the McCarran security laws.[88] Her
fate, Jones argued, was symptomatic of a broader struggle: "If we can be
denied all rights and incarcerated in concentration camps, then trade
unionists are next; then the Negro people, the Jewish people, all foreign-
born, and all progressives who love peace and cherish freedom will face
the bestiality and torment of fascism. Our fate is the fate of American
democracy."[89] Jones's letter to the UN suggests that, while she might
have invoked notions of U.S. global leadership predicated on the Truman Doctrine like other leaders of the period, she retained a strong
sense of internationalism in the face of Cold War isolationist sentiments.[90] The chain of affiliations she establishes in her letter to the UN
between antiracist activists and American democracy in general effectively highlights the danger represented by McCarthy-era purges, which
she quite explicitly compares to Nazism.

Notwithstanding her powerful self-defense, Jones was imprisoned
for several years and eventually deported to Britain in 1955. Once there,
she quickly became involved in radical politics of a decidedly internationalist ilk. In an interview given shortly after her arrival in Britain, for
example, she pointed out the domestic ramifications of U.S. militarism
and imperialism by saying, "I was deported . . . because I fought for
peace, against the huge arms budget which funds [sic] should be
directed to improving the social needs of the people."[91] She also cam-
paigned against apartheid, going on a hunger strike outside the South
African embassy in 1962 to protest the incarceration of Nelson Mandela.
In addition, Jones quickly immersed herself in the cultural life of
Britain's diasporic community. Following the Notting Hill riots of 1958,
she organized the first Caribbean Carnival to help revive the black community's spirits. Perhaps most important, however, was her founding
and editorship of the West Indian Gazette, the first truly community-
based publishing effort of the post-1948 era and the primary political
and cultural organ for black Britons from the late 1950s until Jones's
death in 1964. Jones used the pages of the West Indian Gazette not only
to keep the black community in Britain abreast of political developments in the Caribbean, Africa, and the United States, but also to challenge the turn of the British establishment toward increasingly explicit
forms of racism.

In the pages of the West Indian Gazette, for instance, Jones repeated
the warning given by Dr. Martin Luther King following his visit to
Britain in 1965. Challenging the Commonwealth Immigrants Act, King

argued that "as far as housing is restricted and ghettoes of a minority are allowed to develop, you are promoting a festering sore of bitterness and deprivation to pollute your national health."[92] Jones maintained in her article that the answer to the growth of ghettos in Britain was not, as many members of the political establishment held, the termination of immigration, but rather the banning of discrimination in housing and elsewhere. Despite such calls for institutional reform, Jones, unlike many of her compatriots, was not under any illusions about the beneficence of the British liberal tradition.[93] Instead, she argued that an elaborate ideological apparatus had been constructed to legitimate British imperialism, condemning the British working classes to an insular and racist outlook concerning their brothers and sisters in the colonies:

> All the resources of official propaganda and education, the super-structure of British imperialism, were permeated with projecting the oppressed colonial peoples as "lesser breeds," as "inferior coloured peoples," "natives," "savages," and the like—in short, "the white man's burden." These rationalizations served to build a justification for wholesale exploitation, extermination, and looting of the islands by British imperialism. . . . These artificial divisions and antagonisms between British and colonial workers, already costly in toll of generations of colonial wars and ever-recurrent crises, have delayed fundamental social change in Britain, and form the very basis of colour prejudice.[94]

Jones's sensitivity to the links between culture and imperialism was evident not only in such explicitly political passages as this one, but also in her editorship of the *West Indian Gazette,* which she used as a vehicle for inspiring black pride and autonomy. Crucial to this sense of self-esteem, Jones observed, was pride in the growth of national liberation movements in the colonial territories that many black Britons had until recently called home.[95] Britain's "Afro-Asian-Caribbean peoples," whom Jones saw as increasingly united by their common experience in Britain, therefore promised to reintroduce a radical internationalist consciousness into the parochial world of British politics, challenging several centuries of racist imperial ideology.

The political experiences of the embryonic black British community during the 1960s hammered home the urgency of an internationalist outlook. Pioneering organizations such as the Campaign Against Racism and Discrimination (CARD), established following Dr. King's visit by Jones and other progressives as a multiracial coalition, splintered when the group's black leaders offended white liberals by seeking to establish control of the organization.[96] As such multiracial coalitions foundered, younger leaders of the black community looked to the United States and anticolonial nationalist organizations in the colonies for inspiration. By the time of Stokely Carmichael's visit to Britain in 1967, groups dedicated to the autonomous organization of the black community such as the Michael X's Racial Adjustment Action Society (RAAS) had already been formed.[97] Heavily influenced by Black Power currents in the United States, RAAS and organizations such as Nigerian playwright and activist Obi Egbuna's United Coloured People's Association adopted militant postures of black autonomy, grassroots populism, and anti-imperialist, antiracist unity.[98] Carmichael's visit further underlined the vanguard character of developments in the black communities of America. Yet despite the apparently derivative character of many of these British political groupings, the Black Power imperative to decolonize the mind led to the evolution of genuinely novel cultural initiatives that flowed from the strong ties of Britain's black communities to their former homelands in the Caribbean, Africa, and Asia.

Behind the Mask

Carnival Politics and British Identity in Linton Kwesi Johnson's Dub Poetry

BRITISH DUB POET LINTON KWESI JOHNSON (LKJ) moved to Britain from Jamaica on the cusp of adolescence in 1963. He arrived in the metropolis during a time of tremendous social and cultural ferment. Living in Brixton, South London, LKJ was quickly immersed in the radical currents that circulated throughout the black and Asian diasporic world at the time. The Black Panthers, whose youth wing he joined while still attending secondary school, exposed LKJ to the fertile blend of socialist political-economic analysis and black consciousness that characterizes the internationalist strands of the black radical tradition.[1] In addition, as a young member of the Caribbean Artists Movement (CAM) in London during the early 1970s, LKJ participated in the groundbreaking debates that took place within that organization concerning the appropriate forms and themes of artistic production among members of the Caribbean exile community in Britain.[2] Popular culture acquired increasing significance as these artists struggled, under the weight of the increasingly incendiary political events of the period, to forge a role for themselves as artists and popular leaders.

Following the lead of figures like Edward Kamau Brathwaite, LKJ sought to craft his own poetic language in order to overcome the traditions of linguistic and mental colonization imposed by the educational apparatus in the British colonies of the Caribbean. He found a model for his own work in what he called the *dub lyricist,* Jamaican and black British deejays who would "toast" or invent improvised rhymes over the heavy rhythm tracks of reggae dub records. As he explains in an essay published in *Race and Class* in 1974, LKJ turned to the dub poetry movement that was made into a potent cultural force in Jamaica by Rastafarians such as the poet Bongo Jerry as a way of developing a vernacular aesthetic. Such an aesthetic, he believed, offered a vital connection to the lives of black diaspora youths and responded to the political and aesthetic desires that emerged as West Indians settled in Britain.[3] Although LKJ described the dub lyricist as making "a vital contribution to the oral documentation of the history of Jamaica and to the Jamaican oral tradition," he himself was actively adapting this West Indian tradition to circumstances confronted by black communities in Britain.[4]

LKJ's lyrics reflect, in other words, the shift from a predominantly exilic focus on the Caribbean evident among older members of CAM to one grounded far more closely in the issues critical to young black people born and raised in Britain. His work nevertheless remained responsive to transatlantic cultural currents. In 1979, LKJ released his second full-length album, *Forces of Victory.* The songs featured on this album were published the following year in the collection *Inglan Is a Bitch.* Unlike his previous LP, *Dread Beat and Blood* (1978), *Forces of Victory* successfully integrated spoken word and musical accompaniment, leading to a compositional style far more heavily influenced by the dictates of lyrical performance than is evident in previous compositions.[5] In addition, *Forces of Victory,* and the collection of verse that followed after, for the first time consistently deployed what is now seen as LKJ's characteristic black British vernacular. The album is therefore of particular significance, announcing the arrival of LKJ's mature style as well as offering important accounts of black British experience during the late 1970s.

The LP *Forces of Victory* took its title from the theme developed by the Race Today collective, of which LKJ was a prominent member, for the Caribbean carnival held in London's Notting Hill neighborhood in 1978. According to an editorial statement in the collective's journal, carnival was "central to the developing cultural movement within the West Indian community in the United Kingdom."[6] In fact, Race Today had been deeply involved with the festival since 1976, when running battles broke out between black youths and the London metropolitan police force, presaging the massive riots that convulsed Britain's cities during the next decade. As its title suggests, LKJ's album brings the potent popular tradition of dub poetry to bear in order to memorialize the endangered carnival and to ensure its continuance. LKJ's celebration of carnival raises a number of broad questions concerning diasporic cultural practices in the metropolis. Was the victory celebrated during the carnival not an ephemeral triumph, one with the durability of papier-mâché in a hard London rain? How was it possible for a recreational event like the carnival to take on such a pivotal symbolic place in representations of identity and community in Britain? What enduring conflicts within the national body politic did carnival crystallize, and what fresh debates did it catalyze? How, finally, does LKJ's performance poetry intervene in the complex social circumstances that surround carnival?

THE HISTORICAL ROOTS OF CARNIVAL

The word *carnival* derives from the Latin *carnem levare,* "to put away meat." Carnival, in terms of the traditional Catholic calendar, is an occasion to celebrate the life of the senses one last time before the penance and purgation of Lent. This ecclesiastical context has fueled readings of carnival as a temporary inversion of the dominant order, a brief bacchanalia that engages and canalizes energies that might otherwise have been used to orchestrate a more durable rupture in the status quo.[7] Yet carnival is also one of the central rituals of geographically distant but culturally related African and South Asian diasporic populations, from Port of Spain to Rio, New York, Toronto, and London. The historical origins of the Trinidad carnival and the frequent conflicts that attended its annual celebration suggest that, at least in the context of the African and South Asian diaspora, it plays more than the role of a fleeting catharsis.[8] A Bakhtinian reading of carnival as a kind of cultural safety valve elides the festival's role as an enduring site of social negotiation and conflict. Indeed, behind the breathtakingly beautiful costumes and floats evident during carnival time in locations throughout the Americas and in Britain, behind the relatively evanescent public manifestation of the masquerade that makes carnival so galvanizing for critics and tourists alike, lies an unfolding history of community formation and transformation.[9] The spectacular street festival and its temporary inversion of the political status quo are only the most visible elements of a more elaborate and enduring process of social mobilization.[10]

Carnival's role during the 1970s in igniting conflict between the black community and the state was not a new one.[11] Originally a French creole affair in colonial Trinidad, the predominantly religious celebration quickly changed its racial and class complexion after the emancipation of the slaves in 1838. The freed slaves turned carnival into a celebration and commemoration of their liberation. Having taken Trinidad from the French in 1797, British colonial authorities on the island began seeking to suppress the alarmingly seditious annual festivities. As commentators such as Cecil Gutzmore have noted, in doing so they were merely extending the tactics of state repression that they had brought to bear on popular cultural activities in early industrial Britain.[12] Like such activities, carnival expressed an unruly spirit that challenged the forms of discipline necessary to the rhythms of industrial labor and production. In addition, of course, the Trinidad carnival conjured up the specter of the slave rebellions of the past. For instance, one of the central rituals of Trinidad's carnival during the postemancipation period, canboulay (*cannes brulées,* or burned cane), reenacts the burning of sugar cane fields by rebellious slaves.[13] In addition, carnival traditions helped foster polycultural connections between the creole culture of the island's blacks and the indentured laborers brought by the British to Trinidad from South Asia following the end of slavery.[14] Aside from the elements of class and race satire and subterfuge that surfaced in carnival costumes and performances, the Caribbean carnival thus also contains a sedimented history of directly confrontational cultural traditions. Attempts by colonial authorities to suppress such traditions led to repeated instances of extremely violent rioting in Trinidad in the late nineteenth and early twentieth centuries.[15]

True to this Caribbean tradition, carnival in Britain has been a crucial vehicle of what Kobena Mercer calls the vernacular cosmopolitanism of Britain's diaspora populations.[16] Indeed, the particularly synthetic quality of the carnival, which involves virtually every possible medium of creative expression, marks it as a central site for the creation of such a composite aesthetic. One source of the tensions surrounding carnival is the failure of the British establishment to accept the validity of carnival as an art form. During the yearlong period when the diverse carnival themes are developed, costumes created, funds raised, and preliminary celebrations attended, a repertoire of popular cultural identities is elaborated within black communities throughout the diaspora. These identities are grounded in a spatial and cultural geography that interweaves the local and the global. Moving from the mas' (masquerade) camp to the calypso tent to the streets of Notting Hill, participants in the carnival celebration carve out sites that help cement the bonds of social cohesion uniting local communities of Caribbean origin in Britain.[17] Mas' themes are carefully debated and researched during the year before the parade, creating an important participatory educational forum for participants that translates into a blend of didacticism and spontaneous pleasure for parade spectators.[18] Indeed, the carnival has played a central role in establishing the meaning of black community and identity in Britain. It offers a defiantly public site for Caribbean immigrants and their children and grandchildren to affirm both their diasporic affiliations and local connections. Today, the Notting Hill carnival is the largest street festival in Europe, attracting approximately two million revelers to a largely peaceful celebration. During the 1970s, however, the agents of the state perceived carnival as an incendiary disruption of public order.

As an event that took place in the streets of the capital city, the Notting Hill carnival was a particularly intense flash point in struggles over spatially embedded definitions of British national identity during the middle to late 1970s. In his seminal work on the character of nationalism, Tom Nairn characterizes the nation-state as Janus-faced.[19] Nairn uses this reference to the Roman god of the threshold to describe the temporal double consciousness of nationalist projects. In order to legitimate the disruptive work of modernization implicit in nation building, nationalist leaders characteristically turn to images—ironically often of quite recent vintage—that signify the archaic, organic identity of the people.[20] Yet as Ernst Renan observed, there is another side to nationalist projects. In addition to the construction of collective memories, nationalist projects also engage in acts of strategic forgetting. In the case of Britain, nationalists must forget the remarkably mongrel character of national identity as well as the imperial history that is responsible for postcolonial migration to Britain. Postwar British public life has been characterized by a superabundance of nostalgic images of national identity, many of which achieved unparalleled presence in public life shortly after the 1970s through heritage films such as *Chariots of Fire* and *A Passage to India*.[21] Such icons of national unity are all, of course, secured by the ultimate figurehead, the reigning monarch.[22]

However, postwar British history saw these images of national identity take on a predominantly geographical character.[23] Place became central to national identity. Britishness was represented more than ever as a homogenous affair, the pure product of a proudly autochthonous island race. The racial implications of such insular rhetoric were immediately apparent, and had dramatic impact, as the racially motivated changes in Britain's citizenship laws during the period make clear. In 1971, the right of domicile within Britain that had been extended to colonial subjects by the Nationality Act of 1948 was definitively rescinded. Notting Hill's Caribbean carnival, which began to attract massive crowds of revelers in precisely this period, was an inflammatory reminder of the contradictions inherent in the exclusionary definitions of national identity that had gained a legislative seal of approval by the 1970s. The carnival offered dramatically visible evidence of the transnational, postcolonial connections of a significant number of British subjects. In 1976, more than fifteen hundred members of the London police force tried to shut down the carnival after attempts to move the festival to a sports stadium or to split it into a number of smaller events failed. The police met with fierce resistance from black youths. This event and the carnivals that followed it in 1977 and 1978 are generally regarded as the coming-of-age ceremonies of the second generation of black Britons.

The Notting Hill carnival also has specific historical links to the black community's resistance to neofascism in Britain. The carnival celebration began as a response to one of the first significant postwar public expressions of racist hostility toward the presence of Britain's nonwhite citizens. In the summer of 1958, white working-class youths whom the press labeled *teddy boys* because of their eccentric attire descended on the dilapidated precincts of London's Notting Hill.[24] Organized by Oswald Mosley's Union Movement (a revival of Mosley's prewar organization, the British Union of Fascists), crowds of up to four thousand white youths roamed the city streets for four days, assaulting any West Indians they could lay their hands on.[25] The police did nothing to impede their hooliganism until members of the black community began to organize themselves to counter these attacks. Shortly, coordinated resistance to racial attacks was organized, and the police force moved to reestablish public order. While these events could hardly be said to constitute the origin of a black public sphere in Britain, they did establish the confidence of Britain's black community in its ability to turn back racial terror.

To help heal the many wounds caused by these experiences, Claudia

Jones, a Trinidadian radical active in the Communist Party and anti-colonial circles, organized the first Caribbean carnival in Britain.[26] Bringing together musicians from Trinidad such as the calypso singer Lord Kitchener with activists such as Amy Garvey, former wife of Marcus Garvey, Jones articulated a cultural politics predicated on the political significance of diasporic cultural institutions such as the carnival. Indeed, Jones wrote in the introduction to the 1959 carnival souvenir brochure: "If then, our Caribbean Carnival has evoked the whole-hearted response from the peoples from the Islands of the Caribbean in the new West Indies Federation, this is itself testament to the role of the arts in bringing people together for common aims, and to its fusing of the cultural, spiritual, as well as political and economic interests of West Indians in the UK and at home."[27] As envisaged by Jones, carnival in Britain was to unify the heretofore isolated immigrants from diverse islands such as Barbados, Jamaica, and Trinidad, creating a popular cultural front through which to resist the rise of fascism in the "motherland."

Following Jones's death in the early sixties, the Caribbean carnival went into a decade-long period of hibernation. By the early 1970s, however, a second generation of black Britons began resuscitating the festival. Following a study trip to Trinidad by carnival organizer Leslie Palmer in 1973, a Caribbean-style carnival was revived in Britain.[28] There was a surge in the popularity of steel pan bands, which provide the rhythmic backbeat that allows revelers to "jump up" during the carnival procession. By the mid-1970s, steel band music had become a massive popular movement in Britain, with as many as one hundred bands organized in the London metropolitan area and formal instruction becoming a regular part of the curriculum in city schools.[29] Mas' camps, where the thematic focus of particular mas' bands or groups in the parade are planned, coordinated, and eventually constructed, also began to proliferate. Since these mas' camps are practically a year-round affair, they play a significant role in consolidating neighborhood Caribbean communities around the metropolis. In addition to these competing mas' camps, a group of indigenous British calypso singers began to add their topical ballads to fare imported from Trinidad. The carnival was becoming less the ritual of an exiled Caribbean community and more a celebration of the hybrid cultural forms created by black Britons.

Popular Authoritarianism and Black Autonomy

By the mid-1970s, the neofascist National Front (NF) had become a significant force at the polls and on the streets. Racial harassment escalated, and increasingly homicidal attacks on black and Asian people became a regular aspect of life in Britain's decaying inner cities. The NF often tried to polarize communities by organizing marches through poor neighborhoods with a high percentage of nonwhite residents. NF goons were protected during these marches by a police cordon.[30] Antiracist groups that sought to repulse such neofascist incursions were often arrested or attacked by the police, offering a graphic example of the state's fundamental racial bias to anyone in doubt. As a result of the police failure to challenge the National Front's inflammatory tactics, black communities revived the independent self-defense organizations that had sprung up during the 1958 white riots. The defiant assertion of autonomy found throughout LKJ's *Inglan Is a Bitch*, the book where lyrics from his previous two albums were collected in 1980, is a product of this conjuncture during the 1970s. Violence by neofascist groups at the time produced a militant practice of counterviolence within the black community recorded by LKJ in his poem "Fite Dem Back."

In addition to neofascist cadres, the black community also had to contend with quotidian assaults by the forces of the state during this period. In *Policing the Crisis*, Stuart Hall and his colleagues at the Birmingham Centre for Cultural Studies anatomized the transformation of the state that occurred in the 1970s.[31] Drawing on the work of political theorist Nicos Poulantzas, Hall provides a structural analysis of the new form of state that evolved in reaction to the crisis of hegemony within the social-democratic nations of Western Europe during the 1970s. According to this analysis, a breakdown of the hegemonic consensus in these countries occurred as a result of the state's inability to reconcile the competing interests—private accumulation and public consent—that it had absorbed in the course of the second half of the twentieth century. During the countercultural movement of the 1960s, the superstructures of the liberal postwar welfare state had come under attack from new social movements such as feminism, Black Power, and the student movement, which indicted the forms of institutional discrimination and hypocrisy that characterized postwar social democracy. At the same time, the increasingly flexible forms of accumulation and the transnational organizational structures that were coming to characterize the capitalist system during the 1970s overwhelmed the state's mechanisms of social engineering.[32] By 1976, British capitalism was in full-blown crisis. The OPEC oil embargo had decimated the nation's manufacturing sector, massive strike waves were toppling ineffectual governments with increasing frequency, and the International Monetary Fund had imposed a regime of fiscal austerity on the country that augured the notorious structural adjustment policies meted out to underdeveloped countries during the 1980s.[33] Consent, as Hall and his colleagues put it, was exhausted. For Hall, the securing of public consent through the popular ideology of "law and order" became, as a result, the state's sole basis of legitimacy.[34] Coercion against "ethnic minority" populations secured the consent of the white majority for the state. This "popular authoritarianism," as Hall called it, thus had an inescapably racial upshot. The principle elements of Enoch Powell's race-baiting "Rivers of Blood" speech of 1968, in which the future of the nation was tied to its racial purity, came, during the 1970s, to be part of mainstream discourses that operated through a symbolic politics of prophylaxis. British public discourse was suffused with a racism that, as Étienne Balibar has argued, consisted of a conflictual relation to the state that was "lived distortedly" and "projected" as a relation to the racial Other.[35]

The popular authoritarian ideology that characterized the 1970s cast Britain's black and Asian communities, the great majority of whom lived in the most economically marginal urban areas of the nation, as the greatest threat to the nation's tranquility. Of course, this ideology effectively obscured the structural components of Britain's economic and social crisis. If racist ideologues like Powell used the presence of blacks in Britain to explain the nation's postwar economic decline, the ideology of law and order blamed the social crises ignited by this decline on the very people who were its greatest victims. Reviving the Victorian-era "sus" laws that allowed police to arrest those they suspected of criminal intent without any evidence, the police force became an increasingly aggressive presence in the decaying urban areas where blacks had been forced to settle during the postwar period. Tensions inevitably escalated between the police and black communities, providing greater justification for the ideology of "law and order" in official eyes. As the British police adopted the military-style strategies developed by their American colleagues during the urban conflagrations of the late 1960s and early 1970s in the United States, black neighborhoods came to seem increasingly like battle zones, subjected to the "heavy manners" of an occupying army. Black youths in particular could not walk openly on the streets of British cities without courting arbitrary arrest.[36]

Perhaps the most powerful poem in *Inglan Is a Bitch*, "Sonny's Let-tah" conveys the damage wrought by the "sus" laws on black communi-ties during this period. In this poem, LKJ adopts the persona of Sonny, a young black man writing a letter to his mother from Brixton prison after being arrested in an altercation that followed the police's unwarranted attempt to arrest his younger brother.[37] Countering the stereotypical views of black criminality and violence that were essential components of the moral panic that attended popular authoritarianism, LKJ human-izes Sonny by narrating his devotion to his mother. Just as in "Fite Dem Back," LKJ underlines the refusal of members of the black community to accept British state violence meekly by describing Sonny's response to the police attack. Unlike the former poem, however, "Sonny's Lettah" acknowledges the oppressive impact of institutional racism within the police force and the judicial system.[38] Sonny is now locked up in Brixton jail with little apparent hope of appeal against the biased system that landed him behind bars. This poem is the first one included in the col-lection *Inglan Is a Bitch*, where it is printed next to a photograph of LKJ in front of a "Free Darcus Howe" poster. The poster's motto—"self-defense is no offense"—suggests that the black community not only experienced repeated attacks from both police and neofascists, but that they were engaged in campaigns during this period to challenge the bias of a judiciary that refused to acknowledge the legitimacy of resistant counterviolence.[39] Nevertheless, the tone of triumphant resistance found in later poems like "Fite Dem Back" and "Forces of Victory" is modulated in this poem by the note of somber reflection introduced through Sonny's meditation on his failure to protect his younger brother. LKJ's poem provides us with a poignant insight into the painful emotions felt by Sonny as he sits isolated in his cell. His signature, which LKJ of course speaks aloud on the album, suggests his stoic endurance in the face of state racism: "I remain, / your son, / Sonny" (9).

THE POLITICAL AESTHETICS OF SOUND SYSTEM CULTURE

Within this embattled context, activists in the black community came to see the carnival as a crucially important instance of collective solidarity and resistance. Adopting the Fanonian analysis that had inspired Stokely Carmichael and the Black Panthers in the United States, groups such as the Race Today collective described black neighborhoods as internal colonies.[40] Identification with the colonial condition meant, in this context, the articulation of a political analysis of the underdevelopment, oppression, and superexploitation that affected racial minorities in developed urban capitalist conditions.[41] To overcome the colonized mentality and police brutality that prevailed under these conditions, activists such as the Black Panthers in the United States and Race Today in the UK developed a politics of militant resistance within the defensive space of the ghetto. For the Race Today collective, the carnival route consequently became a "liberated space," an autonomous zone within which the black community could assert its prerogative to occupy public space in Britain.[42] The historical connection between the carnival and the white riots of 1958 lent support to this perception. In addition, the massive and belligerent police presence following the 1975 carnival seemed to confirm the argument that the state saw black culture per se as a threat.

Spitting out defiance of the popular authoritarianism that victimized black communities in the 1970s, the title track of LKJ's *Forces of Victory* serves both as a remembrance of black people's historical resistance to the racist state and as an active performance of a counterhegemonic black aesthetic. "Forces of Victory" demonstrates the clear understanding among radical sectors of the black population that their struggle is ultimately against the state.[43] The battle to preserve carnival in Britain made the role of the state in catalyzing other forms of oppression such as neofascist violence completely clear. LKJ's poem reenacts the black community's triumphant defeat of police efforts to shut down the carnival in 1976 and 1977, using this triumph as a broader symbol of black resistance to the oppressive conditions established by popular authoritarianism.

The emphasis on public performance that characterizes all of the poems in *Inglan Is a Bitch* is particularly evident in "Forces of Victory." For instance, the poem's speaker adopts a defiant tone toward the unnamed "y'u" of the poem, a second-person plural that can only refer in this context to the police forces. There is nothing, as the speaker proclaims, that these forces can do to stop the carnival performers from parading along their planned route, a route that traces—at least for a couple of days—the geography of collective black solidarity. The ability to trace a path round the entire neighborhood of Notting Hill is an instance of what the geographer Neil Smith has called "jumping spatial scales" as a mode of empowerment.[44] As Smith explains, the hierarchical production of spatial scale means that individuals and communities are deprived not simply of movement from place to place, but of access to the broader spatial scales where power is choreographed. If the British state increasingly sought to contain black communities spatially through aggressive policing practices that curtailed their geographical mobility and criminalized certain forms of dress, hairstyle, and even ways of walking, the carnival allowed these communities to reoccupy their streets and neighborhoods. The Caribbean origins of carnival also suggest another form of scale jumping, this time through repossession of the resources of hope embedded in diasporic histories of resistance and rebellion.

LKJ's poem in fact effects a metaphorical inversion of the internal colonization suffered by black Britons at this time. The Race Today Renegades mas' band based their costumes in 1978 on the guerrilla outfits of the revolutionary anticolonial movements of the era.[45] Mimicking the popular mobilizations in colonized nations such as Mozambique or Vietnam, the Renegades paraded their defiance of what is seen as an imperial power structure. With their masquerade army, complete with wooden guns and papier-mâché tanks and planes, the Race Today Renegades sought to vanquish the forces of racism (aka "Babylon") using style, parody, and performance. Rupturing the European tradition of separating politics from aesthetics, the "Force of Victory" theme transformed the street fighting of the previous two years into a celebration of black identity.[46] Of course, on an explicit level the mas' theme of the Race Today Renegades refers to the inability of the police to shut down carnival during the two previous years. However, the hyperbolic pantomime of autonomous national identity resonates more broadly with the instances of resistance to state and fascist coercion that proliferated within the black and Asian communities during the late 1970s. By performing an alternative, militantly autonomous set of identities into being, the Race Today Renegades mas' band and LKJ's poetic evocation of their actions challenged the state's arrogation of legitimate violence on a symbolic plane.

The victorious celebration of carnival during the middle to late 1970s was possible largely because of the coalescence of the black community brought about through the integration of sound systems. In

1975, the organizers of the festival, the Carnival Development Committee (CDC), decided to include sound systems along the procession's route for the first time. While steel pan bands, mas' camps, and calypso all originate in Trinidadian culture, sound systems are a characteristic and fundamental component of Jamaican and Jamaican diasporic youth cultures. A sound system is an assemblage of massive, often homemade speakers, a powerful amplifier, a number of turntables, and a DJ who "toasts" or raps over the music she or he is playing. By including sound systems in the carnival procession, the CDC turned the festival into a pan-Caribbean affair. Of course, the kinds of cultural differences that characterized immigrants from different nations in the Caribbean had been mitigated from the start by processes of racialization in Britain that made such differences seem trivial. However, it was not until the carnival of 1975 that this pan-Caribbean unity became a dominant facet of the black public sphere in Britain and facilitated commensurate efforts of political organization. There were initial tensions over the logistics of this pan-Caribbean event. Mobile Trinidadian steel pan bands, for instance, expressed fears that their music would be drowned out by the booming bass tones of the stationary Jamaican sound systems. However, these fears were quickly overshadowed by the police force's attempts to shut down carnival.

Sounds systems and the dance halls in which they thrived were also central components of black youth culture during the postwar period. As Norman Stolzhoff has stressed, dance hall music has roots that go back in Jamaica to the era of slavery.[47] When amplified sound systems were introduced in Jamaican urban areas during the 1950s, they helped catalyze an indigenous musical culture that offered a crucial venue for youths of the Jamaican underclass to articulate counterhegemonic views and aspirations. Sound systems have an equally long history in Britain. Playing in basement blues dances during the early 1950s, artists such as Duke Vine and Count Suckle provided a vital social space that circumvented the color bar, which prevented blacks from attending dances held in established music halls and clubs.[48] Not only did sound systems offer an escape from the racially oppressive venues of dominant popular culture for the black community; they also provided an autonomous space that interrupted the order of waged labor. As a result, sound system culture helped articulate a critique of the worsening economic situation of black youths in Britain's depressed inner urban areas during the 1970s.[49]

By the mid-1970s in Britain, sound systems had begun playing the dread rhythms of reggae. Through their dissemination of the militant ideology of Rastafarianism, sounds systems became a central element in an increasingly radicalized black youth culture. As Dick Hebdige has pointed out, Rastafarianism inverts the values of dominant society, reading texts such as the Old Testament for signs of the righteous suffering of diasporic Africans in order to create an uncompromisingly anticolonial ideology of liberation.[50] The musical aesthetic of the sound system, which Hebdige has termed "cut'n'mix," is itself an example of such a politics of rescripting.[51] Taking existing recordings, deejays would remix or dub these tracks to create new musical forms that offered an implicit commentary on the original.[52] As Paul Gilroy argued in an early essay, the deconstructive aesthetic that underlies dub is a potent vernacular form of ideology critique.[53] By breaking up, distorting, and adding pounding bass to the original versions of popular songs, dub musicians like King Tubby and Lee "Scratch" Perry created a performative mode that meshed well with the critique of state power subaltern black communities in both Jamaica and Britain were articulating at the time.[54]

Moreover, during the 1970s, popular Jamaican deejays such as U-Roy, Big Youth, and Prince Far I also began "toasting," inventing their own rhymed lyrics over the musical dub. These lyrics offered a comment not simply on the music but also on contemporary social events, very much as rap music came to do during the 1980s in the United States.[55] Like the calypso singers of Trinidad whose lyrics featured acerbic commentary on contemporary social and political events, deejays and other talkover artists, responding to their audiences in a dialogic manner, helped focus and shape local opinion concerning public events. Although the primary role of sound systems remained the creation of danceable music, the rise of toasting meant that deejays could function to a certain extent as community griots, organic intellectuals of the dance hall. Thus, in addition to offering a site for the radical musical experiments of the dub aesthetic, sound systems also helped establish a vernacular black public sphere in Britain. Individual sound systems typically developed a devoted local following, a support base of youths who would travel with the sound systems as they moved to another community to engage in musical competitions.[56] These competitions often led to violent clashes between supporters of hostile sound systems, establishing an unhappily fratricidal element in black youth culture.[57] However, when the sound systems were incorporated along the route of the carnival procession for the first time in 1975, they brought with them literally hundreds of thousands of highly politicized black youths.[58] This was the first significant collective public appearance of the second generation of black Britons, and it caused panicky overreaction among the forces of law and order.

NEW ETHNICITIES AND POLYCULTURAL POLITICS

The militaristic theme adopted by the Race Today Renegades suggests a level of uniformity and homogeneity within the black community against which the structure of the carnival militates. Carnival is, after all, made up of a number of competing mas' bands, each adopting its own theme. As a result, the carnival is a particularly interesting site to investigate the evolving identities and political strategies that characterized the black community in Britain during this period. Such an examination reveals the extent to which monolithic conceptions of black culture were contested. 1977, for example, saw the organization of the Lion Youth mas' band by a group of women who had grown frustrated by the male chauvinism that characterized carnival culture.[59] As one of the founders of this mas' band stated, women were the predominant organizers and laborers in the mas' camps, and yet they were systematically excluded from the planning of the bands' themes each year. Lion Youth became the first all-woman mas' band. The band was, like LKJ's dub poetry, a product of the forms of cultural reconstruction and transnational linkage that characterize the struggles of the period to forge a vernacular aesthetic. Emerging from the George Padmore and William Sylvester schools, institutions founded by black parents who felt the British school system was purposely under- and miseducating their children, the Lion Youth mas' band transformed the masquerade elements of carnival into investigations of African diasporic heritage.[60] By embracing politicized and carefully researched African and diasporic themes each year, mas' bands like Lion Youth were consciously moving away from the Trinidadian "butterfly" tradition, which had by the 1970s become commodified and touristic.[61] Lion Youth mas' band offers a fascinating instance of the pedagogic role of popular culture, developing mas' themes centering, for example, on the rebellious Saramacen slave communities of Guyana and the syncretic religious practices associated with the Black Madonna.[62] In 1978, Lion Youth adopted a theme similar to that of the Race Today Renegades, using a sound system named Peoples' War to provide musical accompaniment to their marching. Their emphasis on historical research is, however, evident in the African background to their theme: "Guerrilla completing Shaka's task." Moreover, their presence in the streets of Notting Hill marked a significant challenge to the traditional male domination of carnival.

Far from consolidating a monolithic conception of the black community in binary opposition to the forces of white racism, carnival helped to promote dialogue and contestation around black identities. The model of monolithic community implicit in much black nationalist thought of the previous decade was, in other words, actively challenged through the cultural activism of groups such as the Lion Youth mas' band. In his discussion of work produced by black film and video collectives of the Thatcher era such as Ceddo and Sankofa, Stuart Hall theorized this profusion of difference as the advent of "new ethnicities."[63] According to Hall, the undifferentiated black subject constructed in the course of struggles to gain access to representation for marginalized communities needed to be challenged, for this subject was implicitly male and heterosexual. Consequently, Hall proclaims the "end of the essential black subject" and a corollary recognition of "the immense diversity and differentiation of . . . black subjects."[64] Compelling as Hall's account of this shift is, the history of carnival suggests that such challenges to monolithic conceptions of collective identity have a long prehistory. As a form that is grounded in the vernacular aesthetics of the Caribbean diaspora, the Notting Hill carnival has offered a complex politics of identity and spatiality since its inception. The Notting Hill carnival was thus an important venue in the consolidation of new ethnicities in postwar Britain.

A decentralized and participatory performance tradition that helped provoke spontaneous uprisings against state power, carnival also offered an important model for new political practices that evolved within black and Asian communities during the 1970s. Such practices were based on an explicit rejection of the vanguardist philosophy that underpinned many Black Power organizations. In an editorial published in 1976, the Race Today collective articulated the new philosophy of self-organized activity:

> Our view of the self-activity of the black working class, both Caribbean and Asian, has caused us to break from the idea of

"organising" them. We are not for setting up, in the fashion of the 60's, a vanguard party or vehicle with a welfare programme to attract people. . . . In the name of "service to the community," there has been the growth of state-nurtured cadres of black workers, who are devoted to dealing with the particularities of black rebellion.[65]

In turning against the tradition of the vanguard party, groups such as the Race Today collective were not simply rebelling against their immediate predecessors in the Black Power tradition. They were, rather, recuperating a tradition of autonomist theory and practice that extends back to the work of C. L. R. James in Britain during the 1930s. By the mid-1970s, James had returned to Britain, and his brilliant writings on the tradition of radical black self-organization had begun to influence younger generations of activists in the black community there.[66] Of course, for James and other radicals of his generation such as George Padmore, the impatience with vanguardist philosophies stemmed from the failure of the Comintern and the Soviet Union to support anticolonial struggles during the 1930s adequately.[67] In James's case, however, this disillusionment with particular Communist institutions was developed through his historiographic and theoretical work into a full-blown embrace of popular spontaneity and self-organization. From his account of Toussaint L'Ouverture's tragic failure to communicate with his followers during the Haitian revolution in *The Black Jacobins* to his attack on the stranglehold of the Stalinist bureaucracy on the revolutionary proletariat in *Notes on Dialectics*, James consistently championed the free creative activity of the people.[68] In addition, his theories gave activists a way of talking about the complex conjunction of race and class that characterized anti-imperialist struggle in the periphery and antiracist politics in the metropolis.[69] Taking the revolutionary activity of the slaves in Haiti as his paradigm, James articulated a model of autonomous popular insurrectionary energy that offered a perfect theoretical analysis of spontaneous uprisings such as those that took place at the Notting Hill carnivals of 1976–78. He was, indeed, one of the few major radicals to proclaim the inevitability and justice of the urban uprisings throughout Britain in 1981.[70] The impact of James's ideas concerning the autonomy of the revolutionary masses can be seen in the polycultural politics of coalition that mushroomed in response to the violence of the British state during the late 1970s.

Despite the increasing militancy of the black community, the grip of popular authoritarianism on the majority of the British population continued to tighten. If the black community was particularly subject to harassment and violence by the police, the Asian community suffered especially heavily from both organized and impromptu racist violence. In June 1976, eighteen-year-old Gurdip Singh Chaggar was attacked and stabbed to death by a group of white youths opposite the Indian Workers' Association's Dominion Cinema in Southall.[71] Horrified by the lack of official action in response to this violence committed in the symbolic heart of one of Britain's largest Asian communities, the elders of the community gathered to give speeches and pass resolutions against the tide of racist violence.[72] Asian youth in Southall, however, were fed up with this kind of pallid response, and with the accomodationist approach of their so-called leaders. They marched to the local police station demanding action. When the police arrested some of them for stoning a police van along the way, the crowd of youths sat down in front of the police station and refused to budge until their friends were freed. The following day, the Southall Youth Movement was born.[73] Other Asian youth groups followed in its wake around London and in other British cities. These groups were primarily defensive and local in character.[74] Unlike the class-based organizations that traditionally dominated the left wing in British politics, these groups stressed the language of community over that of class. Their struggle tended to turn on immediate goals related to political self-management, cultural identity, and collective consumption rather than on the more ambitious but distant goals of the revolutionary tradition.[75] They shared, in other words, the emphasis on control of local space that characterized the spontaneous uprisings around the Notting Hill carnival during these years.

Like the spontaneous uprisings that took place during carnival, the Asian Youth Movement also led to the development of new political formations that helped forge what Stuart Hall terms new ethnicities. Youth organizations and defense committees that sprang up in one community tended to receive help from groups in other communities, and, in turn, to go to the aid of similar organizations when the occasion arose. In the process, boundaries between Britain's different ethnic communities were overcome in the name of mutual aid. Asian groups like the Southall Youth Movement joined with black groups such as Peoples Unite, and, in some instances, new pan-ethnic groups such as Hackney Black People's Defence Organization coalesced.[76] In addition, blacks and Asians formed political groups that addressed the oppressive conditions experienced not only by racialized subjects in Britain but throughout the Third World at this time. Such groups regarded racism in the metropolis and imperialism in the periphery, in the tradition of C. L. R. James, as related aspects of the global capitalist system. Many of these groups hearkened back explicitly to the Bandung conference of 1955 between African and Asian heads of state by developing a politics of solidarity in the face of state and popular racism in Britain. The polycultural character and ambitions of these groups is evident from the titles of journals such as *Samaj in'a Babylon* (produced in Urdu and English) and *Black Struggle*. While such coalitions always had their internal tensions, they were sustained by their participants' conscious reaction to the divide-and-conquer politics that had characterized historical British imperialism and that continued to manifest itself in the metropolis.

The emotional resonance of this politics of polycultural solidarity is suggested by LKJ's poem "It Dread Inna Inglan." Composed as part of a campaign to free an unjustly imprisoned man from the Midlands, LKJ's poem celebrates the potent affiliations that racialized groups in Britain strove to foster during this period. LKJ's catalog of different ethnic groups in this poem closes with the unifying label "Black British," which unites all the groups that precede it in common resistance to the racism of figures such as Margaret Thatcher. For important radical theorists of the time such as A. Sivanandan, blackness was a political rather than a phenotypical label.[77] Skin color, in other words, only became an important signifier of social difference when it was embedded in power relations predicated on the systematic exploitation and oppression of certain groups of people by others.[78] If this understanding of the social construction of "race" derived from the bitter experiences of colonial divide-and-conquer policies, the politics of solidarity found within local antiracist groups emerged from a tradition of struggle against the racializing impact of state immigration legislation and policing policies in postwar Britain. As the popular authoritarian ideology gained increasing purchase on the British public in the crisis conditions of the late 1970s, such forms of solidarity became increasingly important.

When LKJ published "It Dread Inna Inglan," Margaret Thatcher had just won the general election. Her agenda was, however, already quite clear to Britain's black and Asian communities. In 1978, she had given an interview on Granada TV in which she linked the fears of postimperial Britain to prejudice against black people:

I think people are really rather afraid that this country might be rather swamped by people with a different culture and, you know, the British character has done so much for democracy and law, and has done so much throughout the world, that if there is any fear that it might be swamped, people are going to be really rather hostile to those coming in.[79]

The assumptions behind Thatcher's infamous "swamping" rhetoric are, of course, precisely the insular ones that undergird the increasingly exclusionary immigration legislation of the postwar period.[80] Indeed, Thatcher's painfully sanctimonious voice articulated views held by mainstream politicians of both the Labour and the Conservative parties throughout the postwar period. What had changed was the frankness with which such openly racist views could circulate in the public sphere. Thatcher's speech delivered almost immediately bloody results for Britain's black and Asian communities. The media began running reports about everyday instances of "swamping," and Enoch Powell was offered time on the BBC to discuss "induced repatriation."[81] In an attempt to stave off Thatcher's move to co-opt the burgeoning racist vote, the National Front petitioned to hold an election meeting in the Southall Town Hall in order to establish their legitimacy as the party that was really serious about dealing with the "swamping" threat. The Tory-controlled council gave the NF the green light to meet on 23 April 1979, St. George's Day, in spite of the fact that Southall contains one of the largest Asian communities in Britain. Despite the Southall community's declared intention to hold a peaceful demonstration against the NF, on the day of the NF meeting 2,756 police, including Special Patrol Group (SPG) units with horses, dogs, vans, riot shields, and a helicopter, arrived to crush the protest. A police rampage ensued in which Blair Peach, a teacher and antiracist campaigner, was beaten to death, and hundreds of others were seriously injured when police attacked hemmed-in demonstrators with batons, shields, and even a van. Seven hundred people were arrested, and 342 of them were convicted of disturbing the peace after show trials were held deep in suburban Thatcher territory. The Tory government refused to hold an inquiry into the events. The SPG officer who beat Blair Peach to death was never identified, let alone tried. Metropolitan police commissioner Sir David McNee had the following comment to make about the events: "If you keep off the streets in London and behave yourselves, you won't have the SPG to worry about."[82] Opponents of racism in Britain were not about to cave in to such thinly veiled threats.

The traditions of polycultural solidarity that emerged from autonomous antiracist defense groups like the Southall Youth Movement, from the popular resistance at the Notting Hill carnival, and from organizations such as Rock Against Racism transformed British popular culture for a whole generation.[83] The creativity with which such groups tackled Britain's postimperial legacy helped stimulate a renaissance in the popular arts that would put Britain on the cutting edge of artistic and theoretical innovation during the 1980s and 1990s. The radical culture generated by the antiracist groups of the 1970s remains pivotal to overcoming the toxic contradictions of popular authoritarianism in postimperial Britain. As LKJ was to write in the title track of the album he released after *Force of Victory:* "it is noh mistri / wi mekin histri / it is noh mistri / wi winnin victri."[84]

Beyond Imperial Feminism

Buchi Emecheta's London Novels and Black British Women's Emancipation

IN 1979, THE YEAR THAT MARGARET THATCHER became prime minister of a demoralized and fractious nation, a groundbreaking national feminist group was formed at a conference in London. The Organization of Women of African and Asian Descent (OWAAD) held a series of important annual conferences and generated a great deal of energy among activists before it split apart in 1983 over the group's failure to adopt an inclusive stance towards its lesbian members. Despite the brevity of OWAAD's life and its significant shortcomings, many black feminists now regard the group as a decisive formative influence because of its high profile as the first autonomous national organization for women of color in Britain. Among the organization's resonant position statements was the call for unity between women of African and Asian descent. While embracing expansive notions of solidarity derived from the Black Power movement in Britain, OWAAD nonetheless challenged the oppressive aspects of patriarchal black cultural traditions. In additional to interrogating sexism within the ranks of the antiracist movement, OWAAD activists also mounted a searing critique of the failure on the part of white feminists to address the forms of race and class oppression endured by black women in Britain.[1] The multifaceted nature of OWAAD's criticism angered many within both the antiracist and feminist movements, who believed the organization was creating dangerous divisions that undermined the struggle against racism and sexism at a particularly trying time.[2]

Notwithstanding such opposition, OWAAD and affiliated organizations such as Southall Black Sisters (SBS) made a strong impact not only on the feminist movement but also on progressive politics in general in Britain during the 1980s. Essays like Hazel Carby's "White Woman Listen!" offered a galvanizing challenge to both liberal and socialist feminists in Britain, pointing to the ethnocentrism of analytical terms such as *patriarchy* and to the consequent marginalization of black women's experience.[3] Carby's ringing call for autonomous organizing by black women emerged from and helped legitimate forums like OWAAD. In addition, Stuart Hall's important essay "New Ethnicities," which outlines the "end of the innocent black subject," similarly reflects the rise of black feminism.[4] Hall's response to groups such as OWAAD acknowledges the need for a new theoretical take on the nature of both subjectivity and political movements. Rather than seeing identity, black and otherwise, as a fixed category, Hall's work emphasizes the process of articulation through which diverse elements such as race, class, gender, and sexuality cohered to create composite but continuously evolving selves and political formations. This analytical perspective played an important role in challenging exclusionary definitions of citizenship popularized by politicians such as Margaret Thatcher, suggesting that national identity had to be redefined in terms of cultural difference rather than insular stability.

Yet despite Hall's theoretical recognition of the implications of black feminism and Carby's clarion call for independent organizing, there have been few attempts to engage with the historical lineaments and legacy of the black British feminist movement until very recently. White historians and activists typically worried about why black women were alienated by mainstream feminism rather than concentrating on the autonomous achievements of women's groups like OWAAD.[5] This emphasis reflects the pervasive ethnocentrism that helped spark independent black feminist organizing in the first place. Even less attention has been devoted to the everyday life experiences of black women in Britain that contributed to the formation of feminist groups. If historians have now begun to document the legacy of groups like OWAAD and SBS, what is the prehistory to such organizations of autonomous collective mobilization? What barriers prevented black women from coming together in collective forums prior to the formation of OWAAD and similar groups in the 1970s? Similarly, what links might be traced between the culture of political activism that developed among black women in the 1970s and 1980s and the efforts to discover individual voice and collective solidarity that preceded such activism?

Buchi Emecheta's London novels offer a particularly powerful point of departure to investigate such questions.[6] These novels are explicitly conceptualized as a form of documentary fiction that records the travails and coming-to-voice of a black woman in the metropolis during the late 1960s and early 1970s. In her novels *Second-Class Citizen* and *In the Ditch* and in the memoir *Head Above Water,* Emecheta offers a detailed portrait of everyday life in Britain prior to the emergence of the black feminist movement. Her work should not, however, be taken to represent the experience of all black women in Britain. Of course, there is always a temptation to place a burden of representation on a pioneer such as Emecheta, and to castigate her for depictions that may seem to affirm racist stereotypes of black identity. Some critics have, for instance, attacked this early work of Emecheta's, suggesting that its withering representation of African masculinity is a form of pandering to Western feminism.[7] While it is of course important to acknowledge that the black family is often an important site for refuge from a racist society, such objections tend to ignore the central burden of Emecheta's work—to reject images of black women as passive victims—and impose a homogeneous model of communal solidarity. This reaction foreshadows the nationalist response to black feminist attacks on inequality and gender power within the black community.[8] Emecheta's work and its reception thus anticipates one of the central conflicts faced by black feminism in the following decades.

In addition to challenging the oppressive aspects of certain African traditions, Emecheta is also unsparingly critical of the racism that characterized public life in Britain. Her work therefore offers an important record of the multiple forms of marginalization to which black women in the postcolonial metropolis were subjected. However, this double colonization was effected not simply through encounters with specific individuals, but also through the raced and gendered character of social citizenship in Britain. As the London trilogy documents, the British state sought to regulate poor women through the provision of social welfare benefits in ways that exacerbated gender- and race-based inequalities. As feminist critics were to argue subsequently, the post-1945 welfare state has a two-tiered character, treating men as workers entitled to social insurance and women as "mothers" entitled to welfare benefits.[9] This bifurcated structure reinscribes the dominant organization of gender relations, as well as the public-private split, in family, community, and workforce. In an analogous way, welfare racism splits society along racial lines, denying black families access to even the meager protection offered by the social safety net.[10] Black and Asian women bear the brunt of both of these forms of institutional discrimination, lending extremely concrete definition to the concept of double colonization.

If, in other words, part of the aim of Emecheta's London novels is to depict the efforts of her protagonist Adah to escape victimization within her marriage, an equally significant goal of the trilogy is to indict the institutional structure of social citizenship in Britain. The novels of the London trilogy do this by documenting the inequalities of access to welfare rights experienced by diasporic subjects. In addition, Emecheta's work also depicts the dependency that the paternalistic British welfare state imposes on poor black women such as Adah when they do manage to gain access to benefits. Therefore, although Adah does not participate in any organized social movement, the fictional record of her experience includes a critique of key institutions such as the family and the state that were to figure prominently as targets of black feminist theory and activism in subsequent decades. Buchi Emecheta's documentary fiction thus offers important insights into the way in which the political and theoretical priorities of black feminism emerged from the quotidian concerns of diasporic women in Britain. Implicit in the novels of Emecheta's London trilogy is a critique that calls not simply for a more inclusive model of the imagined community of the nation, but also for the wholesale reformulation of social citizenship in a manner that intended to transform the institutional character of British identity.

Second-Class Citizen: The Struggle to Escape Emotional Dependency

Although the bulk of *Second-Class Citizen,* Emecheta's second novel, is set in Britain, the narrative begins with the birth of Adah Ofili in the growing postcolonial metropolis of Lagos, Nigeria.[11] Almost immediately, Emecheta's narrator Adah informs us that she is not sure of her age. Adah calmly explains on the first page of her narrative that her family had been expecting a boy; their disillusionment was so profound when a girl materialized instead that they failed to record the date of her birth (7). Emecheta uses this striking initial note to convey the sexist character of the Ofili clan's values, which are predicated on thoroughgoing male domination. But the iniquities that Adah endures as she grows up are not simply the product of African patriarchy, as the ideologues of colonialism tended to suggest as they sought to pulverize traditional kinship systems.[12] Ironically, the meritocracy established by the new postcolonial state, in which preference is given to those educated according to European standards, exacerbates the gender-based inequalities of the traditions that Adah's family brings with it when her parents migrate from rural Ibuza to Lagos. As a result, the family mobilizes its relatively scarce resources in order to educate Adah's brother rather than her, since it is assumed that, upon reaching maturity, she will be married off to another family (9). Any economic benefits that might accrue from Adah's education, Emecheta explains, will enrich her husband's family rather than the Ofili clan. Adah's travails therefore offer a postcolonial update of "The Traffic in Women," Gayle Rubin's classic account of the structural logic behind marriage and the commodification of women's reproductive labor in traditional patriarchal kinship structures.[13] Emecheta's narrative demonstrates that, within the terms established by the conjunction of traditional patriarchal kinship patterns and a modernizing postcolonial state, there was an ironclad economic rationale behind women's subordination.

The experiences depicted in *Second-Class Citizen* suggest that structures of gender asymmetry are culturally specific, predicated on specific collisions between local kinship patterns and particular colonial and postcolonial states. It follows, then, that there can be no universal model of women's identity and oppression; Adah's experiences would not necessarily have been the same in another postcolonial country, or even in another part of Africa. This element of *Second-Class Citizen* underlines the distortions created by universalizing categories of women's identity. Dismantling the unitary category of "woman" was one of the central concerns of black feminism in Britain, for this model of identity allowed middle-class, white feminists to purport to speak for their oppressed "sisters" around the world. As Hazel Carby has remarked, such well-intentioned notions of solidarity were an ironic expression of the Enlightenment model of the universal human subject. Though supposedly liberatory, in practice this model of subjectivity legitimated the suppression of all those aspects of culture and identity that did not conform to the norms established by the colonial power.[14] The different varieties of feminism that developed in Britain during the 1960s and 1970 inherited these attitudes, leading many white, middle-class feminists to adopt positions that mimicked colonial discourse. For example, mainstream feminist discourse tended to pathologize the black family in ways that evoked the eugenic discourses of imperial culture. This stance moved dominant feminism disturbingly close to the rhetoric of the right wing during the 1970s. In challenging such imperial feminism, writers like Emecheta and Carby underlined the differential impact of gender- and class-inequality on black and white women.

Imperial feminist models of universal sisterhood obscure the vastly different priorities not simply of affluent women in the developed nations and of poor women in developing countries, but of black and white women in Britain. Such issues are particularly important in the context of quasi-autobiographical work such as Emecheta's London novels since the genre was initially treated as a transparent vehicle for articulating an undifferentiated feminine identity.[15] Yet if Emecheta's depiction of postcolonial African sexism indicts the unified model of subjectivity that undergirded white, middle-class Western feminist models of sisterhood during the 1970s, *Second-Class Citizen* also challenges romantic representations of precolonial African tradition such as those cultivated by prominent advocates of negritude like Léopold Sédar Senghor. During the era of decolonization, Senghor and other male intellectuals advanced an idealized representation of precolonial Africa, one in which women, seen as repositories of inviolable cultural tradition, were consigned to the role of fecund mothers of the nation.[16] Emecheta's depiction of the oppression encountered by Adah lays bare the costs of negritude's ideological subordination of women. In challenging such depictions, Emecheta anticipates the critiques that black feminists were to articulate a decade later when they began to contest representations of their identity not simply in racist discourse but also in the patriarchal traditions of the black community.

The opening chapters of *Second-Class Citizen* offer a veritable pilgrim's progress of obstacles and setbacks. However, while describing the structures of subordination Adah encounters, the novel refuses to represent her purely as a victim. Instead, from the novel's first page, Adah speaks of a mysterious sense of Presence that directs her actions and often inspires her to engage in acts of defiance. We learn later that

Adah's father perceives her as the returned spirit of his beloved mother (13). The Presence that guides her throughout her life can thus be read as a link to previous generations of African women. This sense of a guiding presence prevents Adah from suffering the complete loss of self we witness in a novel such as Joan Riley's *The Unbelonging*, in which the protagonist migrates to Britain as a young woman and, once there, crumbles under the weight of racism and sexism.[17] Unlike Riley's protagonist, whose identity crisis leaves her disoriented and paralyzed, Adah struggles endlessly to assert herself against great odds.

Foremost in the years of her youth is her determination to acquire an education. As a child, she absconds from home, walks to a local school, and defiantly informs the teacher that she's decided to attend classes (11). After her father dies, Adah's mother is inherited by her father's brother—a common practice among Ibos at the time—and Adah herself is sent to live in the household of her mother's elder brother. Here she must work to earn her keep, waking at 4:30 A.M. to fetch water from the public pump. Despite such obstacles, she keeps up her studies, permitted to do so by her uncle since her education will increase the dowry she fetches when she's eventually married off (17). Nevertheless, Adah must still defy authority in order to progress to higher levels of study. By drawing on the religious narratives to which she has been exposed while attending missionary schools, Adah is able to invert her sense of culpability for such defiance into a feeling of heroic martyrdom. Adah's pattern of steadfast striving amid tremendous suffering as a young girl is one that will characterize her experience throughout the novel. In spite of her later assertion that the Bible teaches women passivity and thereby exacerbates patriarchal African traditions (28), Christian tradition can evidently be appropriated in order to license acts of defiance. Adah's self-figuration as a heroic martyr parallels the transformation of biblical narratives that takes place within activist black religious traditions such as Rastafarianism, but this time with an expressly feminist twist.[18]

Adah's inversion of the dominant narrative of womanly submission is also exemplified in her marriage. Once she reaches adolescence, she must endure a barrage of elderly, overweight suitors as a result of the relatively high bride price her greedy family has set. Although they have done nothing to further her education, they now wish to capitalize on her accomplishments by collecting a fat dowry (23). In addition to limning the difficulty of escaping the grip of patriarchal tradition,

Emecheta's depiction of Adah also challenges notions of facile access to
an autochthonous African feminism. Although her sense of an abiding
Presence that guides her rebellion seems to suggest a link to such a feminist essence, it must be remembered that Adah gains this bond through
her father. Similarly, in much of the rest of the novel, we see Adah struggling ceaselessly against structures of male supremacy while nevertheless identifying with and placing her trust in individual men. Indeed, so
deeply does Adah internalize notions of male supremacy that she ends
up directing much of her anger at the women who surround her rather
than at the men who benefit most from the patriarchal structures of the
extended Ibo family. This is due in part to the fact that, among extended
kin groups, it is older women who are charged with social reproduction,
which includes preparing their daughter for lives of domestic servi-
tude.[19] Thus, Adah's rebellion against her allotted place in life initially
targets her mother, whom she sees as complicit in perpetuating her subordination. "If it were not for Ma," Adah says, "Pa would have seen to it
that I started school with Boy" (9). She evinces a surprising degree of
satisfaction when the police, whom her mother has notified after Adah
runs off to school, physically abuse her mother and berate her for her
lax parenting. This incident may seem simply to exemplify Adah's
growing sense of her own power and ability to effect change in the
world. However, her animosity toward her mother is an attitude that is
repeated frequently in *Second-Class Citizen,* contributing to a pattern of
hostility toward other women that leaves Adah isolated and, consequently, far more easily subjected to the whims of her increasingly
tyrannical husband. Emecheta's depiction of Adah thus grates against
idealistic notions of women's inherent orientation toward community
and solidarity with other women.[20] The bonds that Adah forges with
women outside her immediate family in *Second-Class Citizen* are tenu-
ous and extremely hard won.

Adah's isolation is evident as soon as she sets foot in Britain.[21] While
living in Lagos, she has grown used to the life of an elite, educated
woman, with many servants and a great deal of social status, despite her
subordination within the Obi clan. When she arrives in London, however, Adah learns from her husband that British racism has flattened out
the Nigerian class system, and that all postcolonial Africans are thrown
together as second-class citizens in the motherland. Adah is appalled
not simply at the squalid apartment block Francis has found for them to
live in, but also at the fact that she must share these accommodations

with working-class Nigerians. This theme in *Second-Class Citizen* challenges the tendency among some black feminists to treat the black community as undifferentiated in terms of class, and thereby to create a monolithic representation of oppression.[22] Although Francis nearly hits her when she scolds him for not finding a better situation, demonstrating to Adah that, free of the restrains exercised by the extended family, there is little to rein in Francis's abusive behavior, she finds no surrogate kin to turn to for support. Yet if her classism forces her into a self-imposed exile from the working-class Nigerians in proximity to whom she is forced to live by the racism of British landlords, her refusal to internalize racist British attitudes is also a crucial factor in her solitude. If other black Britons are willing to settle for second-class citizenship, Adah kicks valiantly against this designation. For instance, when Francis presses her to seek work in a factory like other Nigerian women, she obstinately refuses and instead applies for jobs in which she can employ her university education. Since there were precious few other educated black people occupying such professional positions in Britain at the time, however, Adah's successful application ironically leaves her isolated from other black women both at home and at work.

Adah's relationship with her husband decays precipitously once she arrives in Britain. Despite her refusal to be subordinated in virtually every other walk of life, she demonstrates a virtually masochistic propensity to put up with the humiliation and abuse meted out by Francis.[23] The night after their stormy reunion, for example, Francis forces Adah to have sex with him in "an attack, as savage as that of any animal" (40). When she becomes pregnant as a result of this marital rape, Francis blames her for the baby and sends her off to a doctor to deal with her "frigidity." Although Adah quickly realizes that for Francis, "marriage was sex and lots of it, nothing more" (41), she not only remains in the marriage, but declares that she has discovered that she loves Francis and wants him to succeed in life (42). Dissatisfied with Adah's failure to service him sexually, Francis begins shopping around for other women to take as lovers; rather than challenging this behavior, Adah encourages it since, she says, in an act of spectacular denial, it means she will have some peace at night. So abject is her subordination that she is quite aware that her husband remains with her simply because she keeps "laying golden eggs" as a result of her qualifications and the well-paying jobs they help her land. Thus, her fierce ambition to escape the oppressive confines of her extended family in Nigeria becomes a vehicle to salvage a hollow and exploitative marriage in Britain.

Despite her apparent strength in other walks of life, Adah conforms to many of the characteristics of the abused woman who clings to her batterer. Women like Adah often remain within abusive relationships because their identity is defined through their attachment to an apparently stronger—but also deeply needy—partner.[24] For example, Adah continues to hand over her pay packet to Francis long after it becomes obvious that he has no real intention of helping to support the family. In addition, despite his blatant philandering, which extends even to an affair with the child-minder Adah hires to help care for their children while she's out working, Emecheta's heroine stays glued in a marriage that she herself admits offers her nothing other than the affection of her children. She represses this knowledge, which comes to her during cyclical explosive crisis points such as the confrontation over the child-minder, continuing her slavish submission to Francis in the grooves of everyday oppression that separate the occasional beatings. When Francis becomes a Jehovah's Witness, he finds a perfect excuse to cut his wife off from contact with the mass media, where she might find examples of women who refuse to endure such subordination. Emecheta writes that Adah "simply accepted her role as defined for her by her husband" (95). Finally, Adah submits to Francis's jealous behavior, internalizing his irrational attacks on her character. When, for instance, she attempts to control the frequent pregnancies for which he blames her by getting access to contraception, Francis attacks her, saying that since she's gone behind his back to get a cervical cap she'll now also find ways to have sex with other men without his knowledge. Despite the injustice of this accusation and the savage beating that follows it, Adah stays with Francis. Indeed, she apathetically resigns herself to the loneliness that follows after Francis writes to his family about her behavior. Like many women in abusive relationships, in other words, Adah's individual passivity is partially a product of the stigma attached to perceptions of inadequate comportment by married women, who are often perceived as upholders of community honor.[25] So defeated is she by Francis's accusations that Adah submits herself to yet another pregnancy when her husband refuses to use the contraceptive devices she has procured (149). It is only when she goes to the hospital to deliver her baby and, while there, begins comparing her situation with that of other women, that Adah begins to adopt a more critical and autonomous attitude towards Francis.

Adah's dependency on Francis is never, however, a purely psychological affair, for their relationship does not occur in a vacuum. As she did when representing the articulation of masculinist African traditions with those brought to Nigeria by the British, Emecheta is at pains to demonstrate the ways in which patriarchal institutions in Britain augment Francis's abusive behavior. For example, from the moment she sets foot on British soil, Adah is aware that the legal system makes her an appendage of her husband (40). The racially inflected changes in British immigration laws during the 1960s thus had a particularly adverse impact on women, who became dependent on their husbands for continued residence in Britain.[26] To leave Francis would mean possible deportation, a risk Adah is not willing to take; as a result, she remains trapped by the state in her abusive relationship. This issue, identified so early by Emecheta, remains a cardinal point in antiracist feminist campaigns.[27] The extent of her legal dependency on her husband is brought home to Adah when she attempts, near the end of the novel, to gain access to birth control. To her consternation, she finds out that she must have her husband's signature on a consent form before she is given the materials. This apparently bizarre state practice is a product of the long-standing British legal principle of coverture, which specifies that women legally owe both their domestic and their reproductive labor to men.[28] If Adah is unable to control her body, in other words, it is not simply because Francis refuses to use birth control, but also because the state legislates that he controls his wife's body. Emecheta's emphasis on basic issues of access to marital and reproductive choice remains highly salient around the world today and should therefore be a primary concern of feminists interested in building transnational coalitions.[29]

The institutional sexism Adah confronts is augmented by the racism of individual Britons. Although Adah is fortunate to have extremely supportive colleagues during her stint as a librarian, her search for housing exposes her to the fear and bigotry with which many Britons reacted to postcolonial immigrants. In a tragicomic scene, Adah disguises her voice while speaking on the phone to a potential landlady in order to arrange an initial interview. When Adah and Francis eventually turn up outside the dilapidated building in a run-down part of town to make their application as tenants, the landlady takes one look at them and has what looks to Adah like an epileptic fit (77). Adah's hopes to salvage her marriage by orchestrating a move into better digs are thereby scuttled. Of course, when she eventually decides to leave Francis, the difficulty of finding accommodation is a significant impediment. As a result of her isolation, Adah is ignorant not simply of her right to state income support for her children, but also of the state's provision of public housing to those in need.[30] Once she is aware of these resources, Adah feels far more empowered to leave Francis, suggesting that her dependency on him is not a function of purely psychological factors but also has a pragmatic material component: poverty.

Adah's ultimate emancipation comes not as a result of the intervention of any beneficent outside forces. Instead, she engineers her own liberation through the rediscovery of her voice. While staying at home to care for her recently born fourth child, Adah writes a novel, which she regards as a literal brainchild (166). Francis of course refuses to read the novel and tells her scornfully that she will never succeed as a writer because she is an African woman. Although Adah once again demonstrates her subordination to Francis by accepting his criticism, she is pushed out of her thralldom when Francis maliciously destroys her manuscript. When he burns Adah's book, Francis seeks to immolate what he perceives as a threatening expression of her autonomy. His perception is quite accurate. Adah's writing is an important site through which she can reengage with the independent identity—her Presence—that was so prominent during the years of her childhood. As feminist theories of women's writing have long stressed, narratives, particularly autobiographical ones, offer a space for self-discovery through which women—traditionally marginalized from the public sphere—may stake claims as speaking subjects.[31] For Adah, however, this process of emancipation is defined not simply as the discovery of an autonomous, sovereign self. Instead, since her conception of writing explicitly parallels the act of intellectual creation to childbirth, her self-discovery takes place through development of her caring powers. By emphasizing this maternal creativity, Emecheta's protagonist explicitly repudiates the denigration of black women's life-giving capacity that characterizes social relations in contemporary Britain.[32] In subsequent writing, Emecheta has questioned not simply the moral panic over single black mothers, but also the distaste of many affluent white feminists for women's caring work.[33] As Eva Kittay has written, Western political theorists have largely failed to acknowledge dependency and the care of dependents in their conceptions of equality and justice.[34] When he burns her manuscript, Francis attempts to destroy this fundamental aspect of Adah's identity as an African woman. If she is willing to forgive

Francis all his other forms of soul-killing behavior, Adah will not condone this attack on the nurturing role through which she defines herself. One page after narrating this incident, Adah describes her departure from her husband's life with nothing but her four children, a box of clothes, and a broken finger.

In the Ditch: Working-Class Women's Solidarity and the Welfare State

Published two years before *Second-Class Citizen*, Emecheta's novel *In the Ditch* first appeared in serial form in the leftist monthly *New Statesman*.[35] This success came after years of failure for Emecheta, who tirelessly submitted fiction based on her African experience to British publishers with nothing to show for her efforts. At the time, Emecheta later wrote, mainstream British publishers felt there was no market for narratives set in Africa, and by a woman to boot.[36] Among members of the New Left, however, the publication of *The Making of the English Working Class*, E. P. Thompson's landmark history of British working-class formation, had opened avenues for exploration of the everyday life experience of the nonelite segments of British society.[37] Groups such as the History Workshop at Oxford's Ruskin College began pioneering new nonhierarchical educational practices based on the recording of history by members of the working class themselves.[38] When Buchi Emecheta decided to begin documenting her own life experience among the British lumpen following her escape from her marriage, radical groups such as History Workshop had prepared the ground for the publication of her work by drawing attention to the many silences in the official historical record. Emecheta's work may therefore be seen as intimately linked to the tradition that bore fruit in postcolonial initiatives such as the Subaltern Studies Group in India.[39]

Emecheta's *In the Ditch* was particularly groundbreaking, however, in its focus on the lives of poor women. If *Second-Class Citizen* documented the forms of control exerted within the context of a patriarchal marriage, Emecheta's first-published novel records her struggle to retain a sense of dignity and autonomy as a single parent subjected to the ministrations of the welfare state. This focus on institutional issues is an important supplement to the apparently personal problems highlighted in *Second-Class Citizen*, for it underlines the need to tackle the articulation of patriarchal family patterns with the discriminatory state structures that help consign black women to second-class citizenship in Britain. Furthermore, *In the Ditch* highlights the extent to which the struggles of significant numbers of black women in Britain take place not through organized political groups but around issues of family and social reproduction. The attempts of Emecheta's protagonist Adah to carve out a sense of autonomy and to establish community in the midst of great poverty offer important insights into the regulatory maneuvers of the British welfare state.

In the Ditch's documentation of poor women's experience opened important new lines of feminist inquiry. Even as feminists in Britain began to recuperate the life histories of important foremothers such as Virginia Woolf, Sylvia Pankhurst, and Rosa Luxemburg, scant attention was paid to the plight of less illustrious women. Ironically, at precisely the moment when the neoliberal onslaught on the post-1945 social contract was being prepared, the experience of poor women at the hands of the welfare state was highly underrepresented and ill understood. The predominantly middle-class, white leaders of the feminist movement were relatively unaware of such issues, despite their heavily socialist orientation in Britain.[40] The struggle of poor women for entitlement remains underacknowledged by mainstream (middle class) feminism, which, having insisted on women's autonomy, continues to have difficulty engaging the issue of women's dependency on the state. Welfare "reform" and the attendant war on poor women over the last twenty years has consequently been largely ignored by mainstream feminist organizations and theorists in both Britain and North America.[41]

This lack of solidarity helps perpetuate the enduring preoccupation among policymakers and other elites with the family ethic.[42] According to the precepts of this sacrosanct ethic, women's proper role was to marry and have children while being supported by and subordinated to a male breadwinner. If social welfare policy dictated to men that their proper place was in the labor market, regardless of the prevailing wages and work conditions, it sequestered women in the domestic sphere irrespective of their safety there and punished those who threatened to disrupt the nuclear family.[43] Although feminists subjected the family ethic to withering critique, their predominantly middle-class origins led them to largely ignore the role of the family ethic and social welfare policy in regulating the lives of poor women. As a result, little attention was devoted to the oppressive aspects of the welfare state, and an opportunity for solidarity with those subjected to its disciplinary mechanisms was lost. The history of the everyday struggle for survival recorded by *In the Ditch* therefore offers an important record of poor women's resistance to the family ethic and to the welfare state's attempts at oppressive regulation. As the social safety net is ruthlessly cut back, women's autonomy from abusive relationships and domestic violence is increasingly curtailed, a point that Buchi Emecheta's documentary fiction drives home with great force.

In the Ditch begins with a scene of squalor, as Adah struggles to protect her newborn baby from a huge rat who boldly reconnoiters near the infant's cot. Having fled her husband's oppressive behavior, Adah is subjected to yet another tyrannical male figure: her Nigerian landlord. Taking advantage of her weak position as a single parent, her landlord has doubled the rent he charges normally, berates Adah for even the slightest noises made by her children, and even switches off her electricity when he learns she has applied for public housing.[44] Although Emecheta relates in a comic vein her landlord's ultimate turn to magical incantations in the middle of the night in order to expel her from his building, her underlying point is a serious one. Without access to state housing resources, Adah, pregnant again after Francis breaks into her apartment and rapes her, stands little chance of establishing her autonomy. As a result of the racism of most British property owners, a single parent such as Adah is cast back on the untender mercies of landlords such as her juju-practicing compatriot.[45] Therefore, when the local council eventually finds her an apartment in the run-down Pussy Cat Mansions, Adah says that, though the place looks like a prison, it brought her three essential things: independence, freedom, and peace of mind (15).

But Adah quickly learns that Britain's socialized housing schemes come with strings attached, particularly for single parents. Pussy Cat Mansions, Adah finds out shortly after moving in, is reserved for "problem" families (17). This categorization implies that women engaged in single parenting are aberrant, a thorn in the foot of the social order that needs to be plucked out as soon as possible. Such autonomous women represent a danger to any society that predicates its smooth functioning on the subordination of women to a family ethic. In the course of the twentieth century, however, conflicting demands for women's home and market work led to the creation of government programs that shifted the locus of patriarchal authority from the male head-of-household to the state. As it gained control of efforts to mediate women's reproductive and market labor, the state developed a panoply of regulatory mechanisms that intervened in the lives of women who challenged the family ethic.[46] Such women were subjected to social stigmatization as well as strict government supervision of their lives and sexuality. These trends came to a head during the 1970s, when broader preoccupations caused by the social crises of the previous decade and by the faltering of Britain's economy led to the emergence of a moral panic over child abuse.[47] Deep anxieties about the decline of the traditional family and the crisis of conventional morality fostered a creeping state paternalism, which took the explicit form of strong child protection legislation that encouraged social workers to intervene actively in the parenting practices of poor women.

As the head of just such a "problem" family, Adah is subjected to many of the disciplinary controls of the regulatory paternal state. Thus, in short order after her arrival at Pussy Cat Mansions, the complex's "family adviser," Carol, pays a visit to Adah. "People here," Carol informs Adah, "say that your children make too much noise, and that you leave them all by themselves in the evenings" (24). Adah immediately understands that her aggressively racist neighbors have reported her to Carol. Assuming the worst, Adah replies to Carol's accusation, "So you come to take them away from me, lady?" (24). Faced with Carol's probing questions, Adah caves in completely, wondering with resignation whether the social worker is going to take her to jail. Carol's behavior, however, is more difficult to predict than Adah initially suspects. Rather than punishing her, Carol adopts a conciliatory if patronizing attitude towards Adah. After establishing her role as a minatory authority, Carol adopts the guise of state aid worker and offers to help find sitters to look after Adah's children during the evenings. Adah is well aware of the disciplinary role inherent in this apparently beneficent stance.[48] She therefore observes of Carol that "the lady was a true diplomat, a trained and experienced social worker, one of a race of women whom one was never sure whether to treat as friends or as members of the social police" (25).

For Adah, Carol's offers of aid are a poisoned chalice. Despite her difficult economic circumstances, Adah is determined to avoid the dole, the state aid provided in Britain to women with children. This resistance to state charity is partially a result of Adah's internalization of classist stereotypes concerning those who are forced to accept state aid. When she first arrives in Pussy Cat Mansions, where almost all the women are on the dole, Adah initially views those who depend on state aid as lazy and parasitic (33). Yet this is not the sole reason for her resistance. Having only just escaped a crippling dependency on her husband, Adah is loath to lean on anyone else, the welfare state included. Such dependency of course exacerbates perceptions of poor women as problems, subjected to the state's remedial programs, thereby shifting attention away from the discriminatory behavior and structures that marginalize poor women in the first place. While Adah may not be aware of this political background, the condescension with which Carol speaks to her and her ability to strip Adah of her children make the power dynamic inherent in her relation with Carol quite clear. As a result, like many women, Adah views dependency on either a man or state benefits as equally damaging to her prospects for self-actualization.[49] Despite her determination to remain autonomous, however, Adah cannot keep up the "double shift" called for by waged and domestic labor.[50] Scolded again by Carol for leaving her kids early at school so that she has time to get to work, Adah gives up her job and resigns herself to life "in the ditch."

Adah learns quickly that staying alive while on the dole is a full-time occupation. Although the welfare state helps poor women avoid unsafe and insecure jobs and marriages, in other words, aid programs are implemented in a manner designed to minimize the social costs of such women. This makes survival on the dole extremely arduous. After queuing for her first payment, for instance, Adah goes shopping, only to find that the weekly allowance for groceries does not cover the items she's placed in her shopping basket during this single excursion. The money to pay for her groceries, she decides, will have to come from the allotment given her for heating (38). The indignities to which the dole's inadequate payments reduce poor women had hardly figured in Adah's views of dole recipients as lazy parasites. As she settles into dependency, however, Adah learns first hand about the daily doses of humiliation dispensed by Britain's welfare state. Since there is no fixed allotment, women like Adah have to beg ministry officers for funds to adequately clothe their children. On one such occasion, Adah sits at home all day waiting for the officials to visit her to see about a shoe allowance for her children. While she waits, Adah explains that her children frequently wet their beds since it's too cold to get up and go to the bathroom. Adah has been buying paraffin on credit and cannot afford to heat her kids'

rooms. In addition, although her children are fed at school, Adah herself is not so lucky. By ten o'clock, she is experiencing pangs of hunger
as she waits for the officials, and decides to cook the ration of rice that
she had been saving for dinner. "Blast balanced meals! You can think of
balancing meals when you have enough food," she comments bitterly
(51). Finally, Adah has been allowing herself only three baths per week
in order to save money on gas. In order to be presentable before the
ministry officials arrive, she takes one of these carefully rationed baths.
When her friend Whoopey arrives to find her getting dressed up for the
officials' visit, she advises Adah that this is precisely the wrong course of
action: "We are poor, and the bastards want us to look poor" (53). As
Whoopey explains, the dole requires poor women to abandon their
aspirations not simply for material comforts, but also for the forms of
dignity that are taken for granted among less poverty stricken people.
Not only does the dole drain poor women of all their energy as they
carefully ration themselves and struggle to make ends meet on an inadequate social wage. In addition, it also systematically robs them of their
dignity and enforces an infantilizing form of dependency on the stern
authority of the usually middle-class, male state officials who supervise
aid programs.

Adah also finds out that the dole is intended to keep women
trapped in this humiliating dependency. Emecheta's protagonist initially articulates criticism of state aid that anticipates the arguments frequently heard from conservative quarters during the subsequent
neoliberal era: the dole robs people of their dignity by encouraging
them not to work (47). This criticism offers little sense that the dole is a
kind of social wage that puts a floor below wages, a Keynesian welfare
state strategy calculated to tighten labor markets and thereby generate
higher wages for those who are employed.[51] In such a reading, assaults
on the welfare state over the last two decades are not so much an
attempt to reconnect poor people with the ennobling effect of work as
they are ploys to loosen labor markets and depress wages. Emecheta is
not, however, concerned with these structural economic issues so much
as she is with the psychological and emotional impact of dependency on
women. As a result, it is the shame and despair that life in the ditch
encourages that is the principal focus of her attention.

The strength of Emecheta's depiction of life on the dole therefore
lies in its challenge to the pathologizing representations of the poor that
have gained hegemony in discussions of urban poverty. According to

such perspectives, the behavior of the poor is a product of an "under-class" mentality rooted in dependency on welfare.[52] The key to social transformation is not, then, an attack on the structural inequality that encourages dependency on welfare, but a tough-love approach that forces the poor to stand on their own feet regardless of the vicissitudes of the labor market. Against such pathologizing portraits of the poor, Emecheta's rendering of life on the dole demonstrates the tremendous initiative necessary to survive with a modicum of dignity. As Adah points out after a cheap paraffin heater nearly torches her apartment and her sleeping children, the dole keeps poor women on the edge of survival. Although Emecheta's writing acknowledges the demoralizing impact of welfare, it does not support an "underclass" view of poor neighborhoods as isolated, dysfunctional social enclaves, but instead focuses criticism on the inequalities and suffering that the inadequacies of the welfare state help perpetuate.

In the Ditch also dramatizes the hollowness of contemporary rhetoric concerning employment-based self-sufficiency for those rele-gated to the low-wage sector of the labor force. Desperate to earn some money in order to buy Christmas presents for her children, Adah inter-views for a part-time job as a cleaner in a factory. Although she's offered a wage of six pounds a week by the manager who interviews her, Adah is desperately afraid of having her benefits cut if it's discovered that she's working for more than the amount stipulated by Social Security. Of course, if she's booted off the dole, she'll be in far worse economic straits as a result of the inadequacy of the rate initially offered by the manager. Instead of chancing this, she offers to work for two pounds a week. After a month or so of work, however, the physical toll of the labor begins to affect her health and Adah suffers a breakdown. As a result, she's forced to quit the job and return to eking out an existence on the dole alone. Adah's experience with unskilled labor thus demon-strates the fallacy of assuming that jobs for poor people offer a living wage or the economic security necessary to constitute a viable alterna-tive to dependency on state aid.[53]

In addition, Adah's narrative also highlights the anger generated among poor women by the state's paternalistic regulations. As if the supplicatory pose that life in the ditch imposes were not enough, wel-fare authorities also prohibit women such as Adah from engaging in an active sexual and emotional life. As Adah quickly learns, "The women not only had to be poor, but they had to be sex-starved too" (60). The regulation of poor women's sexuality is not, however, simply grounded on an economic rationale. In addition, the proscription of "fancy men" also has an underlying eugenic consideration: the state intends to prevent poor women from reproducing. As Adah points out, such regulations are absurd given the widespread availability of birth control and abortion in contemporary Britain (61). Faced with this seemingly gratuitous discipline, poor women rebel in a variety of ways:

> Living in the ditch had its own consolations and advantages. There were always warm and natural friends. Friends who took delight in flouting society's laws. Some women indulged in having more and more children, a way of making the society that forced them into the ditch suffer. Some enjoyed taking it out on the welfare officers of the Ministry of Social Security, others took to drink. (54)

The state's transparently classist and racist proscriptions on poor women's sexuality turns childbearing into a right to be struggled for rather than a burden to be avoided, as the pro-choice rhetoric of middle-class feminism tends to imply. Emecheta's explanation of women's rebellion highlights the extent to which forms of behavior that are perceived by state authorities as dysfunctional are instead a rebellion against oppressive regulation and social marginalization. The forms of putative ghetto pathology singled out by conservative critics are, in other words, often insurrectionary acts by women whom society keeps in an immiserated state and whose lives the state attempts to regulate down to the most intimate details.

As Emecheta suggests in the preceding quotation, poor women also cultivate strong bonds of solidarity despite their social marginalization. Women like her gregarious neighbor Mrs. Cox remind Adah of "African matrons" who "have that sense of mutual aid that is ingrained in people who have known a communal rather than an individualistic way of life" (65).[54] This sense of solidarity is expressed not simply in the bonds of affection that develop among the women living at Pussy Cat Mansions. In addition, mutual aid extends to collective action against the bullying bureaucrats of the welfare state. In one particularly powerful scene, Adah's friend Whoopey rallies her when she's scolded for rent arrears. Adah's long-standing insecurity emerges in her exchange with the official, whose attempts to extract rent lead her to reflect, "It is a curse to be an orphan, a double curse to be a black one in a white country, an unforgivable calamity to be a woman with five kids but without a husband" (71). Just as Adah is about to cave in and hand over the money, however, Whoopey and another neighbor intervene and demand that the council clean up her apartment before she pays rent. While class solidarity does not overcome racism among all her neighbors, the bonds forged through resistance to poverty and oppression teach Adah a great deal about the need to challenge authority. Adah is frequently encouraged by her neighbors to engage in rent strikes in response to the appalling conditions she must endure in public housing. In addition, she participates as the women organize a protest march in response to the supercilious behavior of Carol, the complex's social worker. As Adah comments, "Women in the ditch were always too ignorant or too frightened to ask for what they were entitled to. People like Carol were employed to let them know their rights, but the trouble was that Carol handed them their rights, as if she was giving out charity" (98).[55] The solidarity Adah witnesses in response to this sort of condescending behavior has a dramatic impact on the hobbling insecurity that she carried with her following her childhood as an orphan and her damaging marriage to Francis.

Adah's increasing strength is most apparent in her reaction to expressions of racism from some of her neighbors in the ditch. When she first arrives at Pussy Cat Mansions, she attempts to placate her aggressively bigoted neighbors by playing dumb. Her assumption is that British people all believe that Africans are ignorant savages, and that the path of least resistance is to play along with this stereotype in order to solicit their condescending aid (18). This strategy is self-defeating, however, for it simply leads to expressions of weakness that encourage increasing abuse. Yet by the end of her stint at Pussy Cat Mansions, Adah has developed the strength to stand up to such bigotry. When a crabby woman tells her to go back to her own country during a conflict in the washroom, for example, Adah shoots back that she doesn't look English herself (110). The woman sputters racist attacks in response, but is defeated and humiliated by Adah's quick comeback.

The gradual development of Adah from insecurity to strength logically culminates in her departure from Pussy Cat Mansions. Yet this transition is by no means an easy one. Adah ironically fails to apply for rehousing for quite some time as a result of her fear of losing the forms of friendship and solidarity that life in the ditch helps foster (91). Paradoxically, then, Adah's life among what she initially perceives as the degraded recipients of state aid becomes highly attractive because of the comradeship it affords in the midst of material deprivation. One final encounter with Carol nevertheless convinces Adah that she is being used by the social worker rather than vice versa. This perception, augmented by Adah's gradually increasing strength, leads her to ultimately overcome her fear of isolation and climb out of the ditch. The novel concludes with Adah relocating to an apartment in a new complex situated in an affluent London neighborhood. As Emecheta documents in her autobiography, this was the beginning of the transition that lead to her degree in sociology and to her successful career as an author. From this increasingly autonomous and fulfilled perspective, Adah is able to regard with suitable skepticism her apparently strong friend Whoopey's pipe dreams for social mobility through the arrival of a wealthy suitor (131). *In the Ditch* thus traces Adah's journey not only from poverty to increasing economic self-sufficiency, but also from emotional insecurity to growing autonomy and resiliency in the face of the systemic racism and classism that characterized British society during the 1960s.

Conclusion

In the powerful introduction to her collection of essays by black British women authors, then-exiled South African author Lauretta Ngcobo writes:

> White Britons want to forget this [imperialist] past, to forget that we once lived in close proximity with them, in their kitchens, caring for their children, being raped by their men and then bearing those tainted babies. It is not surprising that our appearance in the front garden of Britain causes embarrassment. We bring back to life forgotten crimes and immense guilt. This amnesia is the unacknowledged admission that British society still has not come to terms with our presence. We linger in a kind of social limbo and consequently suffer a state of invisibility.[56]

If Ngcobo's analysis of Britain's imperial amnesia suggests that the invisibility of black women was no accident, the last thirty years have witnessed a sustained battle by such women to escape the forms of invisibility to which they were consigned. Such activism led to the articulation of stinging critiques of racism. The feminist movement in Britain was not spared from these critical salvos. Indeed, a great deal of the energy of black British feminism during its initial period of efflorescence was consumed with carving out a space for black women within the broader feminist movement. In works such as Hazel Carby's "White Women Listen!" black feminists drew attention to the myopia of the dominant traditions of feminism, which called for universal solidarity between women while ignoring the very real inequalities fostered by class and race difference. Carby's work, like that of other black feminists, introduced important traditions of transnational cultural and political practice to Britain.

Take the feminist discussion of the family ethic. During the post-1945 period, the terms of debate about women's labor hinged on the impact of work outside the home on British family life. Yet, as Carby points out, little attention was devoted to the effect of large-scale labor force participation among colonized women throughout the century.[57] Indeed, black women were employed in great numbers in Britain's reserve army of labor in the colonies with absolutely no consideration of the impact on the families of colonized subjects. When black women migrated to Britain, these traditions of working a double shift under highly exploitative conditions traveled with them. Rather that striving to protect black families, the state reproduced commonsense beliefs about their inherent pathology. "Black women," Carby argues, "were seen to fail as mothers precisely because of their position as workers."[58] Thus, the pathologization of black families by the state in Britain during the postimperial period has a strong colonial genealogy. For many black feminists, as a result, discussions of women's emancipation unfolded under dramatically different terms from those adopted by the mainstream feminist movement. The consensus view among many white, middle-class feminists that the family was purely a site of oppression could not be adopted by many black women, who had to fight for the right to have children and who often turned to their families for shelter from racist hostility.

As the first successful black woman novelist living in Britain after 1948, Buchi Emecheta clearly is a pioneering figure in overcoming the invisibility to which black British women were relegated. The autobiographically based documentary fiction of her London novels, the first works she published, encompasses three important stages that are often cited as the classic path toward women's empowerment: discovering

voice; establishing forms of collective solidarity; and engaging in political activism. Yet the progress of Emecheta's protagonist Adah along this
path is marked by significant differences from those which would
obtain for the majority of British women. She must, for example, navi-
gate an extended kin system as an orphan, her identity reduced essentially to that of a commodity. Her marriage continues this relation. Yet
when she finally breaks out of her suffocating subordination to her husband, she finds herself, as a poor black woman, locked in another form
of dependency. Emecheta's depiction of her struggle to survive in the
ditch offers a powerful instance of the pathologization discussed by
Hazel Carby, even if her portrait of Adah's dependency on Francis in
Second-Class Citizen seems to challenge some of Carby's assertions
about the distinctions between black and white feminism. In her London trilogy, Emecheta thus evokes many of the central issues around
black women's struggle to forge and maintain identity in Britain that
would concern groups like OWAAD in subsequent years.

In addition to anticipating many of the important issues for black
feminist organizing, Buchi Emecheta's London trilogy offers important
historical perspective on the present. Far from improving, the sexist and
racist devaluation of black women's identity and labor depicted by
Emecheta intensified in the last decades of the century. If black workers
were recruited to facilitate white upward mobility while accepting
wages at a level unpalatable to the indigenous working class, the end of
the postwar economic boom and the imposition of spiraling rounds of
austerity after the 1970s has disproportionately affected black people.
High unemployment and the downsizing of the Keynesian welfare state
made jobs attractive to white workers who previously regarded such
labor as beneath them. As Amina Mama explains, black women are predominantly concentrated in those areas of the British economy that
have been most affected by post-Fordist downsizing, including caring
professions such as nursing, teaching, community and social work, and
service labor.[59] Consigned to such roles by oppressive notions of "femininity" and by racist practices in education and elsewhere, black women
have born the brunt of neoliberal downsizing policies in these areas. In
addition, since they are more often heads of families and are more likely
to have unemployed domestic partners, assaults on black woman's
wages have a disproportionately damaging impact on the black community as a whole. As neoliberal structural adjustment policies have
ripped through the British economy over the last decades, the plight of

poor black women such as the protagonist of Buchi Emecheta's London novels can only have worsened.[60] Indeed, from the vantage point of the present, Adah's heroic effort to pull herself first out of her abusive marriage and then out of the ditch of welfare dependency is particularly poignant. Tragically, the story of Adah's journey toward autonomy is even harder to imagine today than when it was originally told.

Heritage Politics of the Soul

Immigration and Identity in Salman Rushdie's
The Satanic Verses

ON 27 MARCH 1989 A LARGE PROTEST OF TWENTY THOUSAND or more Muslims from around Britain and the rest of Europe marched through central London to condemn Salman Rushdie's affront to Islam in his recently published novel *The Satanic Verses* and to call for the book's banning. This demonstration was one of the most important protests in a season of discontent among British Muslims, whose anger at the shortcomings of British multiculturalism had been brewing for most of the decade. Lofting banners calling for "Equal Rights for Muslims," demonstrators congregated outside the Houses of Parliament to burn Salman Rushdie in effigy. Here, a multiracial clutch of activists from the recently formed group Women Against Fundamentalism (WAF) had set up a picket.[1] Their placards called for the repeal rather than the extension of the Blasphemy Law and voiced support for Salman Rushdie's freedom of expression. Arguments quickly flared up over the women's avowed solidarity with Rushdie. Soon, the WAF picket was being attacked by young men from the march as well as by a group of white neofascists, who had accompanied the protest march to express their support for the integrity of Muslim culture. The ensuing melee, in which riot police had to intervene to protect the WAF activists from the enraged crowd, underlined the incendiary quality of conflicts around religion and identity in Britain.

The WAF picket attracted controversy even before the march. Members of the Anti-Fascist League had decided to march alongside the Muslim protesters in order to support the rights of ethnic minorities to resist racism. WAF's picket seemed to fly in the face of this stance of antiracist solidarity. Indeed, by coming out in opposition to what leaders were representing as the common voice of the British Muslim community, WAF was challenging a long-standing tenet of antiracist politics in Britain. Throughout the 1970s and the first half of the 1980s, antiracist politics had pivoted on internal solidarity in the face of the institutional and quotidian manifestations of racism in Britain. It was consequently taboo for Asian and black women to express criticism of gender relations within their communities outside closed community forums.[2] In tandem with such models of defensive solidarity, antiracist leaders lionized the street-fighting prowess of local youth groups, who were seen as defending Asian and black communities from the hostile incursions of neofascist hooligans.[3] Leftist groups such as the Anti-Fascist League echoed this analysis of the militant, largely male youth groups as the authentic voice of Asian and black communities. Yet, by embracing the street-fighting machismo of militant antiracist groups, radical intellectuals had to avert their eyes from the role of many youth groups in colluding with the most conservative elements of communities by policing the conduct of women.[4] In championing black nationalism in such uncritical terms, in other words, theorists of black British social movements reproduced the problematic gender politics of anticolonial nationalism.[5] WAF's picket against the anti-Rushdie demonstration therefore challenged not simply religious fundamentalism but also the essentialism of many progressives in Britain's antiracist movement. For many radical Asian and black women in Britain, holding one's tongue in the name of antiracist solidarity had come by the late 1980s to be analogous to the traditional injunction to preserve community honor or *izzat* by staying silent in the face of gender oppression.[6]

In addition to challenging antiracist models of communal solidarity, however, the WAF picket also flew in the face of dominant media representations of Muslim communities in Britain as homogeneous and extremist. The day after the demonstration, for instance, the *Sunday Times Magazine* ran a major article whose introduction is obviously connected to the events of the preceding day: "For several decades Islamic militancy existed for Britons only as indignantly reported outbreaks in far-off countries of which we knew nothing. The past few months have shown that it is now a potent, living organism in the body of Britain itself, impossible to wish away or assimilate or suppress."[7] Like much of the rhetoric that circulated in Britain during the Rushdie Affair, the *Times* article tells us more about (non-Muslim) British fears of Muslims than it does about British Muslims themselves. Protests against *The Satanic Verses* suggest to the author that the once hale body of British society has been penetrated by an alien presence, a virus or parasite whose virility explains the alarmed tone of the article's title: "Is Rushdie Just the Beginning?" The article's rhetoric of contamination testifies to a deeply racist conception of the nation as a homogeneous, organic community. Yet it is ironically the presence of the perceived Islamic pathogen that facilitates the retroactive construction of the national body as a sanitary space. The racism inscribed within these metaphors of pollution is one that, in other words, is dependent upon the exaggeration of *cultural* differences, despite the ostensibly somatic rhetoric of disease. As Étienne Balibar argues, this is a racism "whose dominant theme is not biological heredity but the insurmountability of cultural differences, a racism which, at first sight, does not postulate the superiority of certain groups or peoples in relation to others but 'only' the harmfulness of abolishing frontiers, the incompatibility of life-styles and traditions."[8] The image of the nation as diseased site, a once healthy body invaded by a malign cultural virus, legitimates discourses of political prophylaxis designed to reestablish an imaginary healthy state.[9]

As the *Times* article suggests, the Rushdie affair was an opening salvo in what Samuel Huntington, in a much-cited 1993 essay in *Foreign Affairs,* subsequently called a "clash of civilizations" between Islam and the West.[10] Anticipating Huntington's approach, commentators on the Rushdie affair tended to depict Britain as a progressive, secular society whose multicultural, pluralistic values were threatened by bellicose Muslim fundamentalism. This neo-Orientalist binarism is novel to the extent that the Islamic Other is now internal to Europe, rather than, as the *Times* article has it, in far-off countries. Such geographical proximity generates intense anxiety about border crossing and pollution. Indeed, warnings by scholars such as Huntington about the inherently irrational and belligerent character of Islam serve as an *a priori* justification for preemptive measures.[11] These self-fulfilling xenophobic discourses are dependent upon the diminution of both the similarities between "host" and "alien" and the differences within each group. For instance, assertions of British secularism conveniently ignore the fact that Britain retains a Blasphemy Law whose solely Christian provenance makes explicit both the racial formation and the nonsecularity of the state. Despite the fact that they were habitually described as benighted medievalists, British Muslims calling for the equitable application of the Blasphemy Law were in fact appealing to Enlightenment conceptions of an egalitarian legal system. The similarity between protesters' conceptions of religious offense and those of the establishment in Britain was underlined when Dr. Rubert Runcie, the archbishop of Canterbury, called for the extension of the law against blasphemy to cover religions other than Christianity.[12]

The WAF picket in Whitehall was also established with conflicts around rising fundamentalism in South Asia in mind, and, like those conflicts, suggested that the constitutive contradictions of both multicultural state policy and religious fundamentalism are most evident around questions of gender. Feminists working on the interface between nationalism and gender power have long argued that women play crucial roles, both materially and symbolically, in sustaining communities; characteristically, gender difference is used symbolically to define the bounds of national or communal identity.[13] These observations are even more apt in relation to transnational movements such as religious fundamentalism. Fundamentalist movements of all denominations take this reduction of women to the role of icons of collective integrity to an extreme.[14] As WAF defines them, such movements tend to be organized as vanguardist hierarchies that attempt to take over state power in order to enforce a supposedly divinely mandated morality. This morality typically centers on the control of women's sexuality and behavior as a means to preserve collective identity in the face of various pressures.[15] Women are reduced under such circumstances to vehicles for collective honor and theological orthodoxy.

It is no coincidence that WAF's picket was construed as an assault on community honor during a demonstration against a novel that was itself taken as an affront to *izzat*. As Marina Warner has argued, there is a historical homology between control of the word and control of women in religious movements.[16] Indeed, it was precisely these two aspects of Salman Rushdie's novel that were cited as giving offense and legitimating the subsequent fatwa against the author. Yet Rushdie's depiction of the Koran's fallibility and his defiling of the honor of Muhammad's wives take place within dream sequences experienced by his protagonist Gibreel Farishta. These dreams are a response to the unstable social conditions Gibreel encounters in India and Britain during the 1980s. Thus, although the novel has often been seen as sparking a Manichaean clash of civilizations, it in fact simply fictionalizes and critiques the unfolding social conflicts in contemporary Britain and India. Moreover, *The Satanic Verses* suggests that forms of symbolic border policing that turn on representations of feminine purity are central to these conflicts. Thus, although Rushdie has often been taken for a doyen of cosmopolitan hybridity, *The Satanic Verses* explores the conditions that generate fundamentalist assertions of identity, suggesting that diasporic experience generates forms of political bifocality that are just as often conflictual as they are hybrid.[17] Rushdie's focus on the homosocial rivalry that develops between his two male protagonists dramatizes the way in which women's identity and rights have frequently been displaced in the internecine struggles of racialized communities within both Britain and India over the course of the last decades.

After the publication of *The Satanic Verses,* Salman Rushdie was attacked not simply by Islamic fundamentalists but also by many progressive intellectuals who saw his work as complicit with Orientalist representations of Islam.[18] Yet, as Rushdie was quick to point out, his novel is just as critical of British racism as it is of Islamism, and in fact sees the two as intertwined in significant ways. While Islamophobia has only escalated in the West since the publication of *The Satanic Verses,* young Muslim men and women have begun forging a European Islam by developing the tradition of *ijtihad,* or independent reasoning.[19] Despite the controversy that it elicited, *The Satanic Verses* needs to be seen as a pioneering attempt to develop this tradition of *ijtihad.* The work of Women Against Fundamentalism marks a similarly early and important initiative whose critical stance in relation to both British multiculturalism and religious fundamentalism breaks down the facile binaries of culture clash theories. By engaging with communal conflict in South Asia and the racialization of diasporic subjects in Britain, Rushdie's novel highlights the extent to which the control of women and their sexuality is a logical outcome of monolithic, exclusionary representations of identity among both dominant and subordinate groups. Through its analysis of this gendered heritage politics, *The Satanic Verses,* like the protests of WAF activists, underlines the reductive character of the culture clash theories that have occupied an increasingly prominent place in the public sphere since the Rushdie affair.

Of Migrations and Metamorphoses

Migration to Britain is an undeniably violent process, a chaotic birth
into newness, for Saladin Chamcha and Gibreel Farishta, the twin protagonists of *The Satanic Verses*.[20] Blown out of their plane by a Sikh separatist from Canada, the two fall to earth in a big bang that exposes the
fragmented lives of contemporary migrants.[21] For migrants drawn from
underdeveloped nations to fill the most menial positions in the labor
force of metropolitan countries, international travel involves the fearful
negotiation of border controls established precisely in order to regulate
the flow of this new industrial reserve army.[22] As Rushdie's narrator suggests, women and children are the primary objects of the inquisitorial
gaze of this state bureaucracy. Indeed, this surveillance apparatus pene-
trates into the most private spaces and, in doing so, makes citizenship
rights hinge upon questions of gender. The immigration checks that *The
Satanic Verses* itemizes force women to document their marital status
through detailed description of their husbands' genitals, underlining the
state's recognition of their identity solely as legal appendages to their
husbands. In addition, such checks suggest the homosocial bonds and
animosities of the nation-state, for, despite the increasing exploitation
of immigrant women's labor within the metropolis, it is the absent phal-
lus of the male immigrant that is the ultimate object of the state's attention. The paranoid gaze that seeks out these disseminatory objects is, of
course, animated by fear of the growth of Britain's nonwhite population
as a result of the reunion and propagation of Asian and black families.[23]
Finally, such prying examinations emphasize the assumed alterity and
illegality of *all* nonwhite migrants: the "reasonable" facade of the immigration control apparatus obscures the systematic forms of racialization
that it effects upon both immigrants and citizens.

  Discussing the British Nationality Act of 1981, Louise London and
Nira Yuval-Davis argue that the act's implementation of a two-tiered
system that distinguishes between "Patrial UK" and "Commonwealth"
citizens has underlined the gendered nature of access to the rights of a
British subject. The act's increased emphasis on women as reproducers
of the national collectivity—women now being transmitters of citizenship to their children—has gone hand in hand with a campaign involv-
ing the racialized delimitation of the rights of belonging within that collectivity.[24] The Nationality Act culminates a succession of measures that
reframed rights of belonging by limiting citizenship to already estab-

lished resident citizens and to the descendants of white British citizens. As commentators have pointed out, Britain thus aligned itself with the European *gastarbeiter* model, in which the costs of reproducing migrant labor were displaced onto underdeveloped nations through the host country's refusal to grant citizenship rights to the immigrant labor force.[25] Under such conditions, the ethnic and gendered specificity of nationalist ideology becomes ever more apparent.[26]

Having thus shorn itself of its legal responsibilities for its former colonial subjects, Britain had by the Thatcher era become decisively postcolonial. The "debris of the soul"—empty signifiers such as *belonging* and *home*—that plummet down from the shredded fuselage of the *Bostan* jetliner in the opening pages of *The Satanic Verses* are the specific products in the first instance of separatist terrorism. Behind this initial explosion, however, lie the increasingly racist definitions of national belonging codified as Britain's postwar economic boom wound down, emptying words such as *belonging* and *home* of meaning for members of the Asian diaspora in Britain. Fragmentation and double consciousness result, in other words, from the intertwined patterns of globalization and renationalization that Britain has undergone rather than from some vague ontological condition of exile. While this denial of statutory rights does not legally affect the bulk of the postwar immigrant population of Britain, the tendency is for all those who do not *appear* "British" or, worse still, "English," to be treated as possible aliens.

Such state-sanctioned ethnic absolutism brings its institutional power to bear very differently on men and on women. Women, in particular, are frequently represented as the reproducers of threatening forms of internal difference. Indeed, British feminists have expressed fears that, despite the relatively egalitarian postwar state provisioning of reproductive consultation and services, abuses of minority women's reproductive rights may become more widespread given the ongoing moral panic over the pollution of the racial stock of the nation.[27] Contemporary politicians continue to employ the racist rhetoric of national reproduction characteristic of the imperial epoch, despite the exit of Margaret Thatcher and her infamous fear of "swamping."[28]

Notwithstanding the racism Asian and black Britons are likely to encounter within this context, Rushdie's narrator refuses to see migration simply as a condition of deracination. Diaspora in the novel involves not just the discontinuous experience suggested by the *Bostan*'s "debris of the soul," but also processes of mutation that generate "new-

ness." These processes raise the question of whether a notion of essential identity is possible in light of such transformations, and of what attitudes the translated will assume in order to make sense of their disjunctive experience. Rushdie's narrator poses such questions explicitly:
"How does newness come into the world? How is it born? Of what
fusions, translations, conjoinings is it made?" (8). Rushdie asks here not
only what forms of hybridity are generated by diaspora experience, but
also, crucially, what sorts of heritage politics and ethnic absolutism such
displacements give rise to. Despite the dissemination associated with
diaspora, the politics of identity consolidation operate in a tense, dialectical relation to those of hybridization.[29] In the context of the highly
fluid conditions of today's global cultural economy, the assertion of
transcultural affiliation by diaspora populations has become an important strategy for proclaiming the solidarity of racialized national
minorities with transnational communities and their wider horizons
and histories of struggle.[30] Such practices do not, however, necessarily
lead to an embrace of self-consciously hybrid cultural practices and
identities. These changes also antagonize groups intent on consolidating the boundaries between imagined communities using various forms
of ethnic absolutism.

Crashing to earth in the middle of the *Bostan*'s welter of exploded
hopes, Gibreel and Saladin undergo a metamorphosis that suggests the
impact of this new cartography of social space. The pair is initially posed
as antithetical through the songs they sing as they drop toward the
English Channel. Gibreel croons a *ghazal* of reincarnation that embraces
discontinuity and death as well as a ditty from an old Bombay film in celebration of the hybridity of Indian national identity; the assimilated Saladin, by contrast, stolidly replies with the British national anthem. A
polyglot Indian actor floats toward an Anglophile NRI ventriloquist
through the clouds as two diametrically opposed responses to postcolonial experience and migration meet and mix. Despite his Anglophile
resistance to Gibreel's embraces, Saladin finds his identity growing fluid
like that of his companion. The mutation that he feels himself undergo-
ing undermines the English identity he has so carefully constructed for
himself during his years as an expatriate. Saladin is ushered through this
metamorphosis into the double consciousness of the trans-lated, of the
migrant whose physical peregrinations establish the possibility of multiple sites of affiliation. Saladin's celestial mutation fuses him, reluctantly,
with the self-conscious hybridity of Gibreel, the Bombay cinema star.

This scene draws attention to the particularly gendered form of such postcolonial hybridization by pointing to the strains placed upon homosocial bonds within such a context. For Rushdie's twin protagonists fall toward the English Channel in a position whose homoeroticism dramatizes the fear of *unmanning* associated with cultural translation. If, as Robert Young's work has emphasized, hybridity is a fundamentally heterosexual category marked by trepidations over miscegenation, then this opening scene of the novel highlights the homosocial site of bonding normally left unmarked by discourses of hybridity.[31] Just as the turn-of-the-century equation of sexual "deviancy" with racial degeneration marked the instabilities in colonial technologies of sexuality by multiplying the qualifiers for whiteness, so this moment of metamorphosis in Rushdie's text suggests a crisis in the identity of his two protagonists.[32] This crisis turns upon the ambivalence of the homosocial bond that links them. In this scene, the foundational bond that anchors national identity and communal solidarity tips over into a homoerotic relation, one that offers the two protagonists intertwined in an embrace that is traditionally identified with a threat to rather than a pillar of the homosocial order. The sliding of the mimetic desire that marks the homosocial continuum into same-sex desire marks a dangerous supplement to the thematic of doubling traced in Gibreel and Saladin's descent. This errant form of hybridity is connected to a particular set of phobias associated with globalization and migrancy. The product of a mutability that threatens homosocial community, this *degenerate* hybridity is produced by an experience that disrupts stable frontiers, internal and external, personal and political. Resistance to the disseminatory impact of contemporary cultural flows thus tends to take a peculiarly gendered form, one in which fears of the erosion of male identity bring to light the aggression that undergirds the homosocial continuum.

RELIGIOUS COMMUNALISM AND THE RUPTURING OF
NATIONAL ALLEGORY

Gibreel's *ghazal*-chanting during his drop toward the drink may be more charismatic than Saladin's rigid mimicry of British nationalism, but it is no less flawed a response to the traumas of migration. For his celebration of the hybridity of the Indian everyman is predicated on an increasingly hollow representation of national reality. Indeed, in Gibreel's reaction to the *Bostan* disaster, Rushdie is satirizing one of the most powerful representations available of Indian national identity: the Bollywood hero. The song Gibreel sings is, in fact, lifted from a famous Bollywood film that emphasized the adaptive capacity of Indians. As Sumita Chakravarty's work on Indian popular cinema suggests, the malleable persona of the male film protagonist serves as an allegory of the successful fusion of the multiple forms of difference, from class and caste to region and religion, that characterizes the Indian nation.[33] Consciously exploiting the resources of male masquerade and impersonation, the Bombay film star reconciles national binarisms such as the Hindu-Muslim split by suggesting that such differences are merely superficial, that difference is, after all, only skin deep. Drawing on Bombay cinema's textual practice of male masquerade, Rushdie's work initially intimates that such hybridity may serve as an allegory for the identity of the migrant. Yet while the mutability of the hero's body in Bombay cinema may suggest the potential resolution of the intractable contradictions of national identity, it nonetheless also intimates the fear of the disjunction and dissolution that animates essentialist reassertions of communal identity. As recent cultural theory has emphasized, the performative aspect of masquerade underlines the nonessential character of gendered being.[34] While this constructivist approach might provide a convenient unifying allegory for an increasingly fragmented polity, it also makes explicit the experience of instability that affects culture and identity within a globalized world and often acts as the catalyst to various forms of ethnic and cultural absolutism. If Gibreel's celebration of hybrid identity allegorizes Indian national identity, it is a consciousness that is ultimately *not* marked by the easy reconciliations imagined by the cinematic tradition.[35]

But of course the Bombay film industry has been kind to Gibreel, and so it behooves him to embrace the form of hybridity that it purveys. Born of a poor *dabbawalla* (porter) who wears himself out catering to the bloated bellies of film industry moguls, Gibreel climbs to stardom by impersonating the myriad deities of India (17). Rushdie casts Gibreel in the role of the ultimate reconciler, the chameleon onto whom the incredibly various population of India can project its greatest hopes and most intimate desires. By literally incarnating the various belief systems that animate much of the nation's populace, Gibreel becomes a metaphorical embodiment of national identity. In fact, the "theological" genre that Rushdie invents for Gibreel to star in is based on one of the perennial and defining forms of Indian cinematography: the mythological.[36] One of the pioneer genres in early Indian filmmaking, the mythological quickly came to signify the fundamentally *independent* nature of the national imaginary, for it was on this "interior" ground that India's autonomy from the West could be asserted. As the work of the subaltern studies historians has made clear, it was in the religious and cultural spheres that Indian nationalists found alternative principles of autonomy and national integrity to the British-dominated public, administrative sphere.[37] Indeed, the Indian film industry can be said to have played a pivotal role in integrating the popular classes into the project of nation-building through appropriating forms of folk belief and expression in order to suture the former to the anticolonial, nationalist project. In contributing to the representation of the spiritual realm, Indian popular cinema thus asserted its claim as one of the primary representational forms of the imagined community of the nation. In addition, it presented itself as the facilitating form behind the "passive revolution" through which subaltern opinion was mobilized within the anticolonial struggle.

Gibreel's complete identification with the national imaginary turns his misadventures into an allegory of the breakdown of the secular definition of the state, and, ultimately, of the partial, contradictory nature of nationalist ideology. Despite his success at impersonating the various avatars of India's multiple sects, a "Phantom Bug" that has particularly gruesome effects strikes him down at the height of his fame. Adopting the role of amanuensis of national consciousness, Gibreel's body becomes the locus upon which the violent, sectarian disharmony of national reality is written. The symmetry between Gibreel's impersonation of religious figures and popular belief in this incarnation allows Rushdie to analyze the communal violence that tore apart the national fabric during the 1980s. In addition, this symmetry testifies to the intense contradictions always implicit within the project of nation-formation, to the lack of absolute hegemony of the bourgeois, secular class over the other popular elements swept up in the national struggle for self-determination.

The phantom bug that nearly kills Gibreel finds its corollary in the unraveling hegemony of the nationalist project over the various sects and communal groups that together constitute the Indian polity. This crisis became increasingly prominent during the 1980s with the decline of state commitment to the values that facilitated modernization, among which secularism, equal opportunity, and social welfare figured most prominently. Spurred by its flagging electoral prospects, the Congress Party under the leadership of Rajiv Gandhi attempted to make concessions both to the rising forces of Hindu nationalism and to the more militantly fundamentalist elements within the Muslim community.[38] This strategy of conciliating ethnic absolutism appeared to offer an easy resolution to the crisis of the secular Indian state through allowing these two groups to be played off against one another. However, the Shah Bano controversy of the mid-1980s dramatized the impracticality of such a strategy. The Bano affair highlighted the centrality of the question of gender in conflicts over the secular identity of the state and its guarantees of rights to religious minorities. Bano's case turned upon the Indian Supreme Court's ruling in favor of a destitute Muslim woman who sued her husband for support after he divorced her. Muslim leaders interpreted this ruling as a threat to the autonomy of the Muslim community's so-called Personal Laws, which, since independence, have accorded a separate civil code to the Muslim minority. In mobilizing around the question of minority rights, Muslim leaders chose to sacrifice the right of Muslim women to restitution in the name of preserving communal identity. The Indian government's subsequent validation of this position furthered the resulting reification of the question of minority rights by accepting the hard-line fundamentalism of the ulema as the sole representative voice of the minority community. In response to the government ruling, Hindu rightists seized on the notion of "equality" to attack the Muslim community, challenging what they perceived as the government's appeasement of the Muslim leadership. While there was some truth to Hindu rightists' claims that the Personal Laws abrogate the universalistic reach of the constitution by exempting Muslims from the provisions for marriage and divorce codified in the Hindu Code Bill of 1956, these criticisms were hardly made with the good of Muslim women in mind. Conflict between increasingly rigidly defined communal groups thus intensified a form of identity politics in which the question of women's rights was introduced and debated with no concern for ameliorating the conditions of women. Instead, women functioned as pawns in sectarian struggles between incommensurable patriarchies.

In the context of this crisis of the secular nation-state, the status of religion as a folk form that can be appropriated by hegemonic media such as the cinema is put into question. Religion becomes, instead, a "phantom bug" capable of destroying the body politic. If Gibreel's internal hemorrhaging may be said to represent the increasingly violent communal conflicts within India during this period, then his subsequent crisis of faith is a product of the political exploitation of religion. Indeed, Gibreel's crisis is predicated on the hollowing out of spirituality as a result of such exploitation. Not only do Gibreel's prayers for mercy during his sickness go unanswered, but he gets better as soon as it becomes evident to him that there will be no response to his supplications. The departure of God from Gibreel's universe is significant in that it introduces him for the first time to the idea of living a life not only without divine sanction, but without the kind of security and clarity that such sanction introduced. This revelation of his loneliness in the world opens Gibreel to a terrifying and exhilarating world of possibilities and complexities. A heady one for Gibreel: he has momentarily seen through the Manichaean divisions of the social body imposed by orthodoxy. This epiphany prompts him to fall in love with a white woman and decamp to Britain. The resulting mutations and nightmares situate the crisis of the national body in a transnational framework. The seamless ideological interpellation between Gibreel, Bollywood cinema, and popular elements of the nation thus allows Rushdie to analyze the double consciousness of diasporic communities.

The Textual Politics of Fundamentalist Discourse

In his well-known discussion of nationalism, Benedict Anderson asserts that a sacred community such as Christianity or Islam depends upon a notion of the nonarbitrariness of the sign, of the uniquely sacred character of a *particular* truth-language, to bind radically different cultures into a whole.[39] While Anderson argues that historical sacral kingdoms were fragmented and territorialized during the formation of the nation-state, the rise of various forms of religious fundamentalism around the world suggests that it is secular nationalism rather than religious dogmatism that is in crisis.[40] In fact, fundamentalist movements often animate antihegemonic nationalisms today. Yet fundamentalist movements are extremely heterogeneous, of course, and are just as often complicit with forms of neocolonialism—as the example of Saudi Arabia makes evident—as they are with anti-imperialism. In addition, fundamentalist movements manifest themselves among dominant majorities within states as well as in the form of minority movements seeking to promote their beliefs within specific, often ethnically defined constituencies.[41] Finally, although they always repudiate pluralist systems of thought, fundamentalist movements may draw either on experiential values articulated by a charismatic leadership or on the supposedly incontrovertible authority of a sacred text. Ironically, appeals to sacred texts have been an important resource historically for movements seeking to challenge the authority of orthodox religious authorities.[42] In fundamentalism, however, authority lies not in the sacred text itself, despite frequent protestations by leaders to that effect, but rather in the highly authoritarian and almost exclusively male religious figures who claim the right to interpret the text and do so in a selective manner that legitimates their power.[43]

In exercising such interpretive authority, fundamentalist leaders not only evade community sanction through the notion of a God-given interpretive mandate. In addition, leaders' exegetical authority stems from wrenching sacred texts out of the historical continuum in which they were composed and downplaying the complicated generic and aesthetic characteristics of such texts in the name of simplified moral maxims.[44] This co-optation of the text flies in the face of the long-standing interpretive practices that characterize established religious traditions such as Judaism, Christianity, and Islam. In this sense, fundamentalism is *not* a return to tradition, as it is often presented as being, but is instead an abrogation of established bodies of textual knowledge and practice. In addition, fundamentalist reading strategies attempt to arrest the mutability of meaning that characterizes language. As Bakhtin argues, individual consciousness is constituted in language, a social and historical form that is, crucially, an arena of class struggle.[45] Indeed, Bakhtin stressed that the inner dialectical quality of the sign becomes most evident at times of social crisis, when the attempts of socially dominant groups to impart stable interpretations of the sign break down and emergent discourses assert themselves. In other words, the antagonism that prevents any final suturing of the social proliferates during moments of organic crisis in which hegemony is challenged on many levels and in many sites, including through conflicting interpretations of sacred texts.[46]

In the polarized social climate of Salman Rushdie's Ellowen Deeowen (London) during the mid-1980s, hegemonic discourse becomes subject to slippages and inversions that fully dramatize the Janus-faced quality of the sign. As his transformation of the British capital's name suggests, Rushdie's text is filled with puns, double entendres, and other word games that defamiliarize and undermine the claims of hegemonic language to authenticity and authority.[47] While Rushdie's novel delves deeply into the refashioning of the postcolonial metropolis by diasporic residents, it also concerns itself with the disassociation of sensibility experienced by migrants to the metropolis.[48] For many of these migrants, the fetishized authority of the sacred text compensates for the deracinating experiences of migration.[49] In response to what in many instances can be an oppressive textual orthodoxy, *The Satanic Verses* deconstructs the authority of the sacred text of Islam. In highlighting the ambiguity that inheres in the enunciation of divine revelation, Rushdie's fiction hinges not simply on an awareness of language's disseminatory tendencies, but also on the power plays inherent in claims to textual authority.[50] Indeed, Gibreel is quite literally driven mad by the uncontainable heteroglossia of language.[51] The dreams that begin to wrack him shortly after his repudiation of his faith carry Gibreel back to the genesis of Islam. His awareness of the sectarian animus of religion and of the legitimation crisis of national ideology throws Gibreel into an emotional ferment in which he reenacts the Prophet Muhammad's encounter with the angel Gabriel. In rewriting the history of Islam, thereby introducing the Koran's Satanic Verses as well as the pragmatic considerations that impinge upon divine revelation, Rushdie sets out to excavate the forms of *difference* that inhere within the foundation myths of a sacred community.[52] Implicit in this reworking is a critique of the centripetal, hierarchical social structure that the sacred text authorizes. As he had done previously in relation to the nation-state, that is, Rushdie seeks in *The Satanic Verses* to foreground the plural and fragmentary character of a community conceived of, this time, as a transnational sodality.[53]

The central moment within the founding text of a great religion is that of revelation, when the prophet is given the sacred Word that will orient the faithful. Gibreel's dreams on the highjacked airliner *Bostan,* dreams that reenact this moment, raise profound questions concerning the nature of revelation. Gibreel finds himself transformed from the passive witness of the prophet Mahound's experiences to a participant in the drama of revelation as he becomes the angel Gabriel. Faced with the temptation of acknowledging a triumvirate of matriarchal goddesses in order to gain recognition for Islam, Mahound ascends Mount Cone to consult the archangel. Gibreel is understandably unnerved to find himself thrust into this role of divine intermediary (108). Despite having to adopt an unusually active role during this reenactment of Islamic history, Gibreel finds himself ultimately subservient to the prophet's fierce will. In addition to forcing Gibreel to reject the prescripted roles he has taken up in Bombay "theologicals," the novel suggests that revelation is animated by the prophet's own hunger for divine illumination. The moment of epiphany is not, then, a passive one in which truth is imparted like writing on stone tablets, but one in which the prophet's voracious desire for illumination plays a vital, shaping part. In Rushdie's version of the mystical experience, human beings take on a high degree of agency. While such an interpretation of the mystical experience might constitute a refreshingly anthropocentric view of human interactions with the divine, it does raise questions concerning the fungibility of revelation, particularly given fundamentalist movements' typical emphasis on the nonnegotiable veracity of the Word.

Such questions are brought to the fore when the prophet, whom Rushdie names Mahound, recants on the acceptance of the city of Jahilia's matriarchal goddesses that his preceding fit of revelation licensed. Having learned of Hind and her goddess's implacable opposition to Allah, Mahound scales Mount Cone again to find out whether his original compromise and the resulting henotheistic doctrine is truly God's will. Gibreel is once again forced to play the role of the archangel, wrestling the prophet to the ground before imparting the truth. Mahound's second revelation succeeds both in coping with the changed political situation revealed by Hind and in retaining the absolute authenticity of the Word. In order to sanction this shift, however, Mahound is led to adopt a Manichaean perspective that attributes the former revelation to satanic insurgency. Yet, as Gibreel states, he was present at both revelations (123). In addition, it was Mahound's desire for revelation that animated the angel's words in both instances. Mahound's clean separation of good and evil is, in other words, a convenient fiction. The active role played by Mahound in both revelations undermines such neat binarisms by suggesting that he himself harbors both good and evil, both the will to compromise and the adamant monotheism that comes to define Islam. The absolute categories of Manichaean thought offer Mahound an escape from the complexity and contingency that Gibreel's version of the revelation insists on.

In his anthropocentric description of the satanic verses, Rushdie casts his lot with those who would interpret and reinterpret divine writ for human ends. Rather than seeing revelation as some final pronouncement of the truth, this approach opts for a theology alive to the implications of the hermeneutic circle of interpretation through which meaning and truth are constituted. Such an approach of course challenges the agents of textual and political orthodoxy within Islam. This conflict is figured nowhere more prominently than in Mahound's disciple Salman, who rewrites the verses of the Koran as they are dictated to him by the prophet. In yet another of Gibreel's dreams, Salman returns to Jahilia and tells the aging poet Baal of his loss of faith. Acting as scribe for the increasingly powerful Mahound, Salman has become suspicious of the businessman-like acumen displayed by the archangel's pronouncements (364). These suspicions are heightened when he finds the sacred text confirming Mahound's policy of dispossessing women of the prerogatives that adhered to them in the matriarchal society of Jahilia (366). Remembering the incident of the satanic verses from years before, Salman decides to submit Islam to a test by selectively rewriting bits of Mahound's dictation. Like the satanic verses, Salman's substitutions challenge the infallible status of the sacred text. Not only, then, does the site of enunciation shape religious revelation; Gibreel's dreams also depict the proliferation of divinely ordained rules whose role as instruments of Mahound's personal ends is covered by the thinnest of veils. Within this context, the doctrine of infallibility—which once guaranteed the purity of Koranic doctrine when Mahound was tempted by compromise—is quickly translated into a mechanism for policing orthodoxy. Salman's subversion of the sacred verses therefore constitutes an example of what Bakhtin called the Rabelaisian chronotope: the purging of a transcendental worldview, of a unitary language of truth, through a parodic inversion that casts light upon the dialogic quality of language.[54] Of course, Rushdie intended this section of the novel to indict the textual fundamentalism of militant Islamist groups, whose claims of scriptural authority further their control of the public sphere.[55]

Although he was much criticized during the Rushdie affair for advancing models of postmodern doubt that held little appeal for oppressed members of diasporic cultures, the necessity of challenging authority claims made by patriarchal community leaders was echoed at the time by groups such as Women Against Fundamentalism.[56] Despite the elements of misogyny that surface in his previous novels, in *The Satanic Verses* Rushdie foregrounds the homology between control of the Word and control of women that characterizes fundamentalist movements. Rushdie's strategy of parodic inversion therefore culminates in the poet Baal's confrontation with Mahound. Faced with the unstoppable rise of Islam to power, Baal underlines the prophet's hypocrisy by elaborating a profane antithesis to the increasingly deified specifics of Mahound's life. The private life of the prophet is rendered glaringly public when Baal suggests that the whores who have given him sanctuary during Mahound's reign each take on the identity of one of the prophet's wives. The bordello's business booms as a result, the titillation of blasphemous prostitution being all the stronger given the severity of Islamic doctrine (380). The brothel becomes a mirror image of Islam, with Baal taking on the role of the prophet by marrying each of the twelve whores and writing verse inspired by the sensual delights of the resulting life (385). When Mahound eventually discovers Baal's subversive strategy, the tale of this ribald parody breaks the faithful up into uncontrollable laughter. As Baal asserts while conceiving his satirical stratagem, "No imperium is absolute, no victory complete" (378). Baal's inversion of the prophet's life draws attention to the unruly desires that emerge from the popular body to disrupt monolithic definitions of the social.[57] Rushdie thereby suggests that fragmentary, nonsynchronous forms of temporality have been implicit not only within modernity and the nation-state, but also within the sacred empires that preceded them.

The danger inherent in Rushdie's parodic approach lies in the fact that, in underlining the fallibility of Islam's sacred language, the author may not be articulating the specific resistant forms of difference inherent within Islam. Indeed, his work is less a recuperation of subaltern knowledge than a satire of a particular grand narrative, one that foregrounds the agency of the lone creative spirit—embodied in the poet Baal—rather than that of subaltern movements.[58] As a result, the set of binary differences Rushdie establishes in this section of the novel provides a highly schematic contrast between a centralized and monologic form of language and a parodic, deconstructive language that questions all forms of power.[59] In addition, Baal achieves his satirical triumph over Mahound using the bodies of the Curtain's whores. Both men, that is, turn women into relatively passive objects who, as the narrator states, "wished to turn themselves into the oldest male fantasy of all" (384).

The novel's parody of the monologic nature of sacred language thus is achieved through the subordination of women figures, who serve, in stereotypical fashion, as allegories of a form of artifice that undermines stable identity and exacerbates textual indeterminacy.[60] Such forms of instability are a calculated affront to the many religious revival groups that have asserted themselves as secular ideologies have become bankrupt. As one of Rushdie's characters says during a discussion later in the novel: "In India, the development of a corrupt and closed state apparatus had 'excluded the masses of the people from the ethical project.' As a result, they sought ethical satisfactions in the oldest of the grand narratives, that is, religious faith" (537). Contemporary Islamicist movements appeal to the premodern notion of a transnational community unified by a sacred language and text in order to justify the assertion of sub- and supranationalisms of various forms using eminently modern means such as the Internet.[61] Such dissenting movements bring to the fore the contradictions within secular nationalism, the necessarily hegemonizing, comprador nature of its project. As in Rushdie's earlier works of fiction, such movements are represented as attempting to mobilize the subaltern elements that have *resisted* interpellation within the grand narrative of the nation. Despite the polarized positions that emerged during the Rushdie affair, however, it should be evident that few Islamic groups subscribe to the monolithic antirationalism with which they are associated in the Western media. Various movements are engaged in complex struggles for hegemony over definitions of Islam in vastly different Arab-speaking nations. Rushdie's use of the Rabelaisian chronotope simplifies this complexity, presenting a battle for control of the public sphere entirely based on an abstract textual politics.

This ahistorical opposition of two different models of reading fails to connect to the conjunctural political conflicts that are driving the rise of various fundamentalist movements.[62] Within a specifically diasporic context, Rushdie's work is easily construed as a challenge to the ties that bind a heterodox community whose power may derive from the very fragmentation of established forms of the social—foremost among which is the nation—taking place today. Ambiguity inevitably infects the site of enunciation in Rushdie's work. Yet it is just such ambiguity and fragmentation that Islamic movements seek to address. As Aziz Al-Azmeh has stressed, the material grounds of the culturalism that is becoming the dominant mode of discourse of racialized minorities in

metropolitan societies lie in processes of structural and spatial segregation, social involution and ghetto formation. A reaction formation to
the European racism that helps animate such processes, "Religion
under conditions of migration proffers a fetishism of the collective
self."[63] Religion, in other words, takes on the role of a subaltern nationalism in search of a prenational utopia.

(En)gendering Heritage Politics

As Rushdie was quick to remind his antagonists following the publication of *The Satanic Verses*, his novel's deconstruction of Islamic revelation takes place within the dreams of Gibreel, a man who is torn by
doubts concerning the nature of good and evil. The parodic subversion
of authority that takes place in these dreams may therefore be construed
as a reflection of Gibreel's own traumatic *lack* of moral clarity. A product of the culture industry, Gibreel is all too aware of the unsettling
effects of traditional culture's hybridization. Indeed, the temporal discontinuity inflicted on Gibreel by his serial dreams aptly dramatizes the
ideological crisis of the nation.[64] Sacred past, profane present, and
future Armageddon become completely jumbled up, divorcing Gibreel
from the normative linear temporality of the nation. In addition,
Gibreel's profligate past haunts him throughout the novel in the form of
apparitions by Reka Merchant, a former lover and suicide. Reka's ghost,
moreover, works her revenge on Gibreel through undermining the
fixed moral distinctions characteristic of Islam (323). Faced with this
disruption of his moral bearings, Gibreel turns to increasingly
Manichaean visions of the world to gain a sense of identity through
opposition: "Clarity, clarity, at all costs clarity!—This Shaitan was no
fallen angel"(353). Gibreel's frantic moral absolutism is founded on a
rejection of complexity, a willful attempt to separate the world into
binary terms. Such an attempt to demarcate a firm boundary is predicated on an unsettling awareness of a lack of self-identity and of coher-
ence in the social. For example, Gibreel's attempt to redeem London by
turning its weather tropical suggests a form of willful ethnic absolutism
on the part of this nomad who is unable to accept the muggy, ambiguous cultural climate of the diaspora.[65] As such, this transformation
reflects the tendencies toward polarization along racialized lines that
has characterized Britain during the post-Fordist era. Gibreel's meteo-

rological machinations offer a powerful symbol of the embattled reactions often produced by the overlapping, disjunctive global order that migrants must inhabit. Ironically, Gibreel's imposition of Manichaean divisions on the world that surrounds him actively *produces* unsettling forms of hybridity.[66] For instance, his attempts to discern and destroy his satanic antagonist lead him into a struggle that turns upon mimetic desire between him and Saladin for Alleluia Cone. Yet the struggle between these male protagonists over Allie emphasizes their kinship rather than their differences from one another. Both men are engaged in a process of projection that hinges upon Allie's impenetrability. Allie signifies a form of identity for both men that they hope will help them escape from the crises of diasporic double consciousness. This projection of imaginary unity and identity onto an Englishwoman is, as was true of Chamcha's relationship with Pamela Lovelace, based on a misperception of her identity on the part of both protagonists.

The root of this mutual attraction and anger toward Allie lies in her ambiguous position vis-à-vis English identity. As a woman, Allie is both subordinate to the patriarchal social conditions in England, and therefore potentially sympathetic to the antiracist struggles of immigrants, and also in a position of dominance as a result of her race. Indeed, Rushdie goes to great lengths to demonstrate the instabilities and uncertainties that plague Allie Cone. Herself a product of the Jewish diaspora, Allie has been traumatized by the suicide of an older sister victimized by the publicity mill and is, rather like Gibreel, haunted by apparitions connected to her mountain-climbing avocation. The glacial bearing that she projects in order to protect herself from intruding eyes infuriates Gibreel, and is the seed for Saladin's Iago-like envious stratagems. Like Pamela, Allie Cone is an example of the complex and unstable constitution of the putatively hegemonic elements of metropolitan society.[67] Notwithstanding these weaknesses, Allie and Gibreel's relationship represents for Saladin the apogee of cultural identity and distinction that he has always sought. The humiliation that begins with his transformation into a satyr culminates in Chamcha's mistaken perception of Gibreel's welcoming party to Britain. It is here that he perceives Gibreel's "possession" of Allie as the capping example of his antagonist's ability to insinuate himself into the English society from which Chamcha himself has been so devastatingly ejected (428). Ironically, it is at this very party that Gibreel's sense that ambiguity is overtaking him is first publicly expressed in the form of violently uncontrollable jealousy.

Allie, who once seemed to Gibreel to harbor the promise of rebirth into a secular life, becomes the subject of his violent fits of misogynistic jealousy. Saladin's obscene telephone calls, which fan this jealousy, are a product of his attempt to derail this apparently idyllic relationship. If he has been denied the middle-class immigrant's fantasy of perfect assimilation, Chamcha is going to see to it that Gibreel and Allie will not play the allegorical role of multicultural lovers. For both men, self-definition involves the instrumentalization of an imagined femininity whose instability is heightened by the specter of a threatening Other.

As Saladin's treachery bites deeper, Gibreel begins to associate Allie with cunning sexual infidelity. All too quickly, she comes to symbolize the temporal and cultural displacements characteristic of the dreams that dislocate his identity. The solidity of Gibreel's own identity thus depends upon the forceful delimitation of Allie's supposed impurity. Indeed, as he falls ever further into the schizophrenic state in which he imagines himself as the archangel, Gibreel begins to mouth misogynistic pieties in a parodic version of the patriarchial logic that animates political Islam (321). Gibreel's suspicion of Allie reveals a strong anxiety over women's power to define men. This anxiety is connected to the creation of imaginary homelands. In a diasporic situation in which points of both arrival and departure are in constant cultural flux, established traditions are eroded and the desire for continuity is frustrated by global communication and commodification.[68] As Arjun Appadurai— picking up on feminist interventions—has argued, under such conditions, "The honor of women becomes a surrogate for the identity of the embattled communities of males while women, in reality, have to negotiate increasingly harsh conditions of work at home and in the nondomestic workplace."[69] As cultural traits become an ever more important index of group cohesion, increasing pressure is placed upon women to play the role of icons of communal identity. At a time of increasingly prominent forms of disjuncture in traditional, spatially static identities, constraints upon women and female sexuality become increasingly evident. Conflicts between differing definitions of community and of spatial identity on levels ranging from the corporal through the local and the national to the transnational play themselves out through attempts to control the role of women as icons of group identity. Within this context, not only is women's self-expression frequently seen as the passive product of masculine agency, but such expression can become the specific target of forms of regulation.

Moreover, in Britain during the 1980s, the multicultural framework tended to define women's demands for equality as outside a poorly understood "Muslim cultural tradition." Drawing on concepts of communal, religious identity codified during the British Raj in order to further imperial rule, multicultural models of ethnic minority communities were predicated on reified, Orientalist models of identity. As Gita Saghal and Nira Yuval-Davis argue, despite its antiracist orientation when compared to the model of assimilation, multiculturalism ironically conferred authenticity and, perhaps more importantly, state funding on community leaders who best embodied these reified models of collective identity.[70] In the name of pluralism, in other words, intolerant identities were often not only accepted as legitimate, but actively supported through the funding efforts of radical local authorities such as the Greater London Council. As a result of multicultural policies, women's demands for equality were often seen as outside the authentic "traditions" of particular ethnic minority communities. At the same time as the state was subsidizing reactionary segments of the Muslim community, conservative leaders within this community employed canny appeals to culture and religion to attack women's autonomous organizing efforts. Women were seen as the carriers of collective cultural values, and regulation of their behavior, preferably within the boundaries of the patriarchal family, would ensure that conservative values would be reproduced both biologically and symbolically.[71]

Given this symbolic struggle over femininity, it is not entirely surprising that Saladin and Gibreel's visions of Allie are eventually channeled into a form of mimetic desire that brings them into direct conflict. Yet this conflict is one that underlines their mutual interrelation. As Eve Sedgwick has emphasized, the homosocial formation of mimetic desire functions to consolidate the bonds—including antagonistic ones—between men.[72] In *The Satanic Verses*, this bond turns upon the nature of identity within the disruptive conditions characteristic of the diaspora. It is for this reason that Chamcha and Gibreel's competition over Allie ultimately devolves into a battle between two opposite but interwoven senses of the self. The battle between Gibreel and Saladin represents a struggle between two principles: a Manichaean division between good and evil versus an uncertain, fragmentary grip on identity (426). This distinction revolves around the question of the attitude of the self toward change, toward the transformations and hybridizations that accompany migration. Saladin, the man who has chosen Lucretius's doctrine of the discontinuous self to characterize his metamorphosis of identity, represents precisely the kind of ambiguity against which Gibreel is struggling. It is such a tendency toward conflict that leads Gibreel to characterize Chamcha in terms of Fanon's self-hating native, one of the Janus faces of diaspora experience that Gibreel's burgeoning fundamentalism cannot endure (353). Yet the narrator's characterization of the two as conjoined opposites highlights the impossibility of stressing either pure hybridity or pure identity. The two tendencies exist in a tense opposition to one another that frequently leads toward internecine struggle. Gibreel and Saladin thus constitute a specific version of the dialectical relation between tradition and translation. While he engages direct with the models of hybridity advanced by black British cultural studies during the 1980s, Rushdie suggests that an adequate conception of diasporic identity must make space for the mobile identificatory strategies of nomadic subjects. Such subjects are not solely hybrid, but rather inhabit diverse identities, varying from the traditional to the assimilated, depending on the cultural context.[73] It is Gibreel's attempt to purify himself of this performative fluidity of identity that dooms him to increasing disintegration.

Dropping intertextual references to Ahab and Ishmael, Rushdie stages a fiery conclusion in which the two protagonists meet in a showdown at the Shandaar Cafe. Gibreel, hallucinating himself as the angel of the Recitation, bears down on Chamcha, now veritably dripping with evil, in order to avenge the destruction of his relationship with Allie. Despite this seemingly victory of the forces of Manichaean difference, the narrator poses a series of questions that suggest that the self is a heterogeneous entity whose moral proclivities cannot be foreseen (467). Rushdie's sense of the conflicting selves that inhabit each of us allows him this one final moment of grace, a moment in which the trajectories of both men are momentarily reversed. In saving Chamcha from the fires of purification, Gibreel surrenders his zealotry in recognition of the complexity of Chamcha's character. This moment of grace suggests the ultimate futility of attempting to adjudicate the competing claims of essentialism and pluralism on a purely theoretical level. It is only by witnessing the specific performative claims asserted within any particular historical conjuncture that we can clarify our identities and their modes of constitution. In a world in which accession to power is more than ever accomplished through, rather than being a precondition of, making good on claims to identity, this emphasis on the performative brings a salutary specificity to bear. Rushdie's *The Satanic Verses* documents the pivotal role played by gender in the delimitation of identity in a global cultural economy. The increasing pressure placed upon racialized groups to legitimate their claims to ethnic identity necessarily dictates an increasing focus upon the heritage politics of the household. Within such a context, women face increasing pressure to conform as icons of communal identity.

CONCLUSION: CONJUNCTURAL ANALYSIS AND
TRANSNATIONAL FEMINISM

The Satanic Verses initially seemed to have consolidated and polarized communal identities in Britain and elsewhere. For British Muslims in particular, the Rushdie affair was a disaster, as the Ayatollah Khomeini's fatwa against Rushdie led to a dramatic increase in media and popular stereotyping of Muslims following years of struggle for economic and social integration.[74] In addition, *The Satanic Verses* catalyzed the emergence of the racially inflected cultural clash theories that, reanimating the corpse of Orientalism, have led to serious debates concerning the place of Islam in contemporary Europe.[75] Yet the Rushdie affair also ultimately forced British policymakers to reckon with the Muslim presence in Britain more seriously. Galvanized by the bias in British legal statutes such as the Blasphemy Law that became evident in the course of the crisis over Rushdie's novel, British Muslim activists lobbied hard for reform of the legal system. Although the Blasphemy Law has not yet been changed, several significant bills were presented in the wake of the Rushdie affair that would have rectified the anomalous protections against religious discrimination that characterize the British state at present. In addition, the Commission on Racial Equality has called for the extension of laws against racial discrimination to Muslims, whose identity as a religious rather than ethnic group has so far held up implementation of incitement-to-hatred and discrimination laws.[76] These measures and the increasing engagement of British Muslim activists with the public sphere in general betoken their increasing integration and conciliation in formal processes, despite the forms of Islamophobia generated by the Rushdie affair.

The increasing public visibility of Islam in Britain also has a transnational dimension, however, for, from the 1970s on, the oil-rich states of the Persian Gulf began recycling petrodollars into the Muslim infrastructure in Europe through the financing of mosques and other Muslim organizations.[77] The Rushdie affair itself was notably trans-national, with the struggle between Iran and Saudi Arabia within the Islamic world playing a prominent role in the local unfolding of the conflict.[78] As we have seen, in Britain this transnational aspect of Islamic identity was most heavily influenced, however, by diasporic links to South Asia, where the rise of Hindu fundamentalism stoked communal tensions that dated back to the partition. It was, for example, only after an opposition parliamentarian in India, in an attempt to embarrass the ruling Congress Party, called for the banning of Rushdie's novel that the Bradford Council for Mosques began militating for the expansion of Britain's Blasphemy Law. Conflict around the Personal Laws, the sepa-rate body of juridical regulations for Muslim domestic affairs, was at the center of rising communal tensions on the subcontinent during the 1980s. In India as in Britain, feminists brought out the contradictions of both dominant state policies toward religious minorities and funda-mentalist assertions of communal identity. As Gita Saghal points out, when fundamentalist forces cannot control the machinery of state power, control over women, which helps to cement patriarchal power over land and inheritance, becomes crucial.[79]

Perhaps the most signal outcome of *The Satanic Verses* controversy, therefore, was the assertion of dissenting voices within Muslim and other religious communities in Britain. For all the novel's shortcom-ings, the project of contesting conservative religious authorities' control over the Word and women was clearly a central aim of Rushdie's work. During the unfolding of the Rushdie affair, it became all too clear that this aspect of his work was quite prescient. As evidenced by groups such as Women Against Fundamentalism, feminist activists played a key role in articulating critiques of conservative definitions of cultural tradition. Challenging the right of traditionalist leadership to interpretive author-ity, intellectuals such as Elizabeth Schustler Fiorenza and Fatima Mernissi have articulated dissenting, feminist readings of sacred texts such as the Bible and the Koran. Such exegetical practices provide sup-port for the work of feminist activists who seek to carve out autonomous spaces for women. In addition to fostering the traditions of *ijtihad* or critical reasoning that are crucial for the articulation of European Islamic identities, however, groups such as WAF have high-lighted the contradictions in the British state. While they recognize the racial and religious bias of measures such as Britain's Blasphemy Law, WAF activists call not for the extension of such legislation to cover previously marginalized groups, but rather for the creation of a truly secular, nonracial public sphere in Britain. Through their challenges to monolithic construction of both majority and ethnic minority identity, WAF and similar groups are helping blaze the trail toward a truly postcolonial condition in Britain.[80]

Genetics, Biotechnology, and the Future of "Race" in Zadie Smith's *White Teeth*

ON 12 FEBRUARY 2001, THE LEADERS OF TWO COMPETING TEAMS of scientists stood next to President Clinton at the White House to announce the results of their history-making research. With a little help from a private competitor, the multinational Human Genome Project had achieved its goal years ahead of schedule: the creation of the first draft map of the human genome. Few commentators found themselves immune to the hyperbole that characterized this unveiling. Ever since James Watson and Francis Crick created their elegant model of DNA's double helical structure in 1953, the genome has been seen, in the words of Watson, as the "ultimate description of life." According to Crick's so-called central dogma, DNA genes have total control over inheritance in all forms of life. Our genes, in other words, contain the basic molecular code that determines everything from the number of toes on each of our feet to the number of points we score on IQ tests. By the time the Human Genome Project unveiled the draft map of the genome in 2001, expectations surrounding the benefits to be gained from molecular biology and biotechnology had become extremely inflated. For the first time, the lay public was told, human beings would not only be able to read their basic genetic recipe but also begin to make significant changes in this recipe. Yet the draft map of the genome also startled many members of the scientific community and the public. Even today, the extent to which this map challenges the fundamental model of DNA as the "master molecule" has not been fully digested.

Much to everyone's surprise, the work of the Human Genome Project revealed that people have only about thirty thousand genes. Scientists had long predicted a figure over three times as great based on estimates derived from analysis of the proteins manufactured by DNA. The significance of this numerical difference cannot be overstated. Human beings, it seems, have only 50 percent more genes than the roundworm, a humble creature with just 959 cells in its entire body.[1] We are no more genetically endowed than some common weeds. Genetically speaking, there is no more than a whisker of difference between us and our furry rodent relative, the mouse, which has only three hundred fewer genes than we do. Although the chimpanzee genome has not yet been decoded, its successful mapping is expected to deliver an even bigger thumping to human beings' inflated ideas of our unique importance as a species.

In addition to unsettling our elevated place on the Great Chain of Being, the mapping of the genome also challenges Crick's central dogma. Crick argued for a one-to-one correspondence between the nucleotide sequence of the genes and the amino acid sequence of the proteins that genes help produce. Yet if the human gene count is too low to match the number of proteins and the many inherited traits that they engender, then there is more to the "ultimate description of life" than the genes alone.[2] Although we are certainly influenced by our genetic inheritance, in no sense can it be said that our lives are determined solely by these genes. For instance, the isolated genome does not explain the substantial inherited differences between a person and a mouse, despite the striking genetic similarities between the two organisms. The biological determinism on which Crick's central dogma was predicated cannot be sustained in the face of evidence for the complex and interwoven relationship between the genome, the particular organism in which the genome is embedded, and the broader environment that shapes and is in turn shaped by that organism.

Despite such accumulating evidence against Crick's central dogma, biological determinism retains a strong grip on popular imagination as well as on scientific research. In the guise of sociobiology, in particular, such determinism has shaped commonsense perceptions of the genetic causes of intractable contemporary social problems such as crime, mirroring the turn toward dysgenics—the study of racial degeneration—as an explanation for social breakdown a century ago.[3] As Richard Lewontin argues, the mechanistic and atomistic worldview of the central dogma—in which genes make individuals, individuals make society, and, as a result, "selfish genes" determine human affairs—has a long genealogy stretching back through Darwin to Descartes.[4] Such reductionism has long displayed great ideological utility by legitimating the competitive individualist ethos central to capitalist society.

If the decoding of the human genome has challenged our sense of the gulf that separates us from other species, what are the implications for traditional understandings of difference *within* our species? More specifically, what is the likely import of these startling revelations concerning the genome for contemporary representations of racial difference? Critics have recently begun to argue that advances in molecular biology will help produce a new raciological regime.[5] As a result of the gradual diffusion of this research, discourses around "race" are shifting away from the model of population plasticity that characterized neo-Darwinian evolutionary theory during the period after 1945. In place of this social constructionist perspective, biologists are debating the meaning of "race" on the sub- and supraepidermal level of genetic variations and similarities within human populations from distinct parts of the globe.[6] Increasingly, "race" is returning as a biological category, one lodged not in the shape of people's skulls—as phrenologists argued during the nineteenth century—but in the shared intricacies of genetic code that, for instance, make many Ashkenazi Jews predisposed to develop Tay-Sachs disease and many people of African descent susceptible to sickle cell anemia.[7] All too often, however, these similarities at the mitochondrial level are confused with commonsense racial designations that reflect the sociological, economic, and political disparities that disfigure our culture far more than precise demographic epidemiological classifications.[8]

To date, there have been relatively few fictional examinations of the genetic revolution's social implications.[9] A rare exception is Zadie Smith's *White Teeth*. Although *White Teeth* garnered much critical acclaim for its lively embodiment of a supposedly "postracial" London, Smith's work is perhaps most notable for its powerful qualification of optimistic readings of the novel forms that biopower is assuming today.[10] *White Teeth* focuses on the extent to which one's cultural and biological pedigree affect identity and belonging in contemporary Britain. The intersection of genetics and "race" is consequently a con-

sistent theme throughout the novel. In fact, the success of the novel
attests to the enduring fascination with racial mixing and hybridity that
characterizes our supposedly "postracial" epoch. *White Teeth* concludes, for instance, with a scene that mirrors the Human Genome
Project's spectacular announcement at the White House. In this scene,
the many characters who orbit around one another throughout the
novel converge at the Millennial Science Commission to witness the
unveiling of Dr. Marcus Chalfen's FutureMouse©· Chalfen intends to
use his genetically customized "creation" as a site for experimentation
into heredity. His naive belief in the pristine isolation of his enterprise
from the political and social tensions that permeate the rest of the novel
is brought crashing down to earth in this final scene, in which Smith
demonstrates the high stakes associated with inheritance and reproduction. Although explicit racial violence does not figure in *White Teeth,*
Britain's colonial past weighs heavily on the novel's characters, shaping
their sense of identity and ramifying across the generations. The conflict
that disrupts Marcus Chalfen's press conference, leading to the escape
of his FutureMouse and the ambiguous resolution of the novel, underlines the increasing politicization of biological and social reproduction
in postcolonial Britain.[11]

Contemporary discourses of biological determinism are gaining
purchase in societies already saturated by forms of biopower.[12] Individuals make reproductive decisions, for instance, not in isolation but within
the context of national immigration and citizenship legislation that
stringently controls mobility, belonging, and collective identity through
reference to heredity.[13] In the case of Britain, such controls have become
more rather than less racialized over the last half-century.[14] In addition,
the turn toward a post-Fordist mode of economic regulation since the
1970s has meant not simply the shift of production to the underdeveloped world, but also the increasing abandonment of state support for
social reproduction in developed nations.[15] Biological determinist constructions of racial difference in Britain such as those satirized in *White
Teeth* therefore take root in a terrain already riven by racialized conflict.
Within such a context, identification of the material substrate for specific
forms of difference and inequality among human beings through genetic
research is far more likely to lead to revivified forms of eugenic discourse
than to the disappearance of "race." By exploring the contemporary
return of eugenics, Zadie Smith's *White Teeth* offers us a timely warning
that the history of "race" is by no means over.

RACIOLOGY AND THE EUGENIC PAST

White Teeth begins with an epigraph: "What is past is prologue." Drawn from a museum in Washington, D.C., this epigraph highlights the inescapability of the past, a theme that frequently recurs throughout the novel. Why would Zadie Smith choose to emphasize the persistence of history in a novel that devotes much of its attention to the composite culture of second-generation black and Asian Britons? But *White Teeth* does not focus on second-generation youths alone; instead, it offers a salutary reminder of the intractable character of racial inequality by tracing the homologies that link the experience of different generations of black and Asian Britons. This flies in the face of accounts of our "postracial" moment. Despite the demonstrable intensification of stratification and inequality around the world, it has become common-place for critics to argue that racial difference is no longer a salient social phenomenon. Such a perspective has gained credibility, ironically, as a result of the significant victories won by anticolonial and antiracist movements around the world over the last half-century.[16]

In conjunction with this political transformation, massive advances in molecular biology during the same period have established a new site for inquiry into human difference. As Paul Gilroy puts it:

> When the body becomes absolutely penetrable, and is refigured as the transient epiphenomenon of coded invisible information, the aesthetic of epidermalization and its regime of power are irrecoverably over. The boundaries of "race" have moved across the threshold of skin. They are cellular and molecular, not dermal. If "race" is to endure, it will be in a new form, estranged from the scales respectively associated with political anatomy and epidermalization.[17]

According to Gilroy, mainstream genomic research has tended to reduce the body, the traditional scale at which "race" was defined, to no more than a lumbering robot whose every action and appearance is determined by invisible strings of DNA. Despite the reductive character of this genomic discourse, Gilroy has recently suggested that the emphasis on identity as code rather than ideological construct may foster the complete dismantling of racial classification. Gilroy sees a utopian outcome in which "at the smaller microscopic scales that open up the body for scrutiny today, 'race' becomes less meaningful, com-

pelling, or salient to the basic tasks of healing and protecting our-
selves."[18]

While genetic code and physical traits do vary among human populations, such differences do not constitute a subspecies level of genetic
differentiation, the biological definition of "race." In fact, ethnic difference accounts for only 10–15 percent of the genetic variation that characterizes human beings. This means that there tends to be greater
genetic variation between any two individuals of the same "race" than
between people from different continents. There is, in other words, no
empirical biological basis for the view that human beings belong to different "races," a view that has helped legitimate social hierarchy since
the early nineteenth century.[19] Gilroy can therefore draw on significant
empirical evidence to support his call for a radical non- or postracial
humanism. But "race" thinking has had a long history, one in which
shifting scientific paradigms have all too easily been appropriated by
those wishing to perpetuate social discrimination.[20] Zadie Smith's
White Teeth confronts the dystopian possibilities of current research
into genetics by reminding us of this long history.

Using a variety of comic modes, *White Teeth* satirizes the insecurities that beset residents of postcolonial, multiracial Britain near the end
of the millennium, and connects such insecurities to issues of belonging
and "race." The novel begins, however, during World War II, and subsequently traces the history of its two principal protagonists, Samad
Iqbal and Archie Jones, and their families across the half-century in
which the anticolonial and antiracist movements achieved their great
victories. The novel's historical setting allows Smith to examine the history of eugenics, focusing on the moment that seemingly discredited the
movement for good: the Holocaust. Yet by tracing an arc across the following fifty years to the present, *White Teeth* underlines the tenacious
hold that biological determinism has had on the popular imagination.
By the novel's conclusion, the eugenic culture that the so-called
People's War seemed to have obliterated makes an unsettling return.
Sparing no one, Zadie Smith satirizes both the ethically obtuse scientists
who are responsible for this reawakened research as well as their fanati-
cally doctrinaire opponents.

Marcus Chalfen's FutureMouse—the embodiment of the tightly
knit utopian and dystopian possibilities of the new biotechnologies—is
liberated by Archie Jones. While sitting in the audience at the Millennial
Science Commission, this perpetually dithering working-class English-

man overhears Chalfen thanking his mentor, Dr. Marc-Pierre Perret. Perret's name and the sight of his bloody tears, the product of a hereditary diabetic condition, take Archie back half a century to an abandoned mansion in the war-torn Balkans. World War II has ended while Archie and his comrade Samad Iqbal sit ignominiously waiting for relief with their dead comrades in a broken-down Churchill tank. Samad decides to capture Perret after advancing Soviet troops inform him that the diabetic Frenchman ironically turns out to have been an important figure in the Nazi eugenics program. The confrontation with Perret represents not simply a stab at the glory that has eluded Samad on the battlefield but also a decisive rejection of the Nazis' attempts to control the future through racial engineering. Since the Soviet troops have not yet liberated the "work camps" in Poland, Archie and Samad have no idea of the full horror of the Holocaust. Despite his ignorance of the lengths to which the Nazis took their eugenics program, Samad sees Perret's work as the ultimate heresy. For Samad, eugenics is predicated on an intrinsically blasphemous project of wresting control of human destiny away from Allah.[21] Their treatment of Perret, Samad tells Archie, is intimately tied to the larger moral questions at stake in the war against totalitarianism.

Despite their eccentric geographical location in Bulgaria, Samad and Archie's encounter with the man the local villagers call Dr. Sick raises fundamental questions about European culture. *White Teeth*'s focus on eugenics and racial hierarchy reveals the contradictions of the Allied cause, and thereby troubles the dichotomous distinction between Allied democracy and Axis totalitarianism. This model, Smith's novel suggests, helps obscure the historical complicity of the Allies with the raciological doctrines implemented by the Nazis. Following the fall of the Third Reich in 1950, UNESCO issued a now-famous statement shaped by the Holocaust that declared the invalidity of established conceptions of "race." Authored by a student of the antiracist ethnographer Franz Boas, the UNESCO document repudiated a tradition of scientific thinking developed in Europe since the eighteenth century.[22] Yet if the Nazis' genocidal policies catalyzed a sweeping rejection of eugenic thought throughout the Western world, they also concealed the extent to which such policies had become common sense among many segments of the population in the United States and Europe. The history of widespread popular acceptance of eugenics before the war—including the notion that heredity rather than economic, social, and cultural factors determine the status of racial groups—has conveniently been expunged from collective memory over the last half century.

Most significantly, Samad and Archie's encounter with an apostle of Nazi raciology highlights the return of colonial racial doctrines to the European heartland that took place in the first half of the twentieth century.[23] The prominence of eugenic thought before the Second World War was intimately related to the imperial ambitions of the European nations in which raciological science was conducted. As scholars such as Ann Stoler have argued, dominant forms of nineteenth-century European identity were shaped in an imperial landscape where notions of racial purity and sexual virtue were paramount.[24] These discourses of imperial propriety linked conceptions of class, "race," and gendered identity, generating a series of exclusionary social taxonomies that had a profound impact on popular consciousness and the metropolitan state. Fears about the dilution of supposedly pure Aryan bloodlines and culture led, for example, to the construction of micro-sites of identity around issues such as parenting, education, and tropical hygiene.[25] In addition, Gobineau's argument that empires decline because of the racial mixing that accompanies their expansion was widely disseminated and helped foster state policies designed to mitigate the degenerative impact of ersatz citizen-subjects. In the United States, for example, thirty states had adopted sterilization laws for the "mentally defective" by 1924, the year in which Congress passed legislation restricting immigration of "inferior stock" from southern and eastern Europe.[26] Britain, a pioneer in eugenic science during the first half of the twentieth century, only narrowly avoided passing similar measures in the face of almost uniform support from the scientific and political establishment.[27] Such examples of biopower demonstrate the extent to which the modern nation has been produced in conjunction with forms of racial discrimination developed on colonial terrain.

Innovations in the biological sciences played a fundamental role in the advance of eugenics policies during the first half of the twentieth century. These innovations were firmly rooted in genetic determinism, which Richard Lewontin argues has been the baseline ideology within biology except for the brief period after World War II that produced the UNESCO statement on "race."[28] The demonstration by geneticists such as Gregor Mendel and August Weismann of the continuity of the "germplasm" (the contemporary term for DNA) suggested that inherited traits were immune to environmental influences. Consequently, social Darwinists in both Europe and the United States reasoned that no amount of cultural assimilation would eradicate the inherited qualities of purportedly inferior "races" such as the Jews. If geneticists like Ernst Haeckel advocated the elimination of undesirable traits through a positive eugenic program of selective breeding, it was left to the Nazi Party to implement a negative eugenic policy: the systematic elimination of degenerate germplasm through genocide. While there were obviously economic motives behind the expansionism of the Axis powers, doctrines of racial superiority played a decisive role in mobilizing popular support for war. Soldiers from Germany, Italy, and Japan went to war saturated with eugenicist doctrines concerning racial superiority that echoed those used by the liberal democratic nations to legitimate their own colonial projects.

Samad and Archie's confrontation with Dr. Sick at the tail end of the war in *White Teeth* therefore needs to be seen within the context of the racial doctrines mobilized by both the Allies and the Axis powers. In World War I, imperial nations such as France and Britain had employed colonial troops with great reluctance. Military service was equated in these countries with citizenship and manhood. The prospect of colonial troops serving side by side with Europeans in the military consequently threatened to expose and undermine the racial hierarchies that cemented European power in the colonies. In the circumstances of labor shortage that attended "total war," however, colonial workers and troops were drawn into the military. In both of the wars, military service helped generate a feeling of entitlement among colonial soldiers, who saw their sacrifices for the mother country as entailing reciprocal obligations that challenged the forms of economic and political subordination on which colonialism depended.[29] In fact, leaders of the Indian independence movement openly defied colonial authority before World War II by demanding, before they agreed to support the war, the application of the Atlantic Charter's promised "restoration of sovereignty, self-government, and national life" to the colonies as well as Europe.[30] In addition, regular contact with European servicemen and civilians allowed colonial soldiers to trespass the rigid social and sexual boundaries that helped legitimate hierarchies of "race" and class in the colonies.

But Zadie Smith's character Samad is fighting for more than just his rights as a British subject. As was true for many soldiers from the colonies, his quest for glory in the European war is motivated primarily by his desire to sustain family honor.[31] Indeed, Samad is driven by a sense of inheritance that ironically mimics the genetic determinism that burgeoned among Europeans in the colonial context. As the great-grandson of Mangal Pande, the first upper-caste native soldier in the Bengal Army to rebel against British authority in what Victorian imperialists called the Sepoy Mutiny, Samad sees himself as the descendent of the Indian independence movement's progenitor. Yet despite the fact that "nothing was closer or meant more to him than his blood" (83) Samad's attempts to demonstrate the nobility of his bloodline are thwarted at every turn in the novel. Unfortunately for Samad, British colonial historians have represented Mangal Pande in less than the heroic light he deserves, turning him into an intoxicated and incompetent buffoon who unwittingly got caught up in the sweep of history (212). Wittily drawing on the analysis of the subaltern studies collective, Zadie Smith uses the case of Samad's great-grandfather to demonstrate the extent to which the historical record can be manipulated to serve the interests of those in power.[32] Samad's actions throughout the novel are dictated by the consuming drive to wipe away the stain on his family honor perpetuated by colonial historiography.

Tied to this humiliating representation of Samad's forefather as a coward is his dismay at the failure of his illustrious genealogy to manifest itself in his own life. Indeed, the more uncertain Samad grows of his genealogical roots, the more fearful he becomes about his own failure and dissolution. Samad's wartime experience thus undermines genetic determinism by demonstrating that intrinsic hereditary identity seldom triumphs over adverse environmental conditions. After having his hand blown apart by an incompetent Sikh sapper, Samad finds his promising career as an aviator quickly aborted. He ends up as a tank radio operator in the "Buggered Battalion," a collection of misfits whose homophobic nickname underlines the connection between constructions of martial masculinity and national identity. Eugenicists historically associated both racial hybridity and homosexuality with sterility and degeneracy. Samad's internalization of these values is evident when his failure to live up to his ancestor's heroic legacy leaves him feeling like a bastard whose mixed English and Bengali cultural identity has destroyed his masculinity.

This fear of cultural bastardization and illegitimacy overwhelms Samad as he leads the attack on Dr. Sick's mansion. One of the Bulgarians he and Archie are leading up the hill protests that this is a battle of the West, something that has nothing to do with him. Samad flees into

the night on hearing this line. When Archie finds him, Samad is con-
templating suicide: "What am I good for, Jones? If I were to pull this
trigger, what will I leave behind? An Indian, a turncoat English Indian
with a limp wrist like a faggot and no medals that they can ship home
with me" (95). Samad has realized that he has become a mimic man, a
colonial subject attempting to conform to the contradictory dictates of
assimilation set out by the empire. As an Indian, he cannot become an
officer in the British army, despite the uniform he has purloined from
his dead CO.[33] Furthermore, his attempts to win glory fighting for the
British in Europe are hardly in keeping with the anticolonial efforts of
either his great-grandfather or of the contemporary Indian independence movement. Far from finding confirmation of his martial bloodline in the war, Samad is overcome by feelings of displacement and dis-
honor that he immediately equates with the lack of manhood and
sterility traditionally associated with homosexuality. As a result of this
crisis, Samad is unable to execute Dr. Sick himself, and instead pushes
Archie to carry out the act in the name of an aggrieved Europe. This
decision is bitterly ironic given the fact that the Nazis first experimented
with genocidal policies in their African colonies before deploying these
policies in Europe.[34]

The idea that blood will tell was a fundamental conceit in nineteenth-century novels written under the influence of social Darwinism.
Characters like Dickens's Oliver Twist escape the poorhouse and regain
their rightful place in society as their aristocratic blood triumphs over
the destitution into which they have erroneously fallen.[35] Genetic determinism was even more evident in novels written in a colonial context.
European genes alone ultimately redeem the shape-shifting Asian childhood of Rudyard Kipling's *Kim*, for instance.[36] As *Kim* demonstrates,
the ideology of genetic determinism helped legitimate the European
imperial mission during the nineteenth century, while reassuring colonial functionaries that their exposure to non-European social conditions would have limited impact on them as long as they observed the
correct protocols. Focusing on the impact of such colonial racial beliefs
on the European homeland, *White Teeth* returns to World War II in
order to underline the pernicious character of such determinist beliefs
and to stress the impact of social inequality on individual identity.
Although the novel does not directly engage the Holocaust, the specter
of genocide lurks in the background of Samad and Archie's clumsy
attempts at heroism. In addition, Samad's frustrated belief in the inher-

ent nobility of his blood and his contradictory indictment of Nazi
eugenics policies dramatize the extent to which notions of genetics and
identity were a force in the recent past. The return of eugenics in *White
Teeth* suggests that the history of raciology needs to be borne in mind as
new forms of eugenics surface in contemporary culture.

The Pitfalls of Hybridity

Thirty years after this fateful encounter with Dr. Sick, Samad winds up
working as a "curry-shifter" in an Indian restaurant in London's West
End. Through Samad's misadventures in multicultural London, Zadie
Smith interrogates current theories of diasporic identity. Black and
Asian cultures in Britain have been taken by prominent postcolonial
critics to exemplify forms of cosmopolitanism that undermine reified
models of cultural identity.[37] The claims of such critics to be representatives of ethnic minorities have, however, been rendered hollow by the
growth of ethnic primordialism within Asian and black communities.[38]
In addition, although theories of hybridity are intended to challenge
exclusionary models of belonging, they suffer from their own forms of
determinism as a result of their programmatic assertion of diasporic
cosmopolitanism. All too often, this analysis simply inverts the dominant tropes of colonial discourse by representing diasporic populations
as inherently progressive. Such hybridity putatively occurs at the cultural level, but since the approach of critics like Homi Bhabha contains
precious little analysis of differentiating social factors such as class, gender, regional provenance, and religious affiliation, it often appears that
postcolonial migrants are inherently, even biologically, destined to
adopt antiessentialist, cosmopolitan identities.[39] *White Teeth* self-consciously parodies the biological determinism of much hybridity discourse through its depiction of Samad's transformation in Britain.

The temptation of Samad Iqbal begins in his children's school.
Nearly a decade into a marriage with a bride—the pugnacious Alsana—
a quarter-century his junior, Samad has become sexually frustrated. His
attempts to conform to divine dictates by resisting the temptation to
masturbate have failed miserably and he has become an apostate
wanker. His body, he confides to a fellow waiter, has grown mutinous in
an outward sign of his corruption by England (120). This feeling of contamination by the West worsens once Samad initiates a doomed affair

with Poppy Burt-Jones, his sons' music teacher, whose double-barreled name succinctly communicates her exemplary Englishness. Despite the ridiculously extravagant Orientalist stereotypes that attract Poppy to Samad, the affair heightens his sense of corruption to the point that he becomes haunted by the apparition of his ancestor Mangal Pande, whom he increasingly sees as a paradigm of cultural nationalist resistance to the colonial destruction of tradition.

Samad's fear of corruption by the West can be placed within the context of the increasing racialization of culture that has taken place in Britain during the postwar period. Despite the persistence of overt forms of institutional and popular discrimination based on "race," commentators have argued that the predominant trend during the period after 1945 has been toward forms of discrimination based on *cultural* rather than biological difference.[40] As the infamous "cricket test" that Zadie Smith uses as an epigraph to this section demonstrates, national belonging tends today to be judged by cultural criteria such as an individual's loyalty to the English—as opposed to the Pakistani or West Indian—cricket team. However, fears such as those articulated by Margaret Thatcher of "swamping" by "alien cultures" only thinly veil the underlying concern with national reproduction that has been an increasingly important factor in debates about immigration and citizenship during the postwar period.[41] Widespread revulsion against state-based eugenic projects following the Holocaust has tended to occlude the extent to which definitions of national belonging and culture have been racialized in a manner wholly in keeping with longstanding models of population control. Such policies have, however, shifted from a focus on maintaining metropolitan national reproduction in the context of interimperial rivalries during the first half of the twentieth century to one of excluding migration from former colonies during the postcolonial era. Such restrictive immigration policies have been accompanied by the criminalization of blackness through draconian policing strategies.[42] Thus, although ethnic minority populations in Britain after 1945 have not been subjected to official eugenic measures such as methodical sterilization campaigns, it is important to note that their excision from the national body politic has been more than simply a symbolic one.[43]

In reaction to such forms of state biopower, ethnic minority groups have often responded by advancing cultural nationalist counterdiscourses. Although such defensive moves obviously lack the links with

institutional racism that characterizes dominant discourses, all too
often such counterdiscourses reproduce the very homogenizing and
essentialist sense of identity they are reacting against. Samad's fear of
dissolution evokes precisely this replication of dominant values. Indeed,
mirroring classic eugenicist discourse, Samad equates cultural inter-
mixture with corruption and decadence. The failure of his heroic ambitions during the war, the maddeningly humble circumstances of his life
in Britain, and his guilt over the affair with Poppy push Samad to adopt
what Paul Gilroy has termed "ethnic absolutism." For Gilroy, the nar-
row cultural nationalism of some black antiracist groups fragments
broader definitions of blackness grounded in resistance to racism.[44]
Like Gilroy, Zadie Smith challenges this trend toward insular constructions of ethnic identity by tracing Samad's hilariously unsuccessful
attempts to shoehorn himself into the mold of a purified and essentialist cultural identity. Nationalist fears of penetration are, *White Teeth*
suggests, mild in comparison to the immigrant's fear of dissolution
(272). As the novel's narrator comments, Samad's search for his roots
proves increasingly constricting and ultimately corrupting:

> If religion is the opiate of the people, tradition is an even more sin-
> ister analgesic, simply because it rarely appears sinister. If religion is
> a tight band, a throbbing vein, a needle, tradition is a far homelier
> concoction: poppy seeds ground into tea; a sweet cocoa drink laced
> with cocaine; the kind of thing your grandmother might have
> made. To Samad . . . tradition was culture, and culture led to roots,
> and these were good, these were untainted principles. That didn't
> mean he could live by them, abide by them, or grow in the manner
> they demanded, but roots were roots and roots were good. You
> would get nowhere telling him that weeds too have tubers, or that
> the first sign of loose teeth is something rotten, something degener-
> ate, deep within the gums. (161)

Although *White Teeth*'s comic mode encourages the reader to retain a
sense of wry sympathy for alienated characters like Samad, the novel
also uses his misbegotten essentialism to satirize the currents of religious and cultural fundamentalism that have polarized the public
sphere in contemporary Britain.[45]

After beginning his affair with Poppy, Samad's apprehensions over
impurity increasingly center on his twin sons' identity. The more he

feels his own identity fragmenting, the more Samad insists on imposing a rigidly conceived ethnic and religious identity on his sons. He fears, for example, that English cultural forms like the "pagan" Harvest Festival organized by Magid and Millat's school are corrupting his sons. Worse still, Samad finds out that Magid has been telling his schoolmates that his name is "Mark Smith," while Millat dreams of becoming a rock star like Bruce Springsteen. What Samad misses in his consternation at this apparent total assimilation of Western culture by his twin sons is the constant negotiation and code-switching they engage in as ethnic minorities in Britain.[46] Instead of helping them in their struggle to create viable composite identities, he decides to free them of the constant cravings of the West by returning them to the East. Since he cannot afford airfare for both twins, Samad splits his twins apart, sending the more intellectually inclined Magid back to Bangladesh, where he hopes he will become a holy man, while keeping the more rebellious Millat with him in Britain. Unable to remain *halal* himself, Samad tries to determine his sons' identity through transformation of their environment. This strategy is ironic given his earlier rebellion against Dr. Sick's attempt to control human fate through eugenic engineering. As his wife notes, Samad frequently declares that Allah alone determines people's fate, and yet he himself engages in overweening attempts to control the lives of others.

The chapter describing the splitting apart of Magid and Millat is named, appropriately, "Mitosis." Through the division and replication of a single cell, Mitosis produces identical genetic material in each of the new cells. This biological reference highlights the fact that the boys are identical twins, and are therefore indistinguishable in genetic terms. Similarities and differences between the two of them as they grow up in isolation should reflect the countervailing effects of, respectively, heredity and environment. When he separates his twin sons, Samad is unwittingly engaging in an experiment similar to that used by biologists over the last half-century to assess the impact of genetic inheritance. Such experiments were initially undertaken by scientists interested in demonstrating the cultural construction of identity, a view that had gained widespread acceptance among social scientists following the turn away from genetic determinism after World War II. Reacting against the environmental determinist dogma of Lysenkoism in the Soviet Union, however, biologists challenged this model during the development of molecular genetics in the 1960s and 1970s by performing experiments with simple organisms whose traits of rapid development tended to minimize the effects of the environment.[47] Although recent trends in biology have emphasized developmental plasticity and thereby acknowledged the key role the environment plays in triggering phenotypical variation, the long-standing repudiation of environmental determinism within the scientific community has had a strong impact. As the controversy over *The Bell Curve* suggested, rigid genetic determinism has regained credibility within the social sciences. Naturally, studies of separated twins are increasingly seen as providing evidence for the role of the genes in determining identity, despite the fact that such studies usually measure cultural similarities in the extended families in which such twins are placed rather than basic genetic determination.[48]

White Teeth satirizes Samad's belief in cultural determinism as well as his dogmatic pride in his lineage by depicting the unexpected maturation of the separated twins. For despite their identical genes, Magid and Millat become polar opposites, as Samad might have hoped, but in exactly the opposite way to what he expected. Growing up in the disaster-prone environment of Bangladesh, Magid is drawn into the orbit of an Anglophile professor and comes to believe that the West alone is capable of imposing order on the chaotic world he finds in the East (239). This transformation upsets Samad's expectation that Magid would mature into a submissive disciple of Islam in the putatively pure environment of the East. As Edward Said has emphasized, imperialism and its postcolonial supplements such as neoliberal globalization have fostered a world of intermixed identities that run counter to fundamentalist or cultural nationalist perspectives.[49] The absolute separation between East and West that Samad dreams of is an illusion, and even after he separates them his sons are constantly constructing new identities based on composites of the interpenetrating cultures of East and West.

If Magid's transformation into an anglophile dandy undermines Samad's illusions of cultural purity, Millat's metamorphosis into a hybrid homeboy emphasizes the constant process of negotiation between different cultures that characterizes second-generation immigrants to an even greater extent:

> Raggastanis spoke a strange mix of Jamaican patois, Bengali, Gujarati, and English. Their ethos, their manifesto, if it could be called that, was equally a hybrid thing: Allah *featured*, but more as a collective big brother than a supreme being, a hard-as-fuck *geezer*

who would fight in their corner if necessary; kung fu and the works
of Bruce Lee were also central to the philosophy; added to this was
a smattering of Black Power (as embodied by the album *Fear of a
Black Planet,* Public Enemy); but mainly their mission was to put
the Invincible back in Indian, the Bad-aaaass back in Bengali, the
P-Funk back in Pakistani. (192)

This bravura description of Millat's "raggastani" ethos draws on cultural studies analysis of youth subcultures in Britain, which has traditionally focused on the symbolic resistance of such subcultures to class-
and age-based forms of social hierarchy.[50] Subcultures, critics such as
Dick Hebdige argue, challenge hegemonic meanings and ideologies
through acts of bricolage that transform and denature the accepted
meanings of commodities and media images.[51] Following this subcultural mode, Millat and his raggastani crew appropriate highly masculinist popular cultural icons such as Bruce Lee and the godfather to articulate a militant sense of Asian pride.

However, there is a nagging contradiction within this act of bricolage: the extremely cosmopolitan pastiche of cultural influences that
constitute "raggastani" identity are used to legitimate an increasingly
essentialist and exclusionary model of ethnic identity. Indeed, despite
their syncretic blend of diasporic cultures, Millat and his friends participate in an event that has been taken as a key flash point in the rejection
of pluralist values: the burning of Salman Rushdie's novel *The Satanic
Verses* in Bradford. As Millat becomes increasingly involved in Islamic
militancy, Zadie Smith dramatizes the clash between the Hollywood
inspiration for his macho identity and the anti-Western orientation of
Islamic fundamentalist doctrine. Millat's tragicomic cultural bastardization also reproduces his father Samad's failure to cleave to his
own ideals of purity. Through this satirical portrait of the instabilities in
Millat's and Magid's cosmopolitan identities, *White Teeth* depicts the
unexpected political outcome of diasporic hybridity and thereby undermines facile models of both genetic and cultural determinism.

The Clash of Fundamentalisms

How are we to gauge the prominence of racial difference in the "posthuman" future that biotech commentators such as Francis Fukuyama

have begun analyzing?[52] One place to start is by examining the enduring salience of "race" in the supposedly postracial present. *White Teeth* comments acidly on the contradictions in contemporary middle-class discourses of multiculturalism through its portrait of the molecular biologist Marcus Chalfen and his wife Joyce. Despite being religious and ethnic minorities, as middle-class intellectuals the Chalfens ironically offer a paradigm of successful Englishness to Archie and Samad's second-generation kids. For the Chalfens, in turn, Archie and Samad's children incarnate titillating forms of cultural, racial, and class difference that inject spice into their otherwise predictable lives. Rather than dwelling on the explicit racism of characters like the aged officer and repugnant bigot J. P. Hamilton, Smith focuses her critique on the far more subtle bias of bourgeois white Britons such as the Chalfens. For example, *White Teeth* pillories Joyce Chalfen's fashionable interest in difference—and the sexual voyeurism that underlies this interest— through the horticultural descriptions in her fictitious book *The New Flower Power:*

> The fact is, cross-pollination produces more varied offspring, which are better able to cope with a changed environment. It is said cross-pollinating plants also tend to produce more and better-quality seeds. If my one-year-old son is anything to go by (a cross-pollination between a lapsed-Catholic horticulturalist feminist and an intellectual Jew!), then I can certainly vouch for the truth of this. (258)

Using Joyce's risibly anthropocentric language of cross-pollination, Zadie Smith mocks postcolonial accounts of hybridity, which *The New Flower Power* apes perfectly. As Robert Young has argued, the currency of *hybridity* as an antiracist term is quite ironic since it is deeply embedded in precisely the kinds of fetishistic classification of difference that characterized nineteenth-century raciology.[53] Joyce's horticultural language underlines this link, allowing Smith to satirize modish talk of racial mixing. In addition, like many recent accounts of hybridity that promote an ahistorical model of diasporic identity, Joyce's description of cross-pollination suggests that hybrid plants have an inherent biological superiority over their thoroughbred competitors that makes them particularly adept at surviving in a rapidly changing environment. As we have seen, although critique of exclusionary models of identity is laudable, sweeping claims for the cosmopolitan and progressive character of diasporic communities seem far too simplistic in the wake of events such as the Rushdie affair.

Because of her interest in cross-pollination and difference, Joyce is transfixed when Millat and Irie Jones, Archie's mixed-race daughter, are sent to the Chalfens' home for tutoring after they misbehave at school. The fetishistic quality of her fascination with otherness quickly becomes apparent, however, as Millat and Irie are integrated into the Chalfen household. Irie is fascinated by the Chalfens' extrovert intellectualism, and does her best to adopt the middle-class manners and mores of the Chalfens. Millat, by contrast, is more interested in gaining access to lazy bourgeois money than intellectual capital. Predictably, the more Irie attempts to conform to what the family calls Chalfenism, the less interesting she is to Joyce. By contrast, the more Millat goes off the rails, the more Joyce becomes fascinated with his problematic identity. As Millat becomes increasingly embroiled with a blundering but militant Islamic group that feeds his teenage dreams of righteous rebellion, Joyce treats his growing cultural nationalism as a curiosity and psychological conundrum rather than a political stance. Joyce's myopic support of Millat offers an implicit comment on the politics of institutional multiculturalism in Britain, whose advocates have a history of taking the most extreme forms of cultural difference to be the most authentic expressions of collective identity. Multiculturalism has therefore become a target of criticism in Britain because of its unwitting tendency to further reactionary currents within ethnic minority communities. As activists with the British group Women Against Fundamentalism have argued, conservative religious leaders have been among the greatest beneficiaries of the adoption of multiculturalist norms since these measures have allowed them to depict challenges to their programs as racism.[54] Joyce's role in abetting Millat's turn to militant Islam despite her putatively progressive outlook underlines the contradictions of multiculturalist dogma.

Like his wife, Marcus Chalfen is deeply invested in questions of hybridization and has a Panglossian belief in the progressive outcome of such processes. As a result, he expresses utter disdain for those who challenge the ethical prerogatives of his genetic experiments: scientific and social progress, Marcus believes, are "brothers-in-arms." Yet *White Teeth* introduces a note of sweeping hubris in its description of Marcus's scientific endeavors:

He went to the edges of his God's imagination and made mice Yah-weh could not conceive of: mice with rabbit genes, mice with webbed feet (or so Joyce imagined, so didn't ask), mice who year after year expressed more and more eloquently Marcus's designs: from the hit-or-miss process of selective breeding, to the chimeric fusion of embryos, and then the rapid developments that lay beyond Joyce's ken and in Marcus's future—DNA microinjection, retrovirus-mediated transgenesis (for which he came within an inch of the Nobel, 1987), embryonic stem cell-mediated gene transfer—all processes by which Marcus manipulated ova, regulated the over- or under-expression of a gene, planting instructions in the germ line to be realized in physical characteristics. Creating mice whose very bodies did exactly what Marcus told them. And always with humanity in mind—a cure for cancer, cerebral palsy, Parkinson's—always with the firm belief in the *perfectibility* of all life, in the possibility of making it more efficient, more logical. (259–60)

Marcus's facile belief in the sanctity of his research skirts the complex ethical questions that Zadie Smith's account of his enterprise raises. By harnessing the awesome but still poorly understood power of recombinant DNA, Marcus is able to engage in forms of cross-pollination that completely eclipse the hybridization processes described in his wife's writing.[55] Human beings have been domesticating and breeding plants and animals for over ten thousand years, but we have always been restrained in our attempts to hybridize our creations by the natural limits imposed by species boundaries. Recombinant DNA overcomes these limits by manipulating genes themselves. In his experiments with mutant mice, Marcus is part of the contemporary attempt to initiate a new biotechnological era in which all life-forms can be transformed into factories for the production of commodities. Indeed, the genetic code of life itself is increasingly being commodified in what critics such as Vandana Shiva see as the final stage of primitive accumulation.[56] By placing himself in this godlike position, Marcus opens a Pandora's box of issues relating to the ramifications of genetic research.

Yet, like many scientists and entrepreneurs in the booming biotech industry, Marcus Chalfen refuses to engage in debate concerning the potential ecological and social perils associated with genetic engineering.[57] Marcus has no time for science studies scholars, who challenge the ideology of scientific objectivity by insisting on the role played by researchers in reflecting and reinforcing the dominant values of their society. He similarly spurns activists who question the ethics of his experiments on animals. His arrogance and insularity are threatened, however, by a young woman he meets at Heathrow airport while waiting for Magid's return from Bangladesh. Her identity as an Asian and a Hindu, she explains to Marcus, make her see some highly dystopian sides to biotechnology. She goes on to amplify this point by describing her fears concerning the potential use of pathogenic organisms by the West against the East, the creation of racial hierarchy through genetic engineering, and the destruction of the sanctity of life (345). Marcus is unhinged by what he sees as the lurid neofascist possibilities the young woman extrapolates from his work. Caught up in the minutiae of scientific research and discovery and in thoughts of the potential medical benefits to be derived from his work, Marcus is unprepared to submit himself to ethical scrutiny by the general public.

Yet as critics like Jeremy Rifkin have argued, genetic engineering technologies are by their very nature eugenics tools.[58] Unlike the eugenics movements of the early twentieth century, the new biotechnology is driven not by totalitarian ideologies of national/racial uplift but by market forces and consumer desire. Nevertheless, reproductive technologies such as prenatal testing that diagnose untreatable genetic disorders already force decisions on families and individuals that are inherently eugenic. Parents will face increasing pressure to use new biotechnologies in order to protect their unborn children from hereditary diseases as these technologies become more widely available. But these pressures are inherently social, and their potentially inegalitarian uses will increase pressure for state intervention.[59] What, for example, will constitute a genetic "defect"? As Rifkin notes, disability rights advocates are already questioning the eugenic implications of such language, wondering whether people like themselves will be seen simply as errors in the code.[60] Likewise, Francis Fukuyama hypothesizes that a genetic "cure" for homosexuality would push individuals to engineer heterosexual children for themselves, leading to greater discrimination against those born queer and to the eventual elimination of homosexuality.[61] The potential for drastic amplification of the already wide race-based disparities of life opportunities as a result of privatized eugenics is just as alarming. In this vein, *White Teeth* examines Irie Jones's self-hatred as a result of her genetic inheritance of kinky hair and a buxom body. Her painful attempts to straighten her hair and to become a Chalfen highlight the difficult questions concerning identity, race, and hegemony that biotechnology will increasingly place before us.

Stung by the complex ethical questions raised by the young woman he meets at the airport, Marcus leans increasingly on Magid, who has arrived in Britain intent on helping him eliminate chaos from the world. The center of this grandiose project is Marcus's FutureMouse, a creature genetically engineered to develop specific cancers in specific tissues at specific times. As Marcus laconically comments in a moment of defensive sarcasm, "You eliminate the random, you rule the world" (283). Notwithstanding such derisive banter, Marcus's project of total control is scientifically unfeasible. As we saw earlier, an organism's environment plays a vital role in determining the expression of its genes. However, even if it were possible to control both the genes of a developing organism and the complete sequence of its environments, one could not maintain total control over the organism because of random variations in the division and growth of cells that occur during development.[62] This chance element, known as developmental noise, undermines the rigid genetic determinism and totalitarian desire for control implicit in Marcus's project.

Despite the fact that Marcus's hubristic experiment is doomed to fail, the public takes the FutureMouse very seriously. In a slap at the commodification of science that has accompanied the biotechnology boom, White Teeth traces the rise of controversy surrounding the FutureMouse as a result of Magid's public relations campaign. In the press releases he gives to Irie to disseminate, Magid describes the creature as the herald of a new phase in history in which human beings will not be "victims of the random but instead directors and arbitrators of our own fate" (357). Magid's desire for control over fate should not be so surprising given his own traumatic life experience. This aspiration, however, is just as doomed as Marcus's genetic determinism. In a hilarious depiction of contemporary clashes over biotech, Marcus and Magid's joint project to win public support for genetic engineering runs afoul of groups whose religious and ethical beliefs are challenged by the FutureMouse.

The press conference at which the mouse was to have made its triumphant debut is disrupted by two such organizations in particular: Millat's posse, the Keepers of the Eternal and Vigilant Islamic Nation (KEVIN), and a militant animal rights group named Fighting Animal Torture and Exploitation (FATE), to which Marcus's son Joshua belongs. As one might imagine from their ludicrous acronyms, Zadie Smith satirizes both of these groups mercilessly.[63] Joshua seems animated more by the cleavage of FATE's sexy female leader than by the group's quasi-theological discussions of animal rights, while Millat's Islamic militancy is more a product of Scorsese films than of the Koran. Nevertheless, despite the personal foibles of both groups' members, *White Teeth* makes FATE and KEVIN the mouthpieces for the two dominant critiques of biotechnology: the theological and the ethical. Although the novel does not dwell on the moral objections of either group in detail, their opposition to the reification and commodification of life represents a potent challenge to the strain of biological determinism evinced most clearly in the FutureMouse. In addition, despite the fact that the clash between these groups and the scientific establishment that takes place at the unveiling of the FutureMouse is not resolved, the renewal of conflict over the control of genetic inheritance reminds us that the legacy of eugenics and raciology is very much alive.

CONCLUSION

Archie's flashback to World War II during the unveiling ceremony for the FutureMouse underlines the legacy of raciological science that lies at the heart of contemporary biotechnology. Through this flashback, we learn that Archie was unable to execute Doctor Perret—aka Dr. Sick—and that this proponent of Nazi eugenics emerged after the war to become Marcus Chalfen's mentor and director of the institute at which the FutureMouse unveiling is taking place. The replication of events during World War II is explicit in the novel's finale. Reenacting the scene in the Balkans, Millat attempts to strike against what he perceives as a blasphemous scheme to wrest control of human fate away from God by putting a bullet into Marcus Chalfen. Once again, Archie chooses clemency, and throws himself in front of Millat's gun at the last second. This time, however, the reader understands more clearly what is at issue in Archie's action. During Archie's flashback to the war, Perret describes his confidence that human perfection can be achieved if only hard decisions concerning who will survive and who won't are made (446). In saving Marcus Chalfen, Archie therefore acts in a manner that contradicts Perret's chilling eugenic philosophy. As he falls to the ground wounded, Archie sees the FutureMouse escape from his cage and, in the midst of the ensuing commotion, head down a nearby mousehole. Chance and human solidarity thereby disrupt the carefully scripted life of the FutureMouse.

The Millennial Science Commission, the dramatic setting for these events, bears more than a passing resemblance to the sensational press conference organized by the Human Genome Project at the White House in 2001. Like the concluding scene of Smith's novel, the White House ceremony revealed more than just scientific research. The map of the human genome released by the government-funded research team was only unveiled at this point as a result of an agreement with their private competitors at the Celera Genomics Corporation.[64] Having decoded the mouse genome in 1999 and made the map available by subscription only, the entrepreneurial director of Celera, Dr. J. Craig Venter, had promised to beat the international public consortium by using a new method of genetic decoding. Competition with Venter's private firm obviously pushed the international consortium to complete its draft far more quickly. However, it also clearly delineated the character of future conflicts over access to the genetic information that helps shape all living creatures. For Celera did not intend to make the map of the human genome available to the public, despite having used information published by the international consortium in its research. Like other companies that are currently engaged in what critics call biopiracy, Celera's research is predicated on the privatization and commodification of the genetic sequences of living organisms. The uneasy truce reached during the unveiling ceremony at the White House in 2001 was thus indicative of future contests over the corporate expropriation of plant, animal, and microbial species.[65]

A number of critics have complained at Zadie Smith's refusal to resolve the final scene of her novel clearly. Having depicted the return of the eugenic past, why does she not take a clearer stand on the impact of this return? Yet this criticism misses the novel's main point: it is impossible to offer any final verdict on the impact of biotechnology at this early date. For while *White Teeth* can warn us against facile liberal models of multiculturalism by highlighting the disturbing return of an age of eugenics, it cannot predict the outcome of this return. How do we balance the closely interwoven utopian and dystopian potentials of the new biotechnologies? What will it mean to be a human being in a world where babies are genetically designed in the womb? How will we retain the sense of common humanity necessary for viable democracy when people are identified, stereotyped, and discriminated against on the basis of their genotype? Will the governments of the world allow a market-oriented wave of eugenics to deepen the already wide chasm that divides the rich and the poor and to expand the brutal exploitation of animals around the world? It is still far too early to answer such questions. Whatever the future holds, we need to face the ethical dilemmas that biotechnology will increasingly place before us with a clear awareness of the dystopian history of such technologies. Zadie Smith's *White Teeth* reminds us of this history and hints at its saliency for conflicts to come.

Conclusion: "Step Back from the Blow Back"

Asian Hip-Hop and Post-9/11 Britain

THE SCALE OF DEVASTATION WROUGHT by the German bombardment of Britain during World War II was immense. During the first month of the Blitz, for instance, seven thousand people died and ten thousand were wounded in London alone. In the face of such devastation, Britons displayed remarkable fortitude. Noel Coward, for example, coolly describes the scene at the Savoy Hotel in his diary of 1941, with the orchestra playing on while the walls of the building bulge as bombs drop nearby. Compare such sangfroid with the state of hysteria provoked by the suicide attacks during the summer of 2005.[1] Although Parliament ultimately scaled back Tony Blair's bid to extend detention without charge to ninety days, plans for national identity cards, secret antiterrorism courts, summary extraditions, the muzzling of free speech, and police "shoot to kill" policies have gone ahead unimpaired by abundant evidence that such policies will do little or nothing to prevent terrorism. Blair's defiant declaration that the July bombers would not destroy the "British way of life" was unnecessary, of course, since the British prime minister, through his increasingly draconian policies, is doing this work himself, unraveling civil liberties that took centuries to establish. What explains the discrepancy between the British stiff upper lip during the Blitz, or, for that matter, during the long years of IRA terrorism, and behavior in today's neoimperial Britain? In addition, why, despite significant mass protests against the invasion of Iraq, have substantial numbers of the British public gone along with Blair's hyperbolic response to attacks that were, after all, quite predictable given Britain's troop deployments in Afghanistan and Iraq?

The response of the British government to the July bombings was not simply a product of Tony Blair's megalomaniacal ambitions, as most journalists have tended to argue, but rather germinated from the deeply racialized manner in which British identity has been framed for the last half-century. While the July bombings and the "war on terror" in general have helped catalyze particularly unsettling forms of discrimination, there are significant continuities between the policies of the Blair government and those of preceding British regimes in the face of real or perceived threats to national security. Although Blair and the members of his cabinet admittedly never articulate explicit racial animus against any groups, their rhetoric and the policies pursued by the Labour government are driven by a *cultural racism* that hinges on the defense of putatively homogeneous national values against an alien threat. This is not, in other words, simply a matter of the individual foibles of particular leaders, but rather of an institutional and ideological racism that is grounded in exclusionary discourses of national identity disseminated across the political spectrum and deeply inscribed in British culture. While the specific members of British society subjected to this cultural racism have changed over the last half-century, the authoritarian populism that it helps catalyze is surprisingly continuous. Not only is this popular authoritarianism unlikely to protect Britons from future terrorist attacks; it is very likely to spark future aggression by underlining the injustice and inequality that lie at the heart of the British body politic.

Four days after the bombings on the London underground and bus system last summer, Blair attempted to reassure British Muslims in a statement made before Parliament in which he argued that "fanaticism is not a state of religion but a state of mind. We will work with you [British Muslims] to make the moderate and true voice of Islam heard as it should be. Together, we will ensure that though terrorists can kill, they will never destroy the way of life we share and which we value."[2] Like George Bush following 9/11, Tony Blair was careful not to suggest that all Muslims are extremists. Despite this apparently antiracist move, Blair at the same time establishes a binary opposition between the enlightened values of "our civilization" and the barbaric behavior of "fanatics." This binary conveniently cloaks the role of Western powers in catalyzing Islamism. Blair cannot admit that his government has helped prosecute a nakedly imperialist war in Iraq that has involved staggering numbers of civilian deaths and regular infractions of the Geneva Convention. So, instead of framing the July bombings as blowback from the imperial adventurism he helped initiate, Blair has recourse to the Manichaean tropes of neo-Orientalist discourse.

In addition to dampening criticism of British imperialist belligerence abroad, such rhetoric sets up a divide between those domestic (and domesticated) "good" Muslims who fall into line behind "our values," including the new antiterrorist legislation, and the "bad" Muslims who explicitly attack government measures in their words or actions.[3] While this kind of rhetoric about national unity might have some political clout for figures like Bush and Blair in the moments of crisis ignited by their policies, it not only fails to clarify the historical context that catalyzes attacks on the imperial homelands, but actively stamps out such analysis by labeling virtually all dissent a form of terrorism. The British government's definition of terrorism is very broad and includes many legal political parties at home and abroad; terrorism, in other words, boils down to pretty much any group the government does not favor.[4] Moreover, fanaticism and terrorism are forms of behavior that characterize only the opponents of Western powers, never those powers themselves. High-altitude bombing sorties against civilian populations by the Atlantic powers have never been seen as terror, despite the similar aims such policies share with those of "terrorists."[5] Given the imperial policies that his government has pursued and his use of reductive stereotypes to represent resistance to such policies, Blair's gestures of inclusion smack of hypocrisy to many in Britain's Muslim communities.

Hostility toward British Muslims has increased significantly over the last decade and a half. As Afro-Caribbeans preponderantly were during the 1970s, Muslims, and, by extension, Asians in general are increasingly seen as an alien threat, the monstrous Other whose presence helps explain Britain's postcolonial decline and current vicissitudes. Although what the Runnymede Trust Commission calls Islamophobia was a factor in the wake of the Rushdie affair and the first Gulf War, hostility toward Asians has ratcheted up significantly after 9/11, with the entire community being reinvented as Muslims of Asian descent and increasingly portrayed by both mainstream as well as neofascist politicians as a potential fifth column. Not surprisingly, this trend has helped to generate significant tensions within Britain's Asian community, with some members of other faiths joining in attacks on Muslims. Moreover, although explicit and even coded racial hatred is proscribed in Britain by laws for which the antiracist movement fought long and hard, Muslims are not protected as a group by such legislation. This is because, unlike religious groups such as Jews or Sikhs, for instance, Muslims are a multiethnic group, and Islam consequently is not shielded from incitement to hatred by antiracist legislation.[6] Neofascist agitators have been quick to take advantage of this loophole in the law, with groups like the British National Party running successful local electoral campaigns organized around overtly xenophobic slogans such as "Islam out of Britain."[7]

The distance between such extreme rhetoric and the nationalist posturing of mainstream politicians has diminished noticeably since 9/11. Shortly after 9/11, for instance, former prime minister Margaret Thatcher issued a blanket condemnation of all Muslims everywhere for the attacks.[8] Moreover, British Muslims are now also blamed for the failure of official British policies of multiculturalism. The bombings, according to this logic, are a symptom of Muslims' failure to integrate adequately into British culture, a failure licensed by multiculturalism's tolerance for diversity. Already in 2002, former chancellor of the exchequer Normal Lamont was warning of the dangers of balkanization created by New Labour's multiculturalist model of a "community of communities." It was quite clear who Lamont was referring to when he inveigled against the moral relativism fostered by multiculturalism. As he put it in an editorial, "Multiculturalism can easily degenerate into moral relativism. Our laws are based on values, and the state has the right to intervene to protect them. Individuals cannot be left alone in their chosen communities, if that involves forced marriages, polygamy, burning books, supporting fatwas or even fighting against our Armed Forces."[9] Lamont's diatribe is part of a renewed push to abandon multiculturalism and enforce assimilation to a homogeneously conceived normative British identity that is picking up steam despite its anachronistic character. Yet notwithstanding Lamont's thinly veiled references to threatening Muslim alterity, the bombers of last July were all seamlessly integrated into British society. As A. Sivanandan points out, Abdullah Jamal, formerly Germaine Lindsay, was married to a white, English woman; Mohammad Sidique Khan was a graduate who helped children of all religions; Shehzad Tanweer, also a graduate, often helped in his father's fish-and-chip shop; and Hasib Hussain's parents sent him to Pakistan because they felt he had fallen into the English drinking-and-swearing culture.[10] These young men took their own lives and those of their fellow citizens not because of an irrational urge to self-destruction but, as Khan stated outright in a video made before he blew himself up, because of their anger at Britain's invasion and subsequent destruction of Iraq.

I obviously do not intend to suggest that concerns about Islamic militants in Britain and elsewhere in Europe are totally unfounded, any more than Stuart Hall and his colleagues intended to argue that there was no criminal behavior taking place when they anatomized racial scapegoating in pre-Thatcherite Britain.[11] In *Policing the Crisis,* Hall and his colleagues argued that sensationalist media representations of black crime combined with invasive U.S.-style saturation policing of black communities and a politically touchy judiciary during the 1970s to create what they called a "moral panic" around the racialized figure of the mugger. In addition, they stressed that the broader context for this moral panic was the organic crisis of social democracy in Britain, a crisis most apparent in the failure of the state to provide means of material incorporation for the spatially and economically marginalized black communities in Britain. Under such circumstances, some members of the black community did indeed turn to the illegal economy, including predatory behavior such as criminality, but the political and media firestorm around mugging was entirely disproportionate to the "real" phenomenon of mugging. Instead, the moral panic concerning mugging was manipulated by politicians such as Enoch Powell and Margaret Thatcher to provide an explanation for the various forms of economic, social, and political dysfunction triggered by the crisis of accumulation that began in the late 1960s and that ultimately precipitated the dismantling of the Fordist-era social contract. Blacks were thus scapegoated for a much broader crisis; their demonization helped cement white working-class consent for the evisceration of social democracy in Britain in the years that followed.

The recent wave of popular authoritarianism regarding British Muslims shares many structural parallels with the moral panic that took place during the organic crisis of the 1970s. Very similar forms of economic and cultural marginalization in the context of a broader crisis are at play. Although some British Muslims, notably those exiled from East Africa during the early 1970s, have done well in economic terms over the last thirty years, the majority of the Asian population in Britain arrived to work in dying industries such as textiles in the Midlands or in the vertiginously downsized service industry. The neoliberal orthodoxy of both Tory and Labour governments since the Thatcher era has kept these groups at the bottom of Britain's economic pile, trapped on run-down public housing estates with often violently xenophobic members of the white working class. It is thus not so much the case that these second- and third-generation British Asians have failed to assimilate as that the neoliberal state has refused to grant them significant access to mainstream British society.

Equally if not more important than this domestic economic cul-de-sac, however, is the global crisis of neoliberal ideology. Although the so-called Washington Consensus has begun to unravel as a result of its own internal contradictions, it is indisputably from within the Muslim world that the strongest resistance to neoliberal policies has come. Hegemonic neoliberal policy during the 1990s took the form of tacit Western support for authoritarian secular regimes in the Muslim world that imposed the West's conditions of structural adjustment and guns-for-oil on their populations with seeming impunity. As these regimes abdicated any autonomous, popular nationalist role, anti-imperialist uprisings such as the Iranian Revolution and the Palestinian intifada, as well as conflicts in Somalia, Bosnia, Chechnya, and, most of all, Afghanistan, helped forge a transnational vanguard of young Islamists.[12] Media networks such as Al Jazeera and the Internet, as well as more low-tech equivalents like newspapers and videocassettes, helped knit Muslims around the world together into an emotionally resonant imagined community. This virtual version of the transnational Arabic community or *umma* transmitted abundant evidence of the horrors of the Pax Americana over the last decade, from the unending nightmare in Gaza and the West Bank, to U.S. military bases near the Holy of Holies and Bush Sr.'s betrayal of the Shiite uprising against Saddam Hussein in 1991. Political Islam is thus a symptom of and response to an organic crisis that, as David Harvey has suggested, has obliterated the legitimacy of secular states in a significant portion of the postcolonial world and, in tandem, has shattered U.S. neoliberal ideological hegemony, leaving nothing but the brutal military power whose bloody overreach we have been witnessing in Iraq.[13]

It should be no great surprise that the contradictions of these neoliberal policies and the even more brutal overt imperialism that has followed in their wake have generated significant ferment within Britain's marginalized Muslim communities. If, as critics such as Tricia Rose and George Lipsitz have argued, hip-hop culture originated in the United States as a response to the displacement caused by "urban renewal," economic recession, and the fiscal crisis of the state in the 1970s, contemporary Asian hip-hop in Britain similarly offers a critical counterpoint to contemporary social and political orthodoxies, including the explicitly imperialist form of neoliberal culture that emerged following 9/11.[14] Indeed, British Asian youth culture is increasingly a vector for a radical anti-imperialist politics. Groups like Fun-Da-Mental and Asian Dub Foundation tackle Islamophobia head-on, asserting a sense of pride in Muslim and Asian identity while also advancing a cultural politics of unity with other racialized ethnic groups in Britain. In addition, these groups have played an important role in dismantling official rhetoric concerning the threat of terrorism following 9/11. Perhaps most significant, however, is the sense of critical transnationalism that emerges from the music of these bands. While tapping into a similar sense of a transnational community as vanguardist Islamist movements, these bands eschew religious dogmatism, and thereby suggest the possibility of alternative forms of politicized Islam working in solidarity with the global justice movement. Such groups may be read as harbingers of alternatives to the fratricidal twins of market and religious fundamentalism.

Fun-Da-Mental is undoubtedly the seminal band in the wave of politicized post-bhangra Asian dance music that took off in the early 1990s.[15] The group released their first LP, *Seize the Time*, in 1994. Although they have often been compared to the United States' Public Enemy, such comparisons tend to obscure the complicated local character of the band's intervention. Formed round core members Aki Nawaz (aka Propa-Gandhi) and Dave Watts (aka Impi D), Fun-Da-Mental appealed to Muslim youths in Britain who were alienated from mosques as well as official community leaders by their opposition to music, dance, and videos, including the popular bhangra music that had become the soundtrack for Asian youth culture in Britain during the late 1980s.[16] In addition to heading up Fun-Da-Mental, group leader Aki Nawaz is a cofounder of Nation Records, probably the most important independent Asian record label in Britain over the last decade. Fun-Da-Mental's music conveys a fierce sense of British Muslim pride, constructing an identity matrix through references to a pantheon of

international black and Asian leaders, including, as the group's first
album title suggests, the Black Panthers, but, above all, Malcolm X and
the Nation of Islam. These references to the Nation of Islam are particularly important in forging black-Asian unity, solidarity enacted in the
multiracial composition of the band itself and, more broadly, in the
British tradition of antiessentialist antiracism. With these references to
the Nation of Islam and its incendiary counterreading of Western history through the lens of white oppression comes a powerful rhetoric of
self-defense that, in the wake of 9/11 and 7/7, seems chillingly prophetic:

> Stop the world 'cause we're living like slaves
> God only knows how I've been managing
> Look at me now, I've got them panicking
> Blood'll be dripping from those headless chickens
>
> This is the world of greed like it never was
> We've had enough, it's time to get tough
> Look who's afraid, not me or mine
> But the devils that worked us in the sunshine
>
> They don't like anybody like me
> X was in the X, Luther King was next
> But they're only two from millions
> My people been treated like aliens
> Los Angeles was just a rehearsal
> First we've been looting, next we'll be shooting
> Here comes another Huey P. Newton
> Making them angry 'cause they can't ban me.[17]

From its opening loping rhythms cut across by an accelerating sample
of Malcolm X's defiant rhetoric, this track oozes anger. Frequent references to the pride instilled by militant self-defense alternate with a catalog of the historical wrongs inflicted on people of color, including slavery and the assassinations of Martin Luther King and Malcolm. In
addition, the group also articulates a critique of the West's domination
by the cash nexus and the moral decadence that such materialism
spawns. Moments of self-defense cited by the group include the Los
Angeles uprising of 1992 following the acquittal of the four white police
officers who beat Rodney King, events that had taken place the year
before *Seize the Time* was recorded. In addition, the singer's citation of

"letting off bombs" suggests a reference to the first Palestinian intifada, which was winding down after six years by 1993. The reference to Malcolm X's famous line about the "chickens coming home to roost" following the assassination of Bobby Kennedy could not, in retrospect, be more ominous an articulation of political Islam's intent to bring neoliberal oppression and militarism home to the imperial heartland.

It is important to note that Fun-Da-Mental's overheated rhetoric has cooled noticeably as "clash of civilization" discourse has come to dominate the public sphere in Britain and the United States. After releasing the inflammatorily titled EP *Why America Will Go To Hell* in July 1999, the group's main subsequent release, the October 2001 album *There Shall Be Love,* is an entirely instrumental recording, bereft of the fiercely condemnatory lyrics of their earlier work. It seems that the group has determined that the militant rhetoric and, most of all, the advocacy of violent resistance in their earlier work may be counterproductive in the struggle for global social justice, a movement in which they have taken an active role since 2001. Yet it is worth taking their earlier work seriously inasmuch as it articulates a sense of righteous anger that is carefully justified in historical terms. This seems significant given the ascription of irrationality that tends to characterize media accounts of Islamism. Such an analysis of Islamism is, of course, part of a long-established Orientalist tradition, anatomized in devastating detail by Edward Said, of representing Islam as the benighted, feminized, unhinged foil for the rational, masculine, and modern West.

It is precisely these stereotypical assumptions that provide an ideological cover for the current Anglo-American project of bringing democracy to the Middle East through the military occupation of Iraq. Yet, as Robert Pape argues in his recent book *Dying to Win,* suicide bombing is not, as Orientalist discourse so often represents it, the product of an irrational self-destructive urge, but rather is a calculated strategic response by vanguardist groups who often have significant support from civilian populations in areas occupied by what appears to them to be a colonial power.[18] Lacking the massive means of military destruction deployed by powers such as the United States, UK, and Israel in their campaigns of airborne extermination, suicide bombers resort to low-tech solutions that purposely target civilian populations. The logic behind such bloody stratagems is that democratic governments are relatively vulnerable to campaigns that massacre civilian populations and, in doing so, bring home the violence of imperial policies abroad, sap-

ping popular support for expansionist policies. Pape's conclusion that
suicide bombing reflects classic anticolonial nationalist struggles rather
than the religious fundamentalism to which it is often ascribed is lent
support by Fun-Da-Mental's lyrics on *Seize the Time,* all of which refer
to struggles for self-determination such as the African-American civil
rights movement and the Palestinian intifada, as well as more local
black British resistance against neofascist hooligans. It is an index of the
power of neo-Orientalist discourse today that Pape's findings and the
anger that smolders throughout Fun-Da-Mental's *Seize the Time* should
continue to seem so startling.

If Fun-Da-Mental have backed away from their radical rhetoric to a
certain extent in the post-9/11 period, their confederates in Asian Dub
Foundation (ADF) have grown more militant. ADF was formed when
the organizers of a community music project in London's predominantly Bangladeshi East End neighborhood decided to form a band with
some of their star pupils. On early albums of the middle to late 1990s
such as *Facts and Fictions* and *Community Music,* ADF focused on
Britain's imperial history in South Asia and on the ways in which this
history overdetermined contemporary social relations and state legislation in postcolonial Britain. Recent albums such as *Enemy of the Enemy*
(2003) and *Tank* (2005) have, however, seen an increasing awareness of
the international contradictions that characterize neoliberalism as it has
evolved from the multilateral, trade-based mode of exploitation in the
Clinton and early Blair era to the military imperialist formation in contemporary Britain and America. While the group has always displayed a
notably composite sense of identity, evident in their syncretic musical
blend of dub, rap, rock, and Asian musical styles such as bhangra, recent
political conditions have pushed their analysis of the nexus of contemporary domestic and international social relations to a new level. In
"Blowback," for example, the group anatomizes the Machiavellian
behavior of imperialist powers like the United States and UK toward
erstwhile client regimes such as that of Saddam Hussein, noting the role
that jingoism plays in legitimating a clamp down on domestic entitlements as well as civil liberties:

> Step Back from the Blow Back
> Plans that were hatched with the strings still attached
> See there's always a catch
> When you're livin' thru a blow back

You're wonderin' why you need places to hide
Keep one eye to the sky when you're waiting for the blowback
Sink into the mud watch out for the scud
Cos oil is thicker than blood in the world of blowback
From ally to madman from client to badman
From Gommorah to Sadaam
Starring in the blowback
Invisible sins Invisible Kings
The shit we're in gonna drown in the spin
Permanent warfare
Burning up welfare
Add up add up
Their share of the hardware
Rights disposed of
Government gloves off
Flick of the wrist
Summary justice
Feel the kiss of the U.S. fist.[19]

By now this sort of analysis has become relatively conventional on the Left, with critics such as Frances Fox Piven noting the important function of neoliberal imperialism in providing domestic legitimation for the Right's agenda.[20] More original, perhaps, is ADF's take on Al Qaeda in "Enemy of the Enemy." Not only does ADF make the link to blowback from the U.S. proxy war in Afghanistan during the 1980s on this track; in addition, the group evokes the double standards that characterize the behavior of imperialist regimes on the international stage. In the name of battling Communism and, now, Islamism, powers like the United States and UK have unleashed campaigns of terror that repeatedly put the lie to pious notions of human rights, suggesting, as ADF puts it, that "what your life is worth depends on where you live." These double standards are all too evident today, as imperial powers engage in devastating saturation bombing campaigns in the name of spreading democracy while ignoring the "collateral damage" inflicted on civilian populations, whose lives never register in the Western media—although they feature prominently in the electronic *umma* that binds together contemporary Muslims.

Running parallel to this hypocritical rhetoric of democratization and human rights abroad are the gaping holes in the political constitution of the European Union. While the EU has conveyed remarkable freedom of mobility and domicile on European nationals and has arguably helped initiate progressive models of international conflict resolution since its consolidation in the early 1990s, it was created with a *cordon sanitaire* thrown round it, one that all too glaringly keeps out the increasingly immiserated and politically oppressed citizens of the predominantly Muslim nations that surround its southern flanks. As Etienne Balibar has pointed out, the exclusionary character of EU citizenship has made the sizable migrant population of the EU, a kind of twenty-sixth member country with a majority Muslim population, into a stateless people.[21] The result, as Balibar observes, has been a recolonization of social relations, one that affects Muslims who have European citizenship almost as much as it affects those who do not have legal residency, since they are all increasingly perceived as part of a potentially hostile fifth column intent on destroying European civilization. Politicized Asian youths such as the members of ADF are only too aware of this new apartheid at the heart of Europe. As the band notes in their song "Fortress Europe," this hard-line policy of sealing Europe off to migrants and the blowback they threat to bring with them ignores the root of the problem: military neoliberalism. The dystopian future of overweening computerized state control ADF outlines in "Fortress Europe" is not that far from being realized; while proclaiming its adherence to a progressive regime of "managed migration," Blair's Labour government has simultaneously normalized policies of long-term detention, deportation, and dispersion that criminalize unwanted (read poor, unskilled) immigrants, reneging on the country's Geneva Convention commitment to rights of political asylum.[22] As ADF's "Fortress Europe" suggests, the popular authoritarianism, hard-line immigration tactics, and antiterrorist legislation that have proliferated in the EU only serve to augment the militancy of young nonwhite Europeans. Recent measures that would permit the expulsion of foreign nationals to countries engaging in torture would abrogate Britain's commitment to the UN Convention Against Torture, giving contemporary critics cause to sneer, as Frantz Fanon did in the context of the Algerian War, at the racialized character of European humanism.[23] Indeed, increasingly virulent attacks on multiculturalism such as those that have saturated the public sphere in Britain following the July bombings and legislative moves to allow expulsion of British nationals who express criticism of the government that can be construed as "condoning terrorism" seem calculated to deepen the alienation and anger that economic, social, and political marginalization have generated among British Asian youths during the neoliberal era.

The anti-imperialist cultural politics of engaged artists such as Fun-Da-Mental and Asian Dub Foundation point toward a radically different and truly postimperial Britain. Of course, social programs to establish genuine economic and political equality within Britain are a basic prerequisite for such a new dispensation. In order for such policies to be implemented, popular authoritarian ideologies that cemented consent during the early stages of neoliberalism would have to be rolled back. But, in tandem with such policies, Britain would need to sever its dependent relation with the United States in order to forge a genuine postcolonial politics. Unfortunately, instead of pursuing such an autonomous direction, Britain's leaders are playing the role of obedient lapdogs to U.S. imperial power. As in the United States, such imperial policies have inevitable and significant domestic ramifications, including the attempt to squelch all dissent.

The antisystemic cultural politics of Islamists are not going to go away by themselves. Indeed, neoliberal imperialism feeds such voices by generating the conditions of endemic economic deprivation and of political oppression that stimulate rebellion. The danger of criminalizing all expressions of political Islam within Britain and Europe more broadly is that it leaves vanguardist Islamists as the only voices of anti-imperialism. Indeed, we only need to look at the policies pursued by Western imperial powers and their indigenous client regimes in the Koran belt over the last fifty years to understand the folly of such a strategy. In addition, as the Blair government's behavior during the "war on terror" makes clear, policies that erode civil liberties in the name of antiterrorism inevitably have wider implications. As George Monbiot recently argued, restrictions on civil liberties that are passed in name of combating "terror" almost without fail are used by politicians such as Blair to silence anyone who questions government policy, no matter how nonviolent their criticism.[24] The popular authoritarianism to which black and Asian Britons have been subjected over the last half-century thus inevitably has ramifications beyond these so-called ethnic minority communities. The voices of activist artists such as Asian Dub Foundation and Fun-Da-Mental offer a potent rebuke to contemporary military neoliberalism, one that will be far more conducive to progressive politics in the long term than current official policies in countries such as Britain and the United States that increasingly seek to silence all dissent. The stinging criticism such groups offer of Britain's imperial legacy makes them part of the chorus of voices that have sought over the last five decades to decolonize Britain and, in so doing, to make of it a truly mongrel nation.

Notes

INTRODUCTION

1. "London Is the Place for Me," Lord Kitchener with Freddy Grant's Caribbean Rhythm, Melodisc 74, London 1951. Available on the compilation *London Is the Place For Me: Trinidadian Calypso in London, 1950–1956*, Honest Jon's Records, 2002.

2. For a discussion of the use of English literature to inculcate loyalty among the colonized in India, see Gauri Viswanathan, *Masks of Conquest: Literary Studies and British Rule in India* (New York: Columbia University Press, 1989).

3. The case of V. S. Naipaul is a particularly dispiriting instance of the potency of such ideas during the final years of the colonial era in the Caribbean. See Rob Nixon, *London Calling: V. S. Naipaul, Postcolonial Mandarin* (New York: Oxford University Press, 1992).

4. According to Edward Pilkington, one-third of those traveling aboard the boat were war veterans. See *Beyond the Mother Country: West Indians and the Notting Hill White Riots* (London: IB Tauris, 1988), 18.

5. Laura Tabili, *"We Ask for British Justice": Workers and Racial Difference in Late Imperial Britain* (Ithaca, N.Y.: Cornell University Press, 1994), 29.

6. Sam King, online interview, 1 January 2001, BBC Windrush History Site, http:www.bbc.co.uk—Windrush—Arrivals, accessed 6 August 2003.

7. The only contemporary of Bennett's whose work came close to her radical embrace of the Creole vernacular and corollary pride in black culture was Roger Mais. For a discussion of of Bennett's creole poetry, see Carolyn Cooper, *Noises in the Blood: Orality, Gender, and the "Vulgar" Body of Jamaican Popular Culture* (Durham, N.C.: Duke University Press, 1993), 39–67.

8. Louise Bennett, *Jamaica Labrish*, ed. Rex Nettleford (Kingston, Jamaica: Sanger's, 1966), 179–80.

9. Compare with notions of decentering advanced nearly four decades later by cultural critics such as Kobena Mercer. See "Recoding Narratives of Race and Nation," in *Welcome to the Jungle: New Positions in Black Cultural Studies* (New York: Routledge, 1994).

10. Cedric Robinson offers what is still one of the most comprehensive overviews of what he terms "racial capitalism" in *Black Marxism: The Making of the Black Radical Tradition* (New York: Zed, 1983). My argument here is also indebted to the work of A. Sivanandan, evident in issues of the journal *Race and Class,* which he edits, as well as in *Communities of Resistance* (New York: Verso, 1992).

11. The classic account of this economic logic in the Caribbean plantation economy is Sidney Mintz's *Sweetness and Power: The Place of Sugar in Modern History* (New York: Viking, 1985). See also Eric Williams, *Capitalism and Slavery* (Chapel Hill: University of North Carolina Press, 1994).

12. On labor militancy in West Africa, see Frederick Cooper's *Decolonization and African Society: The Labor Question in French and British Africa* (New York: Cambridge University Press, 1996).

13. Robert Miles and Annie Phizaclea, *White Man's Country: Racism in British Politics* (London: Pluto, 1984).

14. Penny von Eschen, *Race against Empire: Black Americans and Anticolonialism, 1937–1957* (Ithaca, N.Y.: Cornell University Press, 1997).

15. Robert J. C. Young, *Colonial Desire: Hybridity in Theory, Culture, and Race* (New York: Routledge, 1995).

16. Anne McClintock, *Imperial Leather: Race, Gender, and Sexuality in the Colonial Conquest* (New York: Routledge, 1995).

17. European modernist literature is filled with examples of concerns about racial degeneration in the colonies. The classic instance, of course, is Joseph Conrad's *Heart of Darkness.* For further discussion of representations of degeneracy in colonial novels of the modern era, see Christopher Miller, *Blank Darkness: Africanist Discourse in French* (Chicago: University of Chicago Press, 1985).

18. Ann Laura Stoler, *Race and the Education of Desire: Foucault's History of Sexuality and the Colonial Order of Things* (Durham, N.C.: Duke University Press, 1995).

19. Daniel Defoe, *The True-Born Englishman,* in *The Novels and Miscellaneous Works of Daniel Defoe* (London: George Bell and Sons, 1896), 441–42.

20. This point is one of the primary hobbyhorses of postcolonial theory. For a representative and exhaustive argument along these lines that discusses specifically British examples, see Floya Anthias and Nira Yuval-Davis, *Racialized Boundaries: Race, Nation, Gender, Colour, and Class and the Anti-Racist Struggle* (New York: Routledge, 1992).

21. Robert Young makes this point effectively in his discussion of theories of hybridity. See *Colonial Desire,* 4.

22. The British isles, of course, have their own internal history of domination and resistance. Resistance to English hegemony resurfaced in the 1990s, although Tom Nairn had predicted the rise of nationalism in Scotland and Wales in the late 1970s in *The Break-Up of Britain: Crisis and Neo-Nationalism* (London: New Left Books, 1977).

23. For a thorough history of the Stephen Lawrence case and the other circumstances leading to the MacPherson Report, see the BBC's detailed site: http://news.bbc.co.uk/1/hi/special_report/1999/02/99/stephen_lawrence/285357.stm.

24. Stuart Hall, Charles Critcher, Tony Jefferson, and John Clarke, *Policing the Crisis: Mugging, the State, and Law and Order* (London: Macmillan, 1978).

25. Few critics have focused consistently on the contact zones where African, Asian, Caribbean, and white British cultures have become entangled and creolized. Paul Gilroy's important study *There Ain't No Black in the Union Jack: The Cultural Politics of Race and Nation* (Chicago: University of Chicago Press, 1991), for instance, deals exclusively with the traditions of African diasporic peoples in Britain, the Caribbean, and the United States.

26. For a discussion of the dynamism of culture in the anticolonial struggle, see Frantz Fanon, *Wretched of the Earth* (New York: Grove, 1963).

27. For a discussion of the performative character of citizenship among diasporic

communities in Britain, see May Joseph, *Nomadic Identities: The Performance of Citizenship* (Minneapolis: University of Minnesota Press, 1999).

28. The concept of the contact zone militates against the traditional model of cultural assimilation. James Clifford, for instance, argues that contact zones "presuppose not sociocultural wholes subsequently brought into relationship, but rather systems already constituted relationally, entering new relations through historical processes of displacement." See James Clifford, *Routes: Travel and Translation in the Late 20th Century* (Cambridge: Harvard University Press, 1997), 7.

29. This figure is derived from the 1991 census, according to which "ethnic minorities" constitute 5.8 percent of the total British population. See Yasmin Alibhai-Brown, *Imagining the New Britain* (New York: Routledge, 2001), x.

30. Approximately 60 percent of Britain's population are foreign nationals. For these nonwhite European residents, the opening up of borders in the European Union has diminished rather than increased mobility. See Les Back and Anoop Nayak, *Invisible Europeans? Black People in the "New" Europe.* (Birmingham: All Faiths for One Race, 1993).

31. Kathleen Paul, *Whitewashing Britain: Race and Citizenship in the Postwar Era* (Ithaca, N.Y.: Cornell University Press, 1997), xi.

32. For an overview of this transformation, see Ian Baucom, *Out of Place: Englishness, Empire, and the Locations of Identity* (Princeton, N.J.: Princeton University Press, 1999), 9–13.

33. Colonial expansion was intimately linked to the growth of antiliberal sentiments at home during the mid–nineteenth century. For a discussion of the race state's origins in this period, see Vijay Prashad, *Everybody Was Kung Fu Fighting: Afro-Asian Connections and the Myth of Cultural Purity* (Boston: Beacon, 2001), 20. Hannah Arendt's discussion of the Holocaust's origins in colonial genocide is also germane to this point. See *The Origins of Totalitarianism* (New York: Meridian, 1951).

34. As Laura Tabili puts it, "To view racist policies as the state's response to popular demand or a reflection of union influences promotes an unwarranted 'consensus' view of a social formation riven by structural inequalities and consequent conflict." See *We Ask for Justice*, 7.

35. For a critique of the pathologizing model that has underwritten "race relations" approaches in Britain since the 1950s, see Jenny Bourne, "Life and Times of Institutional Racism," *Race and Class* 43, no. 4 (2002): 7–22.

36. Paul, *Whitewashing Britain*, xiii.

37. Paul, *Whitewashing Britain*, 119.

38. Paul, *Whitewashing Britain*, 1. This economic and political calculus was quite evident to activists at the time. For an extremely prescient discussion of Britain's postwar strategy, see George Padmore, "Blue Print of Post-War Anglo-American Imperialism," *Left*, October 1943, in which Padmore argues that Britain would cling to its colonies in a vain attempt to head off growing U.S. global hegemony.

39. Paul, *Whitewashing Britain*, 7.

40. For an exhaustive discussion of the racialized disparities in British immigration policy during the postwar period, consult Paul, *Whitewashing Britain*.

41. During the early years of immigration, only about two thousand people arrived from Commonwealth nations per year.

42. Ron Ramdin, *The Making of the Black Working Class in Britain* (Aldershot, Hants: Gower, 1987), 236.

43. Ramdin, *Black Working Class,* 239.

44. Swasti Mitter, *Common Fate, Common Bond: Women in the Global Economy* (London: Pluto, 1986), 1.

45. Paul, *Whitewashing Britain,* 138.

46. Paul, *Whitewashing Britain,* 156.

47. Paul, *Whitewashing Britain,* 166.

48. The 1981 Nationality Act distinguishes between so-called patrial and nonpatrial British subjects. This distinction is patently racial. Despite the argument of critics such as Martin Barker for a "new racism" based primary on cultural rather than explicitly racial forms of difference, the history of immigration legislation suggests an underlying trajectory that is explicitly racial and biological. This approach also tends to obscure Britain's increasingly conformity to pan-European, blood-based models of belonging. For discussion of the "new racism," see Gilroy, *Ain't No Black,* 43.

49. Ranu Samantrai, *AlterNatives: Black Feminism in the Postimperial Nation* (Stanford, Calif.: Stanford University Press, 2002), 24.

50. Samantrai, *AlterNatives,* 81.

51. John Solomos, Paul Findlay, Simon Jones, and Paul Gilroy, "The Organic Crisis of British Capital and Race: The Experience of the 1970s," in Centre for Contemporary Cultural Studies, *The Empire Strikes Back: Race and Racism in '70s Britain* (New York: Routledge, 1982).

52. For a synoptic discussion of post-Fordism and its cultural ramifications, see David Harvey, *The Condition of Post-Modernity: An Enquiry into the Origins of Cultural Change* (Cambridge, Mass.: Blackwell, 1989). In a specifically British context, see Colin Leys, *Politics in Britain: From Labourism to Thatcherism* (New York: Verso, 1989).

53. Bob Jessop, *Thatcherism: A Tale of Two Nations* (New York: Polity, 1988), 87.

54. The introduction to *Black British Cultural Studies,* for example, makes scant reference to the emphasis on theorizing "race" and capitalist hegemony that has characterized this tradition. See Houston A. Baker Jr., Stephen Best, and Ruth H. Lindeborg, "Introduction: Representing Blackness/Representing Britain: Cultural Studies and the Politics of Knowledge," in *Black British Cultural Studies: A Reader,* ed. Houston A. Baker Jr., Manthia Diawara, and Ruth H. Lindeborg (Chicago: University of Chicago Press, 1996).

55. Iain Chambers, *Border Dialogues* (New York: Routledge, 1990), 20.

56. For a discussion of the analogous exclusionary construction of national belonging in the United States, see Alys Eve Weinbaum, "Reproducing Racial Globality: W. E. B. Du Bois and the Sexual Politics of Black Internationalism," *Social Text* 19, no. 2 (2001): 15–41.

57. Quoted in Louis London and Nira Yuval-Davis,"Women as National Reproducers: The Nationality Act (1981)," in *Formations of Nation and People* (London: Routledge, 1984), 217.

58. This interpretation challenges representations of labor migrants as a helpless "reserve army of labor" for imperial capital. For a discussion of the shortcomings of the latter view, see Tabili, *We Ask for Justice,* 11.

59. Edward Said, *Culture and Imperialism* (New York: Knopf, 1993).

60. David Morley, "EuroAmerica, Modernity, Reason and Alterity: Or, Postmodernism, the Highest Stage of Cultural Imperialism?" in *Stuart Hall: Critical Dialogues in Cultural Studies,* ed. David Morley and Kuan-Hsing Chen (New York: Routledge, 1996).

61. Robin D. G. Kelley argues powerfully that progressives need to learn how to con-

nect such nontraditional forms of resistance to established modes of political expression in *Race Rebels: Culture, Politics, and the Black Working Class* (New York: Free Press, 1994).

62. For more on the concept of everyday resistance, see Michel de Certeau, *The Practice of Everyday Life*, trans. Steven Rendell (Berkeley and Los Angeles: University of California Press, 1984).

63. For analysis of hustling and other black strategies for surviving wagelessness, see Hall et al., *Policing the Crisis*, 188–90.

64. There are, of course, a considerable number of other forms of resistance on which I do not focus. For instance, in *Policing the Crisis*, Stuart Hall and his colleagues challenge dominant accounts of crime, seeing law and criminality in long historical perspective as expressions of antagonistic social forces.

65. James C. Scott, *Domination and the Arts of Resistance: Hidden Transcripts* (New Haven: Yale University Press, 1990).

66. Gayatri Spivak has articulated a highly influential critique of methodology employed by Scott and his colleagues of the subaltern studies school of South Asian historiography. In her critique, Spivak suggests that their project of recuperating precolonial cultural forms tends to idealistically ignore the overwriting of such records by the colonial script. While this cautionary note is an important one, taken to an extreme it can suggest that colonial culture gained total hegemony over precolonial culture, a stance that seems both empirically and politically untenable. See Gayatri Spivak, introduction to *Selected Subaltern Studies*, ed. Ranajit Guha and Gayatri Chakravorty Spivak (New York: Oxford University Press, 1988).

67. Black Britons, in other words, developed strategies of contesting power on multiple different spatial scales. This is an important point given Paul Gilroy's sweeping critique of nationalism. Gilroy argues in *There Ain't No Black in the Union Jack* that black Britons abandoned engagement with the British nation-state, concentrating instead on more local and more global forms of cultural expression and activism. The potential elitism and pitfalls of this argument are stressed in Laura Chrisman's "Journeying to Death: Gilroy's *Black Atlantic*," *Race and Class* 39, no. 2 (1997): 51–64.

68. Centre for Contemporary Cultural Studies, *The Empire Strikes Back*, 66.

69. Mercer, "Recoding Narratives," 291.

70. This point has been one of the hobbyhorses of postcolonial theory. For an important early challenge to essentialist theories of ethnic identity, see Henry Louis Gates Jr., ed., *"Race," Writing, and Difference* (Chicago: University of Chicago Press, 1986).

71. Cultural hybridity was equated with the political avant-garde in the work of critics such as Homi Bhabha; see *The Location of Culture* (New York: Routledge, 1994). This emphasis clearly derives from a specifically British context in which racialized minority groups were confronted by exclusionary forms of nationalism. However, neither hybridity nor nationalism should be seen as inherently progressive or reactionary. As James Clifford notes, "There is no reason to assume that crossover practices are always liberatory or that articulating an autonomous identity or a national culture is always reactionary. The politics of hybridity is conjunctural and cannot be deduced from theoretical principles. In most situations, what matters politically is who deploys nationality or transnationality, authenticity or hybridity against whom, with what relative power and ability to sustain a hegemony." See Clifford, *Routes*, 10.

72. The notion of scale jumping comes from Neil Smith's "Homeless/Global: Scal-

ing Places," in *Mapping the Futures: Local Cultures, Global Change*, ed. Jon Bird (New York: Routledge, 1993). According to Smith, geographical scale "defines the borders and bounds the identities around which control is exerted *and* contested." Since power tends to flow down from larger to small spatial scales, the transnational connections and cultural practices of postcolonial migrants in Britain constitute an important challenge to dominant constructions of scale and identity.

73. Hazel Carby's "White Woman Listen!" is the classic articulation of black women's autonomy from the (white, middle class) feminist movement. See Hazel Carby, "White Woman Listen!" in Centre for Contemporary Cultural Studies, *The Empire Strikes Back*.

74. For an overview of the emerging black British queer cinema movement during this period, see Mercer, "Recoding Narratives," 221–33.

75. Stuart Hall, "New Ethnicities," in *Stuart Hall: Critical Dialogues in Cultural Studies*, ed. David Morley and Kuan-Hsing Chen (New York: Routledge, 1996), 441–49.

76. Jenny Bourne, "Life and Times of Institutional Racism," *Race and Class* 43, no. 4 (2002): 7–-22.

77. London and Yuval-Davis, "Women as National Reproducers," 212–18.

78. For instance, despite his landmark "New Ethnicities" essay, Stuart Hall has not written at length on gender or sexuality. Similarly, Paul Gilroy and Ian Baucom largely ignore such issues. Critics such as Pratibha Parmar and Kobena Mercer have contributed important revisionary perspectives concerning discourses of gender and sexuality in Britain, but neither has attempted a historical treatment of these questions.

79. Although innate sexism probably also plays a role. As Gayatri Gopinath notes, critics such as Paul Gilroy have located diasporic identity in sites like the DJ's turntable and the ship that are relatively inaccessible to women. Furthermore, despite its intended critical role in relation to established models of identity, even the term *diaspora* retains a masculinist and heterosexist bent. See Stephen Helmreich, "Diaspora Studies and Patriarchal Discourse," *Diaspora* 2, no. 1 (1995): 25–42; and Gayatri Gopinath, "'Bombay, UK, Uyba City'": Bhangra Music and the Engendering of Diaspora," *Diaspora* 4, no. 3 (1995): 303–21.

80. For a discussion of such "representative coloured men" in the United States, see Hazel Carby, *Race Men* (Cambridge: Harvard University Press, 1998).

81. McClintock, *Imperial Leather*, 232–55.

82. Feminist critics have offered particularly stinging criticism of the tendency of multicultural policymakers to view the most conservative members of the so-called ethnic minority communities as the most "authentic," leading to a highly reactionary funding policy. For a representative critique, see Gita Saghal and Nira Yuval-Davis, eds., *Refusing Holy Orders* (London: Virago, 1992).

83. The tradition of cultural studies has been flawed by an idealistic search for resistance within subcultural formations that has often made it blind to the politically reactionary aspects of many subcultures. In the 1970s, for instance, members of the Centre for Contemporary Cultural Studies investigated working-class motorcycle gangs without acknowledging the rampant sexism and racism articulated by many bikers. For examples of this sort of blindness, see Stuart Hall and Tony Jefferson, eds., *Resistance Through Rituals: Youth Subculture in Post-War Britain* (New York: Routledge, 1993).

84. Alibhai-Brown, *Imagining the New Britain*, xii.

85. For a discussion of the theoretical shortcomings of Gilroy's Atlanticist frame-

work of analysis from a Marxist perspective, see Neil Lazarus, *Nationalism and Cultural Practice in the Postcolonial World* (New York: Cambridge University Press, 1999), 62.

86. Stuart Hall, "Frontlines and Backyards: The Terms of Change," in Kwesi Owusu, ed., *Black British Culture and Society: A Text Reader* (New York: Routledge, 1997), 127–30.

87. Samuel P. Huntington, *The Clash of Civilizations and the Remaking of World Order* (New York: Simon and Schuster, 1998).

CHAPTER ONE

1. The following account is drawn from Pilkington, *Beyond the Mother Country*, 113.

2. Qtd. in Pilkington, *Beyond the Mother Country*, 117.

3. Rules regulating sexuality, marriage, and the family are typically a central component of ethnic/national identity. For an extended theoretical discussion of the relation between gender regulation and ethnic identity, see Anthias and Yuval-Davis, *Racialized Boundaries*. The specifically gendered components of British national identity after 1948 are discussed in Samantrai, *AlterNatives*, 59–101.

4. As Mary Douglas notes in *Purity and Danger* (New York: Praeger, 1966), individual bodies are powerful metonymic models for the body politic. This is particularly true of the female body, subject as it has traditionally been to patriarchal controls designed to guarantee undiluted filiation. Women who engaged in interracial sexual relations were likely to be seen as impure and expelled from their status as symbols of collective racial/national identity.

5. I draw this notion of sexuality as a "transfer point of power" from Ann Stoler's discussion of the pivotal role of discourse of racial purity and sexual virtue in the colonial project of civility. For further discussion, see her *Race and Education*.

6. This suggests that it was neither *ius soli* nor *ius sanguinis* that defined belonging in Britain, but rather what Stoler calls the "fuzzy notions of shared morals and culture" that strengthen the state's right to defend the body politic against degeneration. See *Race and Education*, 134.

7. Qtd. in Samantrai, *AlterNatives*, 79.

8. For a discussion of the cultural essentialism that undergirds what is often called the "new racism," see Gilroy, *Ain't No Black*, 43–69. It should, however, be noted that the notion of "new racism" relies on a typically metropolitan British denial of colonial history, where, as Stoler's work makes clear, the use of discourses of sexual/moral virtue to differentiate colonizer and colonized was quite standard.

9. bell hooks discusses what she calls "phallic misogynist masculinity" in an American context in *Black Looks: Race and Representation* (Boston: South End Press, 1992), 88–112. Of course, such patriarchal attitudes must be put in a global context, a project adumbrated by R. W. Connell's "The History of Masculinity," in *The Masculinity Studies Reader*, ed. Rachel Adams and David Savran (New York: Blackwell, 2002), 245–61.

10. Frantz Fanon, *Black Skin, White Masks* (New York: Grove, 1969), 63.

11. For a discussion of the peculiar "complacency" of West Indians in comparison with African-American men during the 1950s, see George Lamming, *The Pleasures of Exile* (Ann Arbor: University of Michigan Press, 1960), 33–36.

12. Fanon, *Black Skin, White Masks*, 14.

13. Prominent postcolonial critics such as Edward Said and Paul Gilroy are virtually silent on the issue of gender power, as are historians of black Britain like Peter Fryer and Ron Ramdin. Said, *Culture and Imperialism;* Gilroy, *Ain't No Black;* Peter Fryer, *Staying Power: The History of Black People in Britain* (Boulder, Colo.: Pluto Press, 1984); Ramdin, *Black Working Class.*

14. For typical examples, see Rebecca Dyer, "Immigration, Postwar London, and the Politics of Everyday Life in Sam Selvon's Fiction," *Cultural Critique* 52 (2002): 108–44; and Stefano Harney, *Nationalism and Identity: Culture and the Imagination in a Caribbean Diaspora* (New York: Zed, 1996), 91–114. A more sweeping argument concerning the hybridization of Britishness during two hundred–odd years of colonial encounters may be found in Baucom, *Out of Place.* The scholarly inspiration for these arguments comes from Homi Bhabha, whose *The Location of Culture* contains seminal essays on migration and hybridity.

15. As Anne McClintock puts it in *Imperial Leather,* "If colonial texts reveal fissures and contradictions, the colonials themselves all too often succeeded in settling matters of indecision with a violent excess of militarized masculinity" (16).

16. For a critique of misogyny and homophobia in movement literature of the 1950s, see Alan Sinfield, *Literature, Politics, and Culture in Postwar Britain* (Berkeley and Los Angeles: University of California Press, 1989), 79–81.

17. Rap music, of course, is the most important site for such issues today. For discussions of machismo in gangsta rap, see Tricia Rose, *Black Noise: Rap Music and Black Culture in Contemporary America* (Hanover, N.H.: Wesleyan University Press, 1994); and bell hooks, *We Real Cool: Black Men and Masculinity* (New York: Routledge, 2003). These critics owe much to Michelle Wallace's *Black Macho and the Myth of the Superwoman* (New York: Verso, 1999), one of the first important feminist critics of patriarchal values in black culture.

18. Donald Hill, *Calypso Calaloo: Early Carnival Music in Trinidad* (Gainesville: University Press of Florida, 1993), 35.

19. Keith Q. Warner, *Kaiso! The Trinidad Calypso: A Study of Calypso as Oral Literature* (Washington, D.C.: Three Continents Press, 1982), 8.

20. Raymond Quevedo (Atilla the Hun), *Atilla's Kaiso: A Short History of Trinidad Calypso* (St. Augustine, Trinidad and Tobago: University of West Indies Press, 1994), 27.

21. Hill, *Calypso Calaloo,* 73.

22. Many critics have commented on the impact of calypso's themes and styles on *The Lonely Londoners* (Longman, 1989), including Fabre, Nasta, Gikandi, and John Thieme, although few have explored these correspondences in adequate detail.

23. Michel Fabre, "From Trinidad to London: Tone and Language in Samuel Selvon's Novels, " in *Critical Perspectives on Sam Selvon,* ed. Susheila Nasta (Washington, D.C.: Three Continents Press, 1987), 215.

24. Fabre, "From Trinidad to London," 213–14.

25. Selvon is, as a result, often seen as the father of Caribbean literature. See Susheila Nasta, *Home Truths: Fictions of the South Asian Diaspora in Britain* (New York: Palgrave, 2002), 70.

26. For a searching discussion and critique of the unfolding of nationalism in the West Indian literary renaissance, see Harney, *Nationalism and Identity.* On exile and nationalism, see Simon Gikandi, *Writing in Limbo: Modernism and Caribbean Literature* (Ithaca, N.Y.: Cornell University Press, 1992).

27. For a discussion of Selvon's characters' transformation of metropolitan space,

see Dyer, "Immigration," 108–9. On their reinvention of Britishness, see Harney, *Nationalism and Identity,* 91–114.

28. See Eve Kosokovsky Sedgwick's *Between Men: English Literature and Male Homosocial Desire* (New York: Columbia University Press, 1985) for a now-classic anatomy of the role of misogyny and homophobia in facilitating male camaraderie.

29. Critics who pay attention to gender power in Selvon's novel tend to treat misogyny as an unfortunate side issue rather than a central component of the masculine identity depicted. For instance, see Dyer, "Immigration," 121.

30. Warner, *Kaiso!* 95.

31. Qtd. in Warner, *Kaiso!* 99.

32. McClintock, *Imperial Leather,* 6.

33. Warner in *Kaiso!* asserts that these attitudes were challenged by both female and male calypsonians during the Black Power movement of the late 1960s and 1970s.

34. For an illuminating discussion of wagelessness and struggle during the 1970s in Britain, see Hall et al., *Policing the Crisis,* 375.

35. Only 13 percent of migrants from the Caribbean were unskilled manual laborers, according to Pilkington, *Beyond the Mother Country,* 23.

36. Pilkington, *Beyond the Mother Country,* 29–30.

37. Feminist writers have only recently begun exploring the importance of work to masculine identity. For a typical example, see Susan Faludi, *Stiffed: The Betrayal of the American Man* (New York: William Morrow, 1999).

38. *The Lonely Londoners* was published in 1956, the year of the Suez Crisis, the definitive humiliation of British imperial pretensions by the new global hegemon, the United States. This crisis sparked an economic depression that put many black as well as white workers out of jobs and spurred calls for immigration control and repatriation efforts.

39. As bell hooks points out in her critique of Michelle Wallace's seminal discussion of black macho, the urge to homogenize black masculinity must be resisted through careful historical contextualization. The attitudes evident in *The Lonely Londoners* are a product of specific histories of racial slavery and colonial subjugation. Moreover, Selvon's characters have very different reactions to this history. For her critique of Wallace, see hooks, *Black Looks,* 100.

40. Selvon's representation of sexual relations is thus remarkably prescient of Fanon's analysis of black (male) sexuality and alienation in *Black Skin, White Masks.*

41. Note that when Cap does turn up for a clerical job, he is instead offered work collecting garbage in a typical instance of deskilling (52).

42. For a discussion of men's use of predatory sexuality to attempt to create a sense of self-worth, see bell hooks, *The Will to Change: Men, Masculinity, and Love* (New York: Atria, 2004), 75–90.

43. Frantz Fanon is the most important of such theorists, although recent critics such as Anne McClintock have expanded his analysis by adding important insights concerning the articulation of race, class, and gender power.

44. For a discussion of Robert Mapplethorpe's reproduction of these fetishizing strategies in the photographs in his notorious *Black Book,* see Mercer, *Welcome to the Jungle,* 172–218.

45. Colin MacInnes's London novels offer an exhaustive catalog of such avant-garde racial fetishism. See *The London Novels of Colin MacInnes* (New York: Farrar, Straus and Giroux, 1969).

46. As McClintock notes, although colonial women were excluded from the corridors of power, they nevertheless often exercised significant forms of dominion over colonized men and women. See *Imperial Leather,* 6.

47. Mark Simpson, *Male Impersonators: Men Performing Masculinity* (New York: Castell, 1994), 48.

48. Lord Beginner with the Calypso Rhythm Kings, "Mix Up Marriage," Melodisc 1229, London, 1952. Available on the complication *London Is the Place For Me: Trinidadian Calypso in London, 1950–1956,* Honest Jon's Records, 2002.

49. For a historical overview of the significance of exile in Britain for such leaders, see Cedric Robinson, "Black Intellectuals at the British Core: 1920s–1940s," in *Essays on the History of Blacks in Britain: From Roman Times to the Mid–Twentieth Century,* ed. Jahdish S. Gundara and Ian Duffield (Avebury: Ashgate, 1992), 173–201.

50. My account of these events is drawn from Rob Nixon, *Homelands, Harlem, and Hollywood: South African Culture and the World Beyond* (New York: Routledge, 1994), 125–28.

51. Rey Chow, "The Politics of Admittance: Female Sexual Agency, Miscegenation, and the Formation of Community in Franz Fanon," in *Frantz Fanon: Critical Perspectives,* ed. Anthony Alessandrini (New York: Routledge, 1999), 34–56.

52. For a discussion of subsequent black feminist efforts to make precisely this point, see Samantrai, *AlterNatives.*

53. David Ellis, "'The Produce of More than One Country': Race, Identity, and Discourse in Post-Windrush Britain," *Journal of Narrative Theory* 31, no. 2 (2001): 214–32.

54. MacInnes, *London Novels,* 416.

55. Pilkington, *Beyond the Mother Country,* 122.

56. Lamming, *The Pleasures of Exile,* 80–81.

57. Pilkington, *Beyond the Mother Country,* 143.

CHAPTER TWO

1. Stokely Carmichael, *Ready for Revolution: The Life and Struggles of Stokely Carmichael (Kwame Ture)* (New York: Scribner, 2003), 578.

2. Stokely Carmichael, *Stokely Speaks: Black Power Back to Pan-Africanism* (New York: Random House, 1971), 78.

3. David Widgery, "Politics and Flowers: The Anniversary of the 1967 Dialectics of Liberation Conference Is a Reminder That the Sixties Produces Ideas as Well as Music," *New Society,* 10 July 1987, 12.

4. Robert Hewison, *Too Much: Art and Society in the 60's: 1960–75* (London: Methuen, 1986), 134.

5. C. L. R. James was invited to speak on the day after Carmichael's address, although this was, according to Carmichael's autobiography, an afterthought in response to his incendiary speech of the day before. One generation later, Paul Gilroy would repeat Carmichael's stinging attack on the parochialism of the British Left in *Ain't No Black.*

6. Edward Brathwaite, "Timehri," *Savacou* 2 (September 1970): 40.

7. Brathwaite, "Timehri," 40.

8. Brathwaite, "Timehri," 40.

9. Despite the obvious links between internationalist Pan-African traditions and Black Power, theorists of the latter have tended to view the movement's political and aesthetic expressions within an exclusively national framework. The paradigmatic work in this regard is William Van Deburg, *New Day in Babylon: The Black Power Movement and American Culture, 1965–1975* (Chicago: University of Chicago Press, 1996).

10. Theories of a convergence between anticolonial struggles in the Third World and the antihierarchical militancy of workers, students, and ethnic minorities in the capitalist core states were integral to the Third Worldism of the New Left during this period. Although it is important to note the broad similarities among different elements of the New Left, the Black Power movement, I would argue, developed these theories of convergence on both a cultural and political plane to a far greater extent than the rest of the Left at the time, which, as I indicate above, was often highly parochial in its concerns. For a discussion of Third Worldism, see Jan P. Nederveen Pieterse, *Empire and Emancipation: Power and Liberation on a World Scale* (London: Pluto, 1990), 6–7.

11. For a revisionist discussion of the idealist Pan-African tradition, see Sidney Lemelle and Robin Kelley, "Introduction: Imagining Home: Pan-Africanism Revisited," in *Imagining Home: Class, Culture, and Nationalism in the African Diaspora*, ed. Sidney J. Lemelle and Robin D. G. Kelley (New York: Verso, 1994), 2–11. Other important histories include, for the British context, T. Ras Makonnen, *Pan-Africanism from Within* (New York: Oxford University Press, 1973); as well as Wilson Jeremiah Moses, *The Golden Age of Black Nationalism, 1850–1925* (New York: Oxford University Press, 1988); Imanuel Geiss, *The Pan-African Movement: A History of Pan-Africanism in American, Europe, and Africa*, trans. Ann Keep (New York: Africana, 1974); and, of course, Paul Gilroy, *The Black Atlantic: Modernity and Double Consciousness* (Cambridge: Harvard University Press, 1993).

12. Van Deburg, *New Day in Babylon*, 2.

13. Britain's most important integrationist organization during this period, the Campaign Against Racial Discrimination (CARD) was, according to its most prominent historian, founded "to speak for a social and political movement that did not exist." See Benjamin W. Heineman Jr., *The Politics of the Powerless: A Study of the Campaign Against Racial Discrimination* (London: Oxford University Press, 1972), 1.

14. For a discussion of this pedagogical apparatus in South Asia, see Viswanathan, *Masks of Conquest*. Many of her observations apply equally—with obvious historical variation—to the Caribbean.

15. On the "telescope effect," see Heineman, *Politics of the Powerless*, x.

16. The concept of *articulation*, drawn from Stuart Hall's work, is central to the idea of translation between different diasporic nodes in Brent Hayes Edwards, *The Practice of Diaspora: Literature, Translation, and the Rise of Black Internationalism* (Cambridge: Harvard University Press, 2003).

17. On *inter/culturation*, see Edward Brathwaite, *Contradictory Omens: Cultural Diversity and Integration in the Caribbean* (Mona, Jamaica: Savacou, 1974), 5. Brathwaite's theory anticipates postmodern ethnographic work on transculturation, as articulated theoretically, for instance, by James Clifford in *The Predicament of Culture: 20th Century Ethnography, Literature, and Art* (Cambridge: Harvard University Press, 1988). On the influence of transculturation in literature, see Amy Fass Emery, *The Anthropological Imagination in Latin American Literature* (Columbia: University of Missouri Press, 1996).

18. For an account of Michael X's life as a hustler and conversion to Black Power activism, see Michael Adbul Malik, *From Michael de Freitas to Michael X* (London: Andre Deutsch, 1968).

19. Carmichael, *Ready for Revolution,* 577.

20. Carmichael, *Ready for Revolution,* 576. Frantz Fanon grappled with the problem of exclusionary ethnic mobilization in the course of anticolonial struggle most decisively during this period. His consideration of the pitfalls of national consciousness remains seminal. See Fanon, *Wretched of the Earth,* 36–52; and, for a more recent consideration of similar issues, Said, *Culture and Imperialism,* 210–15.

21. By the 1970s, however, moral panic about supposed black criminality had become a key component of consolidating New Right hegemony. For an analysis of this conjunction, see Hall et al., *Policing the Crisis.*

22. Carmichael, *Stokely Speaks,* 83.

23. Brathwaite, *Contradictory Omens,* 25.

24. Robert Carr, for example, argues that "it is the mutually dependent coalition of a middle-class elite with a politicized mass base that gives Caribbean nationalist movements their character." See *Black Nationalism in the New World: Reading the African-American and West Indian Experience* (Durham, N.C.: Duke University Press, 2002), 11.

25. Attacking "whitey" was one of the primary components of Black Power aesthetic works in the United States. See Van Deburg, *New Day in Babylon,* 260–64.

26. For a discussion of Brathwaite's reading and an incredibly useful historical overview of CAM in general, see Anne Walmsley, *The Caribbean Artists Movement, 1966–1972: A Literary and Cultural History* (London: New Beacon, 1992).

27. For an extended discussion of global antiracism's current stalemate, see Howard Winant, *The World is a Ghetto: Race and Democracy Since World War II* (New York: Basic, 2001).

28. "Jamaica's Secession Vote Against Federation: Many Regard Jamaican Vote as a Retrograde Step," *West Indies Gazette,* October 1961.

29. Jan Nederveen Pieterse notes that the convergence model was based on Lenin's problematic model of imperialism, with its relatively vulgar base-superstructure model of economic and political linkages. As the history of the West Indies Federation suggests, economic forces pulled countries in the Third World apart just as often as they united them, making the model of a binary First and Third World rapprochement problematic at best. See Pieterse, *Empire and Emancipation,* 7.

30. Carmichael, *Stokely Speaks,* 86.

31. Carmichael's analysis of U.S. informal apartheid and urbanization has been developed by, among others, Douglas Massey and Nancy Denton, *American Apartheid: Segregation and the Making of the Underclass* (Cambridge: Harvard University Press, 1993); Thomas Sugrue, *Origins of the Urban Crisis: Race and Inequality in Post-war Detroit* (Princeton, N.J.: Princeton University Press, 1996); Arnold Hirsh, *Making the Second Ghetto: Race and Housing in Chicago, 1940–1960* (New York: Cambridge University Press, 1983).

32. For a comparison of black nationalism in the United States and South Africa, see George Fredrickson, *Black Liberation: A Comparative History of Black Ideologies in the United States and South Africa* (New York: Oxford University Press, 1995).

33. Stokely Carmichael and Charles V. Hamilton, *Black Power: The Politics of Liberation in America* (1967; New York: Vintage, 1992), 6.

34. Carmichael was not the first to revive this link to the radical theories of the 1930s.

African-American cultural critic Harold Cruse's seminal essay of 1962, "Revolutionary Nationalism and the Afro-American," had anticipated the significance of anticolonial struggles for black mobilization in the United States, as, of course, had Malcolm X's teachings. For a discussion of Cruse and Malcolm's work in this regard, see Nikhil Pal Singh, *Black Is a Country: Race and the Unfinished Struggle for Democracy* (Cambridge: Harvard University Press, 2004), 186–88. On the history of Cold War–era suppression of black internationalism, see Von Eschen, *Race against Empire.*

35. The Comintern's resolution was a result of Lenin's debate with Indian Communist M. N. Roy concerning the right to self-determination of colonized peoples. See V. I. Lenin, "The Socialist Revolution and the Right to Self-Determination (Theses)," in *Lenin on the National and Colonial Questions: Three Articles* (Peking: Foreign Language Press, 1967), 5.

36. James R. Hooker, *Black Revolutionary: George Padmore's Path from Communism to Pan-Africanism* (New York: Praeger, 1967), 12.

37. Lenin's theses can therefore be seen as an important precedent to Antonio Gramsci's work on linking the revolutionary struggles of the Italian proletariat and peasantry. See Gramsci, *The Prison Notebooks* (New York: Progress, 1967).

38. C. L. R. James, "Black Power," in *The C.L.R. James Reader,* ed. Anna Grimshaw (Cambridge, Mass.: Blackwell, 1992), 374.

39. Carmichael and Hamilton, *Black Power,* 6.

40. For a deconstruction of this "civic mythology of racial progress," see Singh, *Black Is a Country,* 5.

41. Carmichael, *Stokely Speaks,* 87.

42. Étienne Balibar, "Ambiguous Universalism," *Differences,* Spring 1995, 71.

43. Carmichael and Hamilton, *Black Power,* 13.

44. Carmichael, *Stokely Speaks,* 91.

45. Carmichael is here developing a "social imperialist" argument whose cogency is discussed in Pieterse, *Empire and Emancipation,* 20.

46. Carmichael, *Stokely Speaks,* 87.

47. Carmichael's argument anticipates that of James Boggs, who explicitly revisited the CP's "Black Belt" thesis in his theorization of the ghetto uprisings to the 1960s. See Boggs, *Racism and Class Struggle: Further Pages from a Black Worker's Notebook* (New York: Monthly Review Press, 1971), 39.

48. For a discussion of the Black Panthers' theorization of the ghetto, see Singh, *Black Is a Country,* 193–202.

49. Hall et al., *Policing the Crisis.*

50. Jane Schneider and Ida Susser, eds., *Wounded Cities: Destruction and Reconstruction in a Globalized World* (New York: Berg, 2003).

51. On the U.S. prison-industrial complex, see Loïc Wacquant, "From Slavery to Mass Incarceration: Rethinking the 'Race Question' in the US," *New Left Review* 13 (January–February 2002): 41–60; and Christian Parenti, *Lockdown America: Police and Prisons in the Age of Crisis* (New York: Verso, 1999). For the role of "race" and criminality in legitimating Thatcherite hegemony, see Hall, *Policing the Crisis.*

52. Patterson's argument, a more reflective version of V. S. Naipaul's notion of "mimicry," was articulated in both his pioneering historical sociology and his fiction during the 1960s. See, for example, *The Sociology of Slavery: An Analysis of the Origins, Development, and Structure of Negro Slave Society in Jamaica* (Rutherford, N.J.: Fairleigh Dickinson University Press, 1967), and *An Absence of Ruins* (London: Hutchinson,

1967). There is a direct connection between Patterson's existentialist ideas about black cultural nihilism and broader New Left models of the "alienation" produced by late capitalism. For a discussion of theories of alienation, see Sinfield, *Literature, Politics and Culture,* 189.

53. Walmsley, *Caribbean Artists Movement,* 52–54. For a discussion of Patterson's theorization of slavery as social death, see Gikandi, *Writing in Limbo,* 6.

54. Brathwaite was particularly critical of Lamming, whose seminal novel *In the Castle of My Skin* had provided a paradigm for writing the Caribbean experience but toward whose subsequent fictional and nonfictional analysis of the black condition as paradigmatic of existential alienation Brathwaite expressed strong reservations. See Gordon Rohlehr, *Pathfinder: Black Awakening in "The Arrivants" of Edward Kamau Brathwaite* (Port of Spain, Trinidad: College Press, 1981), 14.

55. Brathwaite, "Timehri," 36.

56. Gikandi, *Writing in Limbo,* 6.

57. For the denial of coevalness in ethnographic work, see Johannes Fabian, *Time and the Other: How Anthropology Makes Its Objects* (New York: Columbia University Press, 1984).

58. Emery, *Anthropological Imagination,* 127.

59. Edward Kamau Brathwaite, introduction to Melville J. Herskovits, *Life in a Haitian Valley* (Garden City, N.Y.: Doubleday, 1971), xi.

60. Edward Kamau Brathwaite, *The Folk Culture of the Slaves in Jamaica* (London: New Beacon, 1971), 13.

61. V. S. Naipaul published his important novel *The Mimic Men* in 1967. For a deconstruction of Naipaul's elite ethic, see Nixon, *London Calling.*

62. There are suggestive links between Brathwaite's theory of immanent culture and the use of theories of performance by a later critic such as Paul Gilroy to capture the aesthetic autonomy of black Atlantic cultures. See Gilroy, *The Black Atlantic,* 36.

63. Brathwaite's reference to a "great tradition" and to notions of "dissociation of sensibility" underline his debt to T. S. Eliot's criticism. Notwithstanding the mismatch between Eliot's reactionary modernism and Brathwaite's revolutionary political commitments, Eliot's employment of vernacular forms derived from oral culture had a strong impact on Brathwaite.

64. Brathwaite, *Folk Culture,* 15.

65. Glyne Griffith, "Kamau Brathwaite as Cultural Critic," in *The Art of Kamau Brathwaite,* ed. Stewart Brown (Bridgend, Wales: Seren, 1995).

66. Brathwaite, *Contradictory Omens,* 5.

67. I want to suggest here that Brathwaite's work challenges much of the existing theorization of Caribbean modernism. For a discussion of theories of "cultural schizophrenia" and creolization, see Gikandi, *Writing in Limbo,* 12–13.

68. Brathwaite, *Contradictory Omens,* 16.

69. Brathwaite's biological model of osmosis anticipates the musical metaphor of "contrapuntal ensembles" that underpins Edward Said's attack on cultural insularity and essentialism. See Said, *Culture and Imperialism,* 52.

70. Brathwaite, *Contradictory Omens,* 63.

71. Brathwaite, *Contradictory Omens,* 64.

72. See Bridget Jones, "'The Unity is Submarine': Aspects of Pan-Caribbean Consciousness in the Work of Kamau Brathwaite," in Brown, *Art of Kamau Brathwaite,* 87.

73. Edward Brathwaite, *The Arrivants: A New World Trilogy* (New York: Oxford University Press, 1973). All further references to page numbers are given in the text.

74. Brathwaite drew on then cutting-edge historiographic research such as that of Janheinz Jahn and Basil Davidson in linking these westward migrations. For discussion of these debts, see Rohlehr, *Pathfinder*, 17.

75. For a discussion of black vernacular performative traditions, see Gilroy, *The Black Atlantic*, 36.

76. Black Power activists such as Malcolm X attacked integration-minded leaders of the civil rights movement for being subservient "Toms." See Van Deburg, *New Day in Babylon*, 2.

77. For a discussion of the Black Power critique of blaxploitation films, see Van Deburg, *New Day in Babylon*, 287–90.

78. Edward Kamau Brathwaite, *History of the Voice: The Development of Nation Language in Anglophone Caribbean Poetry* (London: New Beacon, 1984).

79. The influence of Amiri Baraka and the U.S.-based Black Arts Movement is particularly clear here. For his theorization of these experiments, see Edward Kamau Brathwaite, "Jazz and the West Indian Novel" III, *Bim* 113, no. 46 (January–June 1968): 124–25.

80. For a particularly powerful discussion of the ability to popular music to defy space and commodification in order to tie together the diverse nodes of the black Atlantic, see George Lipsitz, *Dangerous Crossroads: Popular Music, Postmodernism, and the Poetics of Place* (New York: Verso, 1994).

81. For a discussion of the theme of exile in Caribbean literature, see Gikandi, *Writing in Limbo*, 36–38.

82. The notion of a genealogy of origins is Simon Gikandi's. See *Writing in Limbo*, 10.

83. If, as Benedict Anderson argues, the novel is a vital site for the articulation of national consciousness, Brathwaite's epic poem strives to embody the transnational linkages of the black diaspora. See Anderson, *Imagined Communities: Reflections on the Origin and Spread of Nationalism* (New York: New Left Books, 1991).

84. Claudia Jones, "The Caribbean Community in Britain," *Freedomways* (Summer 1964), reprinted in Buzz Johnson, *"I Think of My Mother": Notes on the Life and Times of Claudia Jones* (London: Karia, 1985), 137–54.

85. The 1962 Commonwealth Immigrants Act allowed only those with work permits to enter Britain and permitted deportation of those who lost such permits. The call for repatriation was a cornerstone of Enoch Powell's ascendancy during the late 1960s, as well as of explicitly neofascist groups such as the National Front that made significant electoral inroads during the early and middle 1970s.

86. Johnson, *I Think of My Mother*, 145. Jones's discussion of representations of the ghetto anticipates many of the central points made a decade later by Stuart Hall and his colleagues in *Policing the Crisis*.

87. Johnson, *I Think of My Mother*, 12.

88. Jones's appeal to the UN anticipates that of Malcolm X roughly two decades later and flows directly from the internationalism of the post-1945 era. For a discussion of African-American activism in this context, see Von Eschen, *Race against Empire*, 4.

89. Johnson, *I Think of My Mother*, 28.

90. For a discussion of the collapse of internationalism and acceptance of the Truman Doctrine by many leaders of the civil rights movement, see Von Eschen, *Race against Empire*, 97.

91. Johnson, *I Think of My Mother,* 129.

92. Johnson, *I Think of My Mother,* 155.

93. For an ethnographic overview of the enduring hold of utopian ideas about the "mother country," consult Donald Hinds, *Journey to an Illusion: The West Indian in Britain* (London: Heinemann, 1966). For a pathbreaking discussion of the self-alienation imposed on second-generation black Britons, see Chris Mullard, *Black Britain* (London: Allen and Unwin, 1973).

94. Johnson, *I Think of My Mother,* 144.

95. Johnson, *I Think of My Mother,* 146.

96. Mullard, *Black Britain,* 140.

97. For a discussion of RAAS's autonomist campaigns, see Malik, *From Michael de Freitas.*

98. See Obi Egbuna, *Destroy This Temple: The Voice of Black Power in Britain* (New York: William Morrow, 1971).

CHAPTER THREE

1. For a history of these overlapping currents in the black radical tradition, see Robinson, *Black Marxism.*

2. For details concerning LKJ's involvement with CAM, see Walmsley, *Caribbean Artists Movement.*

3. Linton Kwesi Johnson, "Jamaican Rebel Music," *Race and Class* 17, no. 4 (1976): 398.

4. Johnson, "Rebel Music," 411.

5. LKJ's collaboration with Dennis Bovell and his Dub Band did not solidify until *Forces of Victory.*

6. Editorial statement, *Race Today,* May–June 1978.

7. Abner Cohen's definition of carnival is "a cultural mechanism expressing, camouflaging, and alleviating a basic structural conflict between the state and the citizenry" (132). For further details, see his *Masquerade Politics: Explorations in the Structure of Urban Cultural Movements* (Providence, R. I.: Berg, 1993). The seminal expression of carnival's ambiguous social role remains, of course, that of Bakhtin. See his *Rabelais and his World* (Bloomington: Indiana University Press, 1984) as well as work inspired by him such as Peter Stallybrass and Allon White's *The Politics and Poetics of Transgression* (Ithaca, N.Y.: Cornell University Press, 1986).

8. See Kwesi Owusu and Jacob Ross, *Behind the Masquerade: The Story of the Notting Hill Carnival* (London: Arts Media Group, 1988), where carnival is defined as "the celebration of emergence, an affirmation of survival and continuity, the destruction of the imposed semantic mould" (39).

9. My discussion of the cultural context behind carnival is indebted to the critique of theories of carnival and social inversion found in Loretta Collins's *Trouble It: Rebel and Revel Urban Soundscapes in the Caribbean Diaspora, 1970s–1990s* (Ames: University of Iowa Press, 1999).

10. Mas' bands such as Lion Youth and People's War sponsor a serious educational program, including newsletters, slide shows, and talks to elaborate on their chosen theme in the run-up to carnival.

11. The best history of carnival to date is John Cowley's *Carnival, Canboulay, and Calypso* (New York: Cambridge University Press, 1996).

12. Cecil Gutzmore, "Carnival, the State, and the Black Masses in the United Kingdom," in Owusu, *Black British Culture*, 334.

13. David Rudder, *Kaiso, Calypso Music* (London: New Beacon, 1990), 19.

14. For a discussion of Creole participation in the Asian Hosay festival in Trinidad, see Vijay Prashad, *The Karma of Brown Folks* (Minneapolis: University of Minnesota Press, 2000), 141.

15. For a discussion of particular instances of such riots, see Cowley, *Carnival, Canboulay, and Calypso*, 2.

16. This argument is lent weight by contemporary perceptions of "carnival as the most important, independently organized, social and political activity by West Indians in Britain." See Race Today Collective, *The Road Make to Walk on Carnival Day: The Battle for the West Indian Carnival in Britain* (London: Race Today, 1977).

17. It should, however, be noted that carnival was also the occasion for significant infighting within the black community. For example, in an essay on carnival, Cecil Gutzmore accuses Race Today of "perfidy and political opportunism" in their dealings with the different factions vying for control of the carnival during the mid-1970s. See Gutzmore, "Carnival, the State."

18. Carnival is thus a perfect example of the dialogic aesthetic forms that Paul Gilroy argues characterize black diasporic cultures. See *Ain't No Black*, 164–65.

19. Nairn, *Break-Up of Britain*, 32.

20. The groundbreaking anatomy of such atavistic politics is Terence Ranger and Eric Hobsbawm's *The Invention of Tradition* (New York: Cambridge University Press, 1983). For a more focused discussion of these issues in a British context, see Patrick Wright's *On Living in an Old Country* (New York: Verso, 1985).

21. For a discussion of the heritage cinema during the Thatcher era, see Andrew Higson, "Re-presenting the National Past: Nostalgia and Pastiche in the Heritage Film," in *Fires Were Started: British Cinema and Thatcherism*, ed. Lester Friedman (Minneapolis: University of Minnesota Press, 1993), 109–27.

22. See Tom Nairn's *The Enchanted Glass: Britain and its Monarchy* (London: Radius, 1988) for a discussion of the British monarchy's role in perpetuating ruling-class hegemony in the UK through the fetishized image of the monarch that, Nairn argues, prevents collective bonding to a republican national identity.

23. For a discussion of the role of "places of memory" in codifying national identity, see Ian Baucom's *Out of Place*.

24. For a discussion of the deplorable housing stock in Notting Hill, see Owusu and Ross, *Behind the Masquerade*.

25. The white riots of 1958 are discussed in Pilkington, *Beyond the Mother Country*.

26. The origin of the carnival has been the subject of some controversy of late. For a definitive substantiation of the argument that Claudia Jones helped found the carnival, see Marika Sherwood with Donald Hines, Colin Prescod, and the 1996 Claudia Jones Symposium, *Claudia Jones: A Life in Exile* (London: Lawrence and Wishart, 1999).

27. Quoted in Sherwood et al., *Claudia Jones*, 157.

28. Cohen, *Masquerade Politics*, 23.

29. Cohen, *Masquerade Politics*, 93.

30. See David Widgery's discussion of the National Front's "antimugging" march in

Lewisham in *Beating Time: Riot 'n' Race 'n' Rock 'n' Roll* (London: Chatto and Windus, 1986), 44.

31. Hall et al., *Policing the Crisis.*

32. Probably the best overview of the cultural shifts associated with these political-economic changes is Harvey's *The Conditions of Post-Modernism.*

33. For a detailed analysis of these developments, see Leys, *Politics in Britain.*

34. Hall, *Policing the Crisis,* 309–22.

35. Étienne Balibar, "'Es Gibt Keinen Staat in Europa': Racism and Politics in Europe Today," *New Left Review* 186 (1991): 5–19.

36. For example, the paramilitary Special Patrol Group (SPG) stopped fourteen thousand people on the streets of the London borough of Lewisham and made four hundred arrests in 1975. For more information on racist policing practices, see Institute of Race Relations, *Police Against Black People* (London, 1979).

37. "Sonny's Lettah" was based on LKJ's own experiences after he was arrested for trying to take down identification information of a group of police officers he saw choking a man to death on the street in London. LKJ was placed in the back of a police van along with three other people who had been picked up on "suspicion" that they were about to commit a crime. All four were then beaten savagely by the police. For an account of the incident, see Caryl Phillips, "Prophet in Another Land" *Guardian Weekend,* 11 July 1998.

38. After years of resistance to the notion of institutional racism, the Macpherson Report that followed the repeatedly botched investigations into the murder of Stephen Lawrence finally admitted the existence of widespread racial bias within the police force, the judiciary, and other institutional sectors of British society. For a discussion of the report, see Bourne, "Life and Times."

39. "Sonny's Lettah" may also be linked to the landmark case of the Mangrove 9, a group of black activists who successfully defended themselves against police charges of "riot, affray, and assault" after they resisted a violence police attack on a demonstration outside the Mangrove restaurant. Located in Notting Hill, the Mangrove was a vital black cultural center that the police repeatedly raided and ultimately tried to close. For a discussion of this case, see A. Sivanandan, *From Resistance to Rebellion: Asian and Afro-Caribbean Struggles in Britain* (London: Institute of Race Relations, 1986), 136.

40. Race Today Collective, *Road Make.*

41. Hall et al., *Policing the Crisis,* 386–89.

42. In his discussion of Salman Rushdie's representation of the riots of the 1980s in *The Satanic Verses,* Ian Baucom relates this claim to public space to the kinds of English traditions of disorderly conduct described by New Left historians such as E. P. Thompson. Contemporary accounts by groups such as Race Today indicate, however, that there is a far stronger link with anticolonial and diasporic uprisings than with purely English traditions of dissent.

43. A group of residents in the borough of Kensington lobbied councillors and the police to ban the carnival after the disruptions of 1975. Attempts by the Carnival Development Committee to negotiate with this group got nowhere. However, the police proved highly responsive to the group's calls to maintain "British law and order" by banning the carnival. In the context of harassment that pervaded Britain's urban areas, it's clear that the clash with this group was part of a much broader struggle with popular authoritarianism.

44. Smith, "Homeless/Global," 103.

45. This explanation is included on the LP *Linton Kwesi Johnson in Concert with the Dub Band,* Island Records, 1986.

46. Carnival costumes secretary Larry Forde criticized the Social Workers Party for their 1977 float "Victory to Freedom Fighters in South Africa," which featured a frozen scene of black guerrillas pointing their guns at two white settlers in chains, not for the violence of the imagery but for their failure to contribute to the festive atmosphere of carnival. See Larry Forde, "Arresting Changes," *New Society,* September 1977, 441.

47. Norman C. Stolzoff, *Wake the Town and Tell the People: Dancehall Culture in Jamaica* (Durham, N.C.: Duke University Press, 2000).

48. Owusu and Ross, *Behind the Masquerade,* 51.

49. Simon Jones, *Black Culture, White Youth: The Reggae Tradition from JA to UK* (Houndmills, Basingstoke, Hampshire: Macmillan Education, 1988).

50. Probably the most evocative discussion of this process of inversion can be found in Dick Hebdige's *Subculture: The Meaning of Style* (New York: Routledge, 1990).

51. Dick Hebdige, *Cut'n'Mix: Culture, Identity and Caribbean Music* (New York: Routledge, 1990).

52. LKJ himself released a large number of dub tracks of his songs. See the collection *Independent Intavenshun,* Island Records, 1998.

53. Paul Gilroy's essay on dub can be found in the Centre for Contemporary Cultural Studies, *The Empire Strikes Back,* 276–300.

54. For a history of Jamaica's social and political upheavals during this period, see Obika Gray, *Radicalism and Social Change, 1960–1972* (Knoxville: University of Tennessee Press, 1991).

55. Hebdige, *Cut'n'Mix,* 84–89.

56. Cohen, *Masquerade Politics,* 99.

57. Linton Kwesi Johnson comments on this fratricidal element in "Jamaican Rebel Music," *Race and Class* 17, no. 4 (1976): 397–412.

58. Estimated attendance at the 1975 carnival was 250,000.

59. Owusu and Ross, *Behind the Masquerade,* 64.

60. Owusu and Ross, *Behind the Masquerade,* 65.

61. For a critique of the Trinidad carnival's commodification, see Earl Lovelace's novel *The Dragon Can't Dance* (New York: Persea, 2003).

62. The performances of Lion Youth were intended to educate not just spectators but members of the mas' band themselves about their Caribbean and African heritage.

63. Hall, "New Ethnicities."

64. Hall, "New Ethnicities," 443.

65. Race Today Collective, "Self Organization vs Self Help," *Race Today,* March 1976.

66. James's influence is, for instance, very much evident in Paul Gilroy's analysis of the riots of the 1980s in Britain's cities. See *Ain't No Black,* 245.

67. For a detailed discussion of this period in James's life, see Paul Buhle, *C.L.R. James: The Artist as Revolutionary* (New York: Verso, 1988).

68. One of the earliest and most succinct discussions of James's autonomist theory can be found in Robinson, *Black Marxism,* 388–94.

69. See, for instance, Stuart Hall and associates' subtle characterization of race as a modality of class in *Policing the Crisis,* 394.

70. Buhle, *C.L.R. James,* 161.

71. My account is derived from Sivanandan, *From Resistance to Rebellion,* 142.

72. The lack of police reaction to such killings is partially explained by the fact that racial hate crimes were not recognized as a specific category of criminal behavior during the 1970s in Britain. This fact is, of course, a symptom of broader forms of institutional racism in Britain at the time.

73. The radical experiences of youths in self-defense groups such as SYM often led them to question established not just the older generation's leadership but also "established" community values such as sexism. See Widgery, *Beating Time*, 32.

74. As Paul Gilroy has noted, these groups reflect the changing mode of production in the post-Fordist economies of developed nations such as Britain. See *Ain't No Black*, 225.

75. Paul Gilroy attributes these goals, derived from the work of Manuel Castells on urban social movements, to British self-defense groups such as the Southall Youth Movement. See *Ain't No Black*, 230.

76. Additional details concerning these organizations can be found in Sivanandan, *From Resistance to Rebellion*, 142–43.

77. Sivanandan remains one of the most powerful advocates of this political mobilization of the category "black." For his critique of the decline of "black" as a political color, see *Communities of Resistance*.

78. The social construction of "race" has, of course, been one of the central concerns of postcolonial theory. For an early example of this line of thought that draws heavily on the British context, see Gates, *"Race."*

79. Quoted in Widgery, *Beating Time*, 14.

80. Paul Gilroy offers a withering critique of this strategy of "ethnic absolutism" in *Ain't No Black*, 59–60.

81. Sivanandan, *From Resistance to Rebellion*, 145.

82. Quoted in Sivanandan, *From Resistance to Rebellion*, 146.

83. For discussion of Rock Against Racism, see my article, "Love Music, Hate Racism: The Cultural Politics of the Rock Against Racism Campaigns, 1976–1981," *Postmodern Culture* 16, no. 1 (September 2005).

84. Linton Kwesi Johnson, *Mi Revalueshanary Fren* (London: Penguin, 2002).

CHAPTER FOUR

1. Beverly Bryan, Stella Dadzie, and Suzanne Scafe, "The Heart of the Race: Black Women's Lives in Britain," in *Black British Feminism: A Reader*, ed. Heidi Safia Mirza (New York: Routledge, 1997), 42–44.

2. For a discussion of typical reactions by male activists such as A. Sivanandan and Tariq Modood to black British feminism, see Samantrai, *AlterNatives*, 137–44.

3. Carby, "White Woman Listen!" 45–52.

4. Stuart Hall, "The End of the Innocent Black Subject," in Morley and Chen, *Stuart Hall*.

5. Julia Sudbury, *"Other Kinds of Dreams": Black Women's Organizations and the Politics of Transformation* (New York: Routledge, 1998), 14.

6. Buchi Emecheta, *Head Above Water: An Autobiography* (New York: Heinemann, 1986), 58.

7. For a discussion of this criticism, see Christine W. Sizemore, "The London Novels of Buchi Emecheta," in *Emerging Perspectives on Buchi Emecheta*, ed. Marie Umeh (Tenton, N.J.: Africa World Press, 1996), 367–85.

8. For a critique of this nationalist tradition, see Samantrai, *AlterNatives*, 137–44.

9. Important examples of this feminist critique are Mimi Abramovitz's *Regulating the Lives of Women: Social Welfare Policy from Colonial Times to the Present* (Boston: South End Press, 1996); and Linda Gordon's *To Be Pitied But Not Entitled: Single Mothers and the History of Welfare, 1890–1935* (Cambridge: Harvard University Press, 1994). For a discussion of the gender bias of the British welfare state, see Beatrix Campbell, *Iron Ladies: Why Women Vote Tory* (London: Virago, 1987).

10. Gary Mink, *Whose Welfare?* (Ithaca, N.Y.: Cornell University Press, 1999).

11. Buchi Emecheta, *Second-Class Citizen* (New York: George Braziller, 1975).

12. For a discussion of colonialism's disruption of non-Western kinship patterns, see Carby, "White Woman Listen!" 51.

13. Gayle Rubin, "The Traffic in Women: Notes on the Political Economy of Sex," in *Toward an Anthropology of Women*, ed. R. R. Reiter (New York: Monthly Review Press, 1975).

14. Carby, "White Woman Listen!" 45.

15. It was not until the late 1980s and early 1990s that postcolonial theorists began intervening in debates about autobiography that assumed ahistorical, transcultural models of patriarchy and feminine identity. See Sidonie Smith and Julia Watson, eds., *Women, Autobiography, Theory: A Reader* (Madison: University of Wisconsin Press, 1998), 10.

16. Juliana Makuchi Nfah-Abbenyi, *Gender in African Women's Writing: Identity, Sexuality, and Difference* (Bloomington: Indiana University Press, 1997), 4–5.

17. For a discussion of Riley's novel, see Simon Gikandi, *Maps of Englishness: Writing Identity in the Culture of Colonialism* (New York: Columbia University Press, 1996).

18. For a discussion of the Rastafarian reappropriation of biblical narrative, see Hebdige, *Subculture*, 33.

19. For an illuminating discussion of the contradictory role of the mother-in-law, for instance, as both cop and confidant for many young married Asian women, see Southall Black Sisters, *Domestic Violence and Asian Women: A Collection of Reports and Briefings* (London: Southall Black Sisters, n.d.), 17.

20. This interpretation of feminine identity has been one of the mainstays of feminist theories of autobiography, beginning with Nancy Chodorow's characterization of the feminine personality as defining itself through relationality. For a discussion of this tradition, see Smith and Watson, *Women, Autobiography, Theory*, 17.

21. The issue of isolation is not limited to Adah alone, despite the class-related character of her experience. For a discussion of isolation as a key facet of black women's disempowerment, see Meena Patel, "Working with Women," in Southhall Black Sisters, *Against the Grain: A Celebration of Survival and Struggle* (London: Southall Black Sisters, 1990), 65; and Southall Black Sisters, *Domestic Violence*, 22–23.

22. For a critique of this homogenizing tendency among certain black feminists, see Razia Aziz, "Feminism and the Challenge of Racism," in Mirza, *Black British Feminism*, 73.

23. Emecheta's vitriolic portrait of her husband has been attacked by critics as giving unwarranted ammunition to racist stereotypes about black men. It is certainly true that Emecheta does little to represent the obstacles faced by working-class black men in Britain. However, it should be remembered that her husband is *not* working class and that he remains unemployed not because of shop-floor racism but because of his failure on university qualifying exams and, later, because of his parasitic economic dependence on Adah. Thus, Francis can hardly be said to be representative of black men in general, and Emecheta's portrait of him therefore cannot be said to diminish black masculinity.

Attempts to silence criticisms like Emecheta's have been a typical response to feminist and queer attempts to engage in constructive critique. For a discussion of such criticism of Emecheta, see Sizemore, "London Novels." For a discussion of patriarchal attacks on black feminists, see Sudbury, *Other Kinds of Dreams,* 66.

24. David P. Celani, *The Illusion of Love: Why the Battered Woman Returns to Her Abuser* (New York: Columbia University Press, 1994), 92.

25. Muneeza Inam, "Opening Doors," in Southall Black Sisters, *Against the Grain,* 25.

26. For a discussion of the racist assumptions behind immigration laws and their impact on black families, see Pragna Patel, "Third Wave Feminism and Black Women's Activism," in Mirza, *Black British Feminism,* 261–63.

27. Patel, "Third Wave Feminism," 262.

28. Estelle B. Freedman, *No Turning Back: The History of Feminism and the Future of Women* (New York: Ballantine, 2002), 130.

29. Freedman, *No Turning Back,* 267.

30. Lack of information concerning access to entitlements is one important way in which the state has historically regulated the poor. For a discussion of the struggle to gain access to social welfare in a U.S. context, see Frances Fox Piven and Richard A. Cloward's classic book *Regulating the Poor: The Functions of Public Welfare* (New York: Tavistock, 1972).

31. For an overview of this tradition, consult Sidonie Smith and Julia Watson, "Introduction: Situating Subjectivity in Women's Autobiographical Practices," in Smith and Watson, *Women, Autobiography, Theory,* 3–56.

32. For a discussion of attacks on black women's single parenting practices in Britain, see Lauretta Ngcobo, *Let It Be Told: Essays by Black Women in Britain* (London: Virago, 1988), 28.

33. Buchi Emecheta in *Women: A World Report* (London: Oxford University Press, 1985), 217.

34. Eva Feder Kittay, "Dependency, Equality, and Welfare," *Feminist Studies* 24, no.1 (1998), Academic Search Premier, 23 November 2004, http://web17.epnet.com/.

35. Emecheta, *Head Above Water,* 65.

36. Emecheta, *Head Above Water,* 61.

37. E. P. Thompson, *The Making of the English Working Class* (New York: Pantheon, 1964).

38. For a discussion of the History Workshop group, see Dennis Dworkin, *Cultural Marxism in Postwar Britain: History, the New Left, and the Origins of Cultural Studies* (Durham, N.C.: Duke University Press, 1997), 185.

39. Guha and Spivak, *Selected Subaltern Studies.*

40. For the telling autobiographical perspective of a young British radical and feminist in this regard, see Sheila Rowbotham, *Promise of a Dream: Remembering the Sixties* (New York: Verso, 2001).

41. Kittay, "Dependency, Equality, and Welfare," 1. For a discussion of these issues in a British context, see Amina Mama, "Black Women, the Economic Crisis, and the British State," in Mirza, *Black British Feminism,* 36–41.

42. Abramovitz, *Regulating Lives of Women,* 3.

43. Abramovitz, *Regulating Lives of Women,* 2.

44. Buchi Emecheta, *In the Ditch* (Portsmouth, N.H.: Heinemann, 1972), 2.

45. For an account of the importance of escaping the tyranny of private landlords, see Emecheta, *Head Above Water,* 39.

46. Abramovitz, *Regulating Lives of Women,* 4.

47. Brid Featherstone, *Family Life and Family Support* (New York: Palgrave, 2004), 71.

48. In her autobiography, Emecheta notes that her portrait of Carol was one of the most controversial aspects of her novel. See *Head Above Water,* 71.

49. Sudbury, *Other Kinds of Dreams,* 63.

50. For a discussion of the "double shift's" reinforcement of capitalist accumulation and patriarchy, see Abramovitz, *Regulating Lives of Women,* 8.

51. For a summary of this classic Marxist view of welfare, see Sandra Morgen and Jeff Maskovsky, "The Anthropology of Welfare 'Reform': New Perspectives on U.S. Urban Poverty in the Post-Welfare Era," *Annual Review of Anthropology* 32 (2003): 315–38.

52. The concept of the "underclass" was developed by William Julius Wilson in *When Work Disappears: The World of the New Urban Poor* (New York: Vintage, 1997).

53. Much contemporary anthropology of poverty has been engaged in just such a project of contesting welfare "reform" by demonstrating the crisis in social reproduction that it is producing. For an overview of this work, see Morgen and Maskovsky, "Anthropology of Welfare Reform," 324–25.

54. This is perhaps the best instance of Emecheta's blending of communal African values with Western feminism. See Sizemore, "London Novels," 372.

55. Emecheta's observations closely parallel those of Fox Piven and Cloward concerning the battle to spread awareness of welfare rights in the United States in *Regulating the Poor,* 325–38.

56. Ngcobo, *Let It Be Told,* 19.

57. Carby, "White Woman Listen!" 49.

58. Carby, "White Woman Listen!" 49.

59. Mama, "Black Women," 38.

60. I'm drawing here on Morgen and Maskovsky's assertion that neoliberal economic restructuring in the industrialized nations is the equivalent of IMF-imposed structural adjustment policies in the developing world. See Morgen and Maskovsky, "Anthropology of Welfare Reform," 324.

CHAPTER FIVE

1. For an account of the day's events, see Gita Saghal and Nira Yuval-Davis, "Introduction: Fundamentalism, Multiculturalism, and Women in Britain," in Saghal and Yuval-Davis, *Refusing Holy Orders,* 17–18.

2. This taboo was upheld by theoretical work such as Pratibha Parmar's "Gender, Race, and Class: Asian Women in Resistance," in Centre for Contemporary Cultural Studies, *The Empire Strikes Back,* 236–75.

3. For a critique of A. Sivanandan's model of stable antiracist collective identity, see Samantrai, *AlterNatives,* 135. This model of community solidarity is just as evident, however, in the work of Paul Gilroy and Ian Baucom on black antiracism. See Gilroy, *Ain't No Black;* and Baucom, *Out of Place.*

4. Pragna Patel, "Southall Boys," in Southhall Black Sisters, *Against the Grain,* 44–49. See also Gita Saghal, "When I Became Involved . . . ," in Southall Black Sisters, 14.

5. For a discussion of Fanon's flawed theorization of gender and anticolonial nationalism, see McClintock, *Imperial Leather,* 365–68.

6. Saghal and Yuval-Davis, *Refusing Holy Orders,* 18.

7. *London Times Magazine,* 28 May 1989, 22.

8. Étienne Balibar and Immanuel Wallerstein, *Race, Nation, Class: Ambiguous Identities* (New York: Verso, 1991), 21.

9. Balibar develops this notion of prophylactic action in order to explain the retention of concepts of assimilation despite the ostensibly egalitarian framework of differentialist racism. See Balibar, "Es Gibt Keinen Staat in Europa: Racism and Politics in Europe Today," *New Left Review* 186 (March/April 1991): 24–25.

10. For a scathing deconstruction of Huntington's work, see Emran Qureshi and Michael A. Sells, "Introduction: Constructing the Muslim Enemy," in *The New Crusades: Constructing the Muslim Enemy,* ed. Emran Qureshi and Michael A. Sells (New York: Columbia University Press, 2003), 1–29.

11. Qureshi and Sells, *The New Crusades,* 2.

12. *Independent* (London), 22 February 1989, quoted in *The Rushdie File,* ed. Lisa Appignesi and Sara Maitland (Syracuse, N.Y.: Syracuse University Press, 1990), 102.

13. The most developed exploration of these intersecting dynamics in a British context is found in Anthias and Yuval-Davis, *Racialized Boundaries.*

14. I follow WAF here in emphasizing that fundamentalism is a tendency within all major world religions rather than within Islam alone, as media and popular representations in the West sometimes have it.

15. Kate Clark, "Is It Fundamentalism? Patterns in Islamism," *Women Against Fundamentalism* 1, no. 5 (1994): 13.

16. Marina Warner in Appignesi and Maitland, *The Rushdie File,* 193.

17. Tim Brennan originated this take on Rushdie, describing him as a kind of rootless cosmopolitan whose work sold out anticolonial nationalism. See Brennan, *Salman Rushdie and the Third World: Myths of the Nation* (New York: St. Martin's, 1989), 2. Subsequent commentators have also underlined Rushdie's concern with hybridity. See, for example, Ian Baucom, *Out of Place,* 190–218; and Gikandi, *Maps of Englishness,* 205–23.

18. Perhaps the most high-profile such attack came from Edward Said, who lamented that Rushdie was giving Orientalists ammunition in his satire of Islamic fundamentalism. Many other progressives followed this line, arguing that Rushdie's criticism was directed at the defeated rather than at the imperial structure of thought that rules the world. See Said statement made at U.S. Pen Writers' meeting in New York, February 22, 1989, in Lisa Appignesi and Sara Maitland, eds., *The Rushdie File* (Syracuse, N.Y.: Syracuse University Press, 1990), 165.

19. On *ijtihad,* see A. Ahmed, *Postmodernism and Islam* (New York: Routledge, 1992); and, more recently, Irshad Manji, *The Trouble with Islam: A Muslim's Call for Reform of Her Faith* (New York: St. Martin's Press, 2003).

20. Gikandi argues that this opening explosion questions some of the key tenets of modernity, including the unified subject, the logic of historicism, and notions of home and belonging. It should be noted, however, that while Rushdie may be questioning such general concepts, he is also critiquing violent separatist movements (such as Sikh

separatism) that act precisely in the name of such concepts. See Gikandi, *Maps of Englishness,* 206.

21. Salman Rushdie, *The Satanic Verses* (New York: Viking, 1989), 4. Further citations will be incorporated in the text.

22. For an overview of immigration theory and its applicability within the contemporary European Union, see Robert Miles, *Racism After "Race Relations"* (New York: Routledge, 1993), 107–49.

23. See Francesca Klug's "Oh to be in England," in *Woman-Nation-State,* ed. Floya Anthias and Yuval-Davis (New York: St. Martin's Press, 1989), 27.

24. London and Yuval-Davis, "Women as National Reproducers," 215.

25. Sivanandan, *Communities of Resistance.*

26. For a full discussion of gender and nationality law in Britain after 1945, see Samantrai, *AlterNatives,* 59–101.

27. Amina Mama, "Black Women and the British State," in *Racism and Antiracism,* ed. Peter Braham et al. (London: Sage, 1992), 98.

28. In fact, this rhetoric has been dusted off and trotted out once more following the introduction of "managed migration" by Tony Blair's New Labour. For a discussion of these policies, see David Bacon, "Britain's War Over Managed Migration," *Z Magazine,* September 2004, 45–49.

29. The term *DissemiNation* is Homi Bhabha's, from his essay of the same title in *Nation and Narration* (London: Routledge, 1990). Bhabha here suggests that nationalist ideology is ceaselessly deconstructed by that ideology's disseminatory site of enunciation. This emphasis on the lability of national identity needs to be qualified by an examination of particular instances of ethnic absolutism and patriarchal domination. Indeed, the difficulty of overcoming the latter is suggested by the androcentric roots of both *dissemination* and *diaspora.* For a nuanced ethnographic treatment of these points, see Sunaina Marr Maira, *Desis in the House: Indian American Youth Culture in New York City* (Philadelphia: Temple University Press, 2002).

30. For an exemplary analysis of such traditions within transnational popular music, see Lipsitz, *Dangerous Crossroads.*

31. Young, *Colonial Desire,* 25–26.

32. For a detailed discussion of technologies of race and gender in the colonial scene, see Stoler, *Race and Education.*

33. Sumita S. Chakravarty, *National Identity in Indian Popular Cinema, 1947–1987* (Austin: University of Texas, 1993), 4.

34. This argument is, of course, made most forcefully by Judith Butler in *Gender Trouble* (New York: Routledge, 1990). The stakes of gender performance, however, are radically different in a South Asian context, as theorists of postcolonial queer identity have been quick to emphasize.

35. Rushdie discusses the crisis of nationalism and the return of communal riots in *Imaginary Homelands* (New York: Viking, 1989), 385–87.

36. For a fuller contextualization of the mythological genre, see Chakravarty, *National Identity,* 36.

37. Partha Chatterjee, *Nationalist Thought and the Colonial World: A Derivative Discourse* (London: Zed, 1986), 51.

38. For a more detailed discussion of these events, see Zoya Hasan, ed., *Forging Identities* (New Delhi: Kali for Women, 1994).

39. Anderson, *Imagined Communities,* 20–25.

40. Gita Saghal and Nira Yuval-Davis argue that the rise of fundamentalism is linked to the failure of nationalist and socialist movements to achieve liberation from neocolonialism. See Saghal and Yuval-Davis, *Refusing Holy Orders,* 6.

41. Saghal and Yuval-Davis, *Refusing Holy Orders,* 5.

42. For a discussion of the radical biblicist tradition, which stretches from the Levellers of the English Revolution to South American liberation theology and African nationalism, see Sara Maitland, "Biblicism: A Radical Rhetoric?" in Saghal and Yuval-Davis, *Refusing Holy Orders,* 27–43.

43. This is just as true of Islam as it is of Christianity, although it should be noted that in the case of the former, fundamentalism manifests itself in the form of a return either to the Koranic text or to the sharia, the body religious laws set down after the Prophet Muhammad's death.

44. Maitland, "Biblicism," 38.

45. V. N. Volosinov, *Marxism and the Philosophy of Language,* trans. Ladislav Matejka and I. R. Titunik (New York: Seminar Press, 1973), 11.

46. For an analysis of social antagonism and the impossibility of final suture of the system of differences of which the social consists, see Ernesto Laclau and Chantal Mouffe, *Hegemony and Socialist Strategy* (London: Verso, 1985).

47. Rukmini Bhaya Nair and Rimli Bhattacharya, "Salman Rushdie: The Migrant in the Metropolis," *Third Text* 11 (Summer 1990): 18–29.

48. Ian Baucom emphasizes the former to the relative neglect of the latter in his reading of the novel's focus on rioting and migrancy. See Baucom, *Out of Place,* 190–218.

49. Malise Ruthven, *A Satanic Affair: Salman Rushdie and the Wrath of Islam* (London: Hogarth Press, 1991), 141.

50. On the instability of the site of enunciation as a constitutive characteristic of nationalist discourse, see Bhabha, *Nation and Narration,* 251.

51. Rushdie refers explicitly to his opposition to imposing religious orthodoxies that stress purity of the word and the self in *Imaginary Homelands,* 394–96.

52. Rushdie is quite obviously influenced here by poststructuralist theories of language and identity. He discusses the hybridity of the self discovered by Gibreel and Saladin in *Imaginary Homelands,* 144.

53. For an analysis of Rushdie's two previous novels in terms of national allegory, see Brennan, *Salman Rushdie.*

54. M. M. Bakhtin, "Forms of Time and Chronotope in the Novel," in *The Dialogic Imagination,* ed. Michael Holquist (Austin: University of Texas Press, 1981).

55. See Aamir Mufti, "*The Satanic Verses* and the Cultural Politics of 'Islam,'" *Social Text* 31–32 (Summer 1992): 277–82.

56. For a summary of the critiques of Rushdie from the perspective of Islamic reformists, see Nair and Bhattacharya, "Salman Rushdie," 28–29.

57. This definition of the popular is influenced by William Rowe and Vivian Schelling's *Memory and Modernity* (New York: Verso, 1991), in which the popular is posed as a set of dispersed sites that disrupt definitions of the nation as a unified body.

58. Compare with Raymond Williams's discussion of the social isolation of avantgarde artists in *The Politics of Modernism: Against the New Conformists* (New York: Verso, 1989), 50–62.

59. According to Malise Ruthven, this failure to offer more than a binary opposition was key to the conflict over the novel in the UK. See *A Satanic Affair,* 159.

60. Gayatri Chakravorty Spivak, "Reading *The Satanic Verses*," *Third Text* 11 (Summer 1990): 45–60.

61. Rushdie himself makes a similar argument concerning fundamentalism and nationalism in *Imaginary Homelands*, 380.

62. This point is highlighted by Talal Asad's critique of liberal analysis of Rushdie's novel, which tended to defend the author's freedom of expression with no consideration of the embedding of texts in particular social contexts. See Asad, *Genealogies of Religion: Discipline and Reasons of Power in Christianity and Islam* (Baltimore: Johns Hopkins University Press, 1993), 283, and "Multiculturalism and British Identity in the Wake of the Rushdie Affair," *Politics and Society* 18, no. 4 (1990): 457–75.

63. Al-Azmeh Aziz, *Islams and Modernities* (New York: Verso, 1993), 7.

64. For a discussion of Islam and temporality, see Rushdie, *Imaginary Homelands*, 381–82.

65. In construing this act of meteorological tropicalization as an example of salutary diasporic hybridity, Ian Baucom completely misreads Gibreel's increasing fundamentalism. See Baucom, *Out of Place*, 209–18.

66. For a discussion of the production of hybridity through attempts to establish pure identity, see Stallybrass and White, *Transgression*, 193.

67. This point is saliently taken up by L. Liu, who criticizes Partha Chatterjee for theorizing the hegemonic discourse of the West as a totalized one that constitutes the native in a manner that leaves no room for alternative subjectivity. See Liu, "The Female Body and Nationalist Discourse," in *Scattered Hegemonies: Postmodernism and Transnational Feminist Practices*, ed. Inderpal Grewal and Caren Kaplan (Minneapolis: University of Minnesota Press, 1994).

68. For a discussion of the vesting of community honor in women, see Ruthven, *A Satanic Affair*, 73.

69. Arjun Appadurai, *Modernity At Large: Cultural Dimensions of Globalization* (Minneapolis: University of Minnesota Press, 1996), 336.

70. Saghal and Yuval-Davis, *Refusing Holy Orders*, 15.

71. Saghal and Yuval-Davis, *Refusing Holy Orders*, 8.

72. For a structural analysis of the homosocial continuum, see Sedgwick, *Between Men*.

73. For a discussion of this form of what she terms "identity dub," in which the binaries of essentialism and fluidity are navigated depending on the context, see Maira, *Desis in the House*, 195.

74. Ruthven, *A Satanic Affair*, 118; and Steven Vertovec, "Islamophobia and Muslim Recognition in Britain," in *Muslims in the West: From Sojourners to Citizens*, ed. Yvonne Yazbeck Hadded (New York: Oxford University Press, 2002), 19–33.

75. For an analysis of contemporary European fears about loss of cultural homogeneity as a result of Muslim immigration, see Hadded introduction to *Muslims in the West*, 4–15.

76. Vertovec, "Islamophobia," 26.

77. J. Nielsen, *Towards a European Islam* (Basingstoke: Macmillan, 1999).

78. Ruthven, *A Satanic Affair*, 107.

79. Saghal, "Secular Spaces," in Gita Saghal and Nira Yuval-Davis, eds., *Refusing Holy Orders: Women and Fundamentalism in Britain* (London: Trafalgar Square, 1993), 170.

80. For an extended theoretical discussion of the impact of black feminist interventions in redefining the public sphere in Britain, see Samantrai, *AlterNatives*, 30–56.

CHAPTER SIX

1. Nicholas Wade, "Reading the Book of Life," *New York Times,* 13 February 2001, F1, LexisNexis http://web.nexis-lexis.com, accessed 21 February 2003.

2. Barry Commoner, "Unraveling the DNA Myth: The Spurious Foundation of Genetic Engineering," *Harper's,* February 2002, 39–47.

3. Joseph Graves, *The Emperor's New Clothes: Biological Theories of Race at the Millennium* (New Brunswick, N.J.: Rutgers University Press, 2001), 90.

4. Richard Lewontin, *Biology as Ideology: The Doctrine of DNA* (New York: Harper-Collins, 1992), 14.

5. Paul Gilroy, *Against Race: Imagining Political Culture Beyond the Color Line* (Cambridge: Harvard University Press, 2000); and Donna J. Haraway, *Modest_Witness@Second_Millenium FemaleMan_Meets_OncoMouse* (New York: Routledge, 1997).

6. Nicholas Wade offers an account of this debate by comparing the work of Dr. Neil Risch, who contends that racial and ethnic differences do relate to genetic code, and that of others such as Dr. David Goldstein, who finds such differences too sweeping and imprecise. See his article "Race is Seen as Real Guide to Track Roots of Disease," *New York Times,* 30 July 2002, F1. For a representative example of how this debate is polarizing the medical community, see Sally Satel, *PC, M.D.: How Political Correctness is Corrupting Medicine* (New York: Basic Books, 2000).

7. Probably the most notorious instance of the return of iniquitous biological determinism is Richard Herrstein and Charles Murray's *The Bell Curve: Intelligence and Class Structure in American Life* (New York: Free Press, 1994).

8. Patricia J. Williams, "Racial Prescriptions," *The Nation,* 3 June 2002, 9.

9. The same surprisingly holds true in the realm of popular culture in general. The film *Gattaca* (dir. Andrew Niccol. Columbia Pictures, 1997) is perhaps the most notable attempt to date to dramatize the dystopian implications of genetic engineering for an American public that regularly encounters products of the biotech revolution such as genetically modified food.

10. For a discussion of "postracial" London, see Yasmin Alibhai-Brown, "A Magic Carpet of Cultures in London," *New York Times,* 25 June 2000, B1.

11. For analysis of these issues in an American context, see Weinbaum, "Reproducing Racial Globality."

12. The term *biopower* is drawn from Foucault. For a detailed assessment of the racial and colonial resonance of Foucault's late work, see Stoler, *Race and Education.*

13. For a discussion of the gendered implications of recent immigration legislation in Britain, see London and Yuval-Davis, "Women as National Reproducers."

14. On Britain's shift from *ius soli* to *ius sanguinis,* see Baucom, *Out of Place.*

15. Neil Smith, "New Globalism, New Urbanism: Gentrification as a Global Urban Strategy," *Antipode* 34 (2002): 434–56.

16. Winant, *World is a Ghetto,* 1.

17. Gilroy, *Against Race,* 47.

18. Gilroy, *Against Race,* 37.

19. Graves, *The Emperor's New Clothes,* 43.

20. See, for instance, Robert Young's discussion of the malleability of raciology in the nineteenth century in *Colonial Desire.*

21. Zadie Smith, *White Teeth* (New York: Vintage, 2000), 100. Further citations will be incorporated in the text.

22. For an overview of this raciological tradition, see Nancy Stepan, *The Idea of Race in Science: Great Britain, 1800–1960* (Hamden, Conn.: Archon, 1982).

23. For a discussion of the return of the racist doctrines and exterminism policies experimented with in German South-West Africa to Europe by the Nazi elite, see Arendt, *The Origins of Totalitarianism,* 206.

24. Stoler, *Race and Education,* 10.

25. Stoler, *Race and Education,* 11. For a detailed discussion of the poisonous interweaving of "race," class, and gender prompted by dysgenic fears, see McClintock, *Imperial Leather.*

26. Graves, *The Emperor's New Clothes,* 119.

27. Matt Ridley, *Genome: The Autobiography of a Species in 23 Chapters* (New York: HarperCollins, 1999), 291–96.

28. Lewontin, *Biology as Ideology,* 26.

29. Tabili, *We Ask for Justice,* 17.

30. Von Eschen, *Race against Empire,* 28.

31. Tabili, *We Ask for Justice,* 19.

32. For a discussion of the theoretical implications of the Subaltern Studies Collective's work, see Spivak's introduction to Guha and Spivak, *Selected Subaltern Studies.*

33. One of the primary goals of the War Office during this period was to ensure that nonwhite officers would never be placed in control of European troops. See Marika Sherwood, *Many Struggles: West Indian Workers and Service Personnel in Britain, 1939–45* (London: Karia, 1985).

34. Sven Lindqvist, *Exterminate All the Brutes* (New York: New Press, 1997).

35. Lewontin, *Biology as Ideology,* 23.

36. For a discussion of *Kim* as colonial fantasy, see Said, *Culture and Imperialism,* 160.

37. The most prominent example is Bhabha, *The Location of Culture.*

38. For a useful discussion of the trend toward "primordialism" among ethnic minority communities, see Pnina Werbner, introduction to *Debating Cultural Hybridity: Multi-Cultural Identities and the Politics of Anti-Racism,* ed. Pnina Werbner and Tariz Modood (New York: Zed, 1997).

39. Ali Nobil Ahmad's critique, for example, underlines the biological determinism of hybridity theory in the following terms: "Steeped in biological determinism and deeply imbued in the teleology of essentialist colonial discourse, Bhabha's hybrids are a master race of Nietzschean übermenschen equipped with special powers to transcend problems of racism." See his article "Whose Underground? Asian Cool and the Poverty of Hybridity," *Third Text* 54 (Spring 2001): 81.

40. Gilroy, *Ain't No Black,* 43.

41. For an extended discussion of the contradictions of postwar immigration policy, see Paul, *Whitewashing Britain.*

42. Michael Rowe, *The Racialization of Disorder in Twentieth Century Britain* (Brookfield, Mass.: Ashgate, 1998).

43. For a discussion of the use of birth control provision in a manner that smacks of population control, see London and Yuval-Davis, "Women as National Reproducers," 218.

44. Gilroy, *Ain't No Black,* 65.

45. For a sensitive discussion of fundamentalism, liberalism, and the legacy of the *Satanic Verses* controversy in Britain, see Alibhai-Brown, *Imagining the New Britain,* 266–69.

46. On the cultural cosmopolitanism of the second generation, see Hall's "New Ethnicities"; and Marie Gillespie, *Television, Ethnicity and Cultural Change* (New York: Routledge, 1996).

47. Jennie Dusheck, "The Interpretation of Genes," *Natural History,* October 2002, 54.

48. For an overview of the debates concerning twins and the environment that reflects the return of genetic determinism, see Ridley, *Genome,* 82–85. For a challenge to this view, see Lewontin, *Biology as Ideology,* 32–33.

49. Said, *Culture and Imperialism,* 336.

50. The classic example of such work is Hall and Jefferson, *Resistance Through Rituals.* For analyses of recent Asian music in subcultural studies vein, see Sanjay Sharma, John Hutnyk, and Ashwarni Sharma, eds., *Dis-Orienting Rhythms: The Politics of the New Asian Dance Music* (New York: Zed, 1997).

51. Hebdige, *Subculture,* 103.

52. Francis Fukuyama, *Our Posthuman Future: Consequences of the Biotechnology Revolution* (New York: Farrar, Straus and Giroux, 2002).

53. Young, *Colonial Desire,* 10.

54. Sahgal and Yuval-Davis, "Introduction: Fundamentalism, Multiculturalism, and Women in Britain," 16.

55. For a discussion of the uncertainties and hazards associated with the now-widespread practice of creation transgenic crops, see Commoner, "Unraveling the DNA Myth," 45–46.

56. Vandana Shiva, *Biopiracy: The Plunder of Nature and Knowledge* (Boston: South End Press, 1997).

57. Jeremy Rifkin, *The Biotech Century: Harnessing the Gene and Remaking the World* (New York: Putnam, 1998), xiii.

58. Rifkin, *The Biotech Century,* 116.

59. Biotechnology is, for example, almost certain to destroy the present privatized American health care system. See Bryan Appleyard, *Brave New Worlds: Staying Human in the Genetic Future* (New York: Viking, 1998), 23.

60. Rifkin, *The Biotech Century,* 147.

61. Fukuyama, *Our Posthuman Future,* 40.

62. Lewontin, *Biology as Ideology,* 26–27.

63. While Smith's satire of Islamic fundamentalism is clearly a courageous rejoinder to positions that became public in the context of the Rushdie affair, her parody of animal rights groups is a little less easy to understand. However, the Left in Britain has a tendency to dismiss animal rights campaigns despite their wide appeal. See Ted Benton and Simon Redfearn, "The Politics of Animal Rights—Where's the Left?" *New Left Review* 215 (1996): 45–53.

64. Steve Connor, "Rival Genome Teams Squabble as they Publish the Ultimate 'Book of Life,'" *Independent,* 12 February 2001, A1, LexisNexis http://web.nexis-lexis.com, accessed 21 February 2003.

65. Jonathan King and Doreen Stabinsky, "Biotechnology under Globalization: The Corporate Expropriation of Plant, Animal, and Microbial Species," *Race and Class* 40, nos. 2–3 (1998–99): 73–89.

CONCLUSION

1. Charles Glass, "The Last of England: Churchill Gave Londoners Courage, Blair is Serving Them Fear," *Harper's,* November 2005, 43–49.

2. Tony Blair, address to Parliament, 11 July 2005, http://www.number-10.gov.uk/output/Page7903.asp.

3. Saree Makdisi, "Brutality that Boomerangs," *Common Dreams,* 23 January 2006, http://www.commondreams.org/views05/0729–26.htm.

4. James Quinney, "The World's Best Kept Secret," *Znet,* 23 January 2006, http://www.zmag.org/content/showarticle.cfm?itemid=9007.

5. On the history of high-altitude bombing, see Sven Lindqvist, *A History of Bombing* (New York: Norton, 2003).

6. Chris Allen, "From Race to Religion: The New Face of Discrimination," in *Muslim Britain: Communities Under Pressure,* ed. Tahir Abbas (New York: Zed, 2005), 49–65.

7. Allen, "From Race to Religion," 60.

8. BBC, "Thatcher Comments Encourage Racism," 23 January 2006, http://news.bbc.co.uk/1/hi/uk_politics/1578377.stm.

9. Norman Lamont, "Down with Multiculturalism, Book-Burning, and Fatwas," *Daily Telegraph,* 8 May 2002.

10. Sivanandan, "Why Muslims Reject British Values," *Observer,* 16 October 2005, http://observer.guardian.co.uk/comment/story/0,6903,1593282,00.html, accessed 23 January 2006.

11. Hall et al., *Policing the Crisis.*

12. Retort, *Afflicted Powers* (New York: Verso, 2005), 163.

13. David Harvey, *The New Imperialism* (New York: Oxford University Press, 2003).

14. Rose, *Black Noise;* and Lipsitz, *Dangerous Crossroads.*

15. For an overview of Asian music with an emphasis on developments in the UK, see Sharma, Hutnyk, and Sharma, *Dis-Orienting Rhythms.*

16. Ted Swedenburg, "Islamic Hip-Hop versus Islamophobia: Aki Nawaz, Natacha Atlas, Akhenaton," in *Global Noise: Rap and Hip Hop Outside the USA,* ed. Tony Mitchell (Middletown, Conn.: Wesleyan University Press, 2001), 57–85.

17. Fun-Da-Mental, "Seize the Time," *Seize the Time,* Beggar's Banquet/Mammoth Records 92421–2.

18. Robert Pape, *Dying to Win: The Strategic Logic of Suicide Terrorism* (New York: Random House, 2005).

19. Asian Dub Foundation, "Blowback," *Enemy of the Enemy,* Universal Music 724358128321.

20. Frances Fox Piven, *The War at Home: The Domestic Costs of Bush's Militarism* (New York: New Press, 2004).

21. Étienne Balibar, *We, The People of Europe? Reflections on Transnational Citizenship* (Princeton, N.J.: Princeton University Press, 2004), 123.

22. Alice Bloch and Liza Schuster, "At the Extremes of Exclusion: Deportation, Detention and Dispersal," *Ethnic and Racial Studies* 28, no. 3 (2005): 491–512.

23. Tony Solo, "Making Excuses for Sid Snake," Znet, 23 January 2006, http://www.zmag.org/content/showarticle.cfm?ItemID=8547.

24. George Monbiot, "Protesters As Criminals," Znet, 23 January 2006, http://www.zmag.org/content/showarticle.cfm?ItemID=8866.

Index

Abdul Malik, Michael (aka Michael X, Michael de Freitas), 46, 52, 72
Absolute Beginners, 45–46
Afghanistan, invasion of, 176, 185
Afrocentrism, 23
Al-Azmeh, Aziz, 139
Algeria, 186
Ali, Muhammed, 52
Alienation, 19, 30, 39, 65, 127
Al Jazeera, 180
Al Qaeda, 26, 185
Anderson, Benedict, 133
Angry Young Men, 31
Animal rights, 170–71
Anti-Fascist League, 122
Antiracism, 7, 14
Apartheid, 42, 56, 60, 67
Appadurai, Arjun, 142
Asian Dub Foundation, 181–88
Asians: communal conflict and, 24; invisibility and, 24
Asylum legislation, 7
Atlantic Charter, 5, 157
Attlee, Clement, 9
Autonomous organizing, 88–89

Balibar, Étienne, 123, 186
Bakhtin, M. M., 75, 134, 137
Bamangwato, 42
Bandung Conference (1955), 91
Bangladesh, 164
Bano, Shah, 132
Beacon Group, 18
Bell Curve, The, 164
Bennett, Louise, 3, 13, 14, 18, 22
Bhabha, Homi, 160

Biopower, 25, 151–73
Birmingham Center for Contemporary Cultural Studies, 6, 80
Black, as political category, 19–20, 91
Black Atlantic, 20, 24, 65, 68
"Black belt" thesis, 56–57
Black British cultural studies, 14, 144
Black Jacobins, The, 89
Black Panther Party, 59, 73, 83, 182
Black Power, 20, 47–48, 51–72, 95
Black Power, 56–57, 67
Black republic scheme, 57
Blair, Tony, 25, 26, 175–76, 186
Blasphemy Law, 121, 124, 145
Blitz, 175
Boas, Franz, 155
Bollywood film, national imaginary and, 130–32
Bostan, 135
Botswana, 42
Brathwaite, Edward Kamau, 20–21, 50, 52, 54, 60–68, 73
British Broadcasting Corporation (BBC), 3
Brixton, 73
Bush, George W., 176

Calypso, 1–2, 18, 30–36
Campaign Against Racism and Discrimination (CARD), 72
Canboulay, 31, 76
Carby, Hazel, 23, 96, 99, 117–18
Caribbean Artists Movement (CAM), 20, 60, 64, 73–74
Caribbean Renaissance, 18, 33

Carmichael, Stokely (Kwame Ture), 20–21, 49–60
Carnival, 21, 32, 70, 74–79, 83–93
Carnival Development Committee (CDC), 85
Celera Genomics Corporation, 172
Chaggar, Gurdip Singh, 90
Chantwell, 32
Chieftain Douglas, 33
Churchill, Winston, 5
Civil liberties, 25, 187
Civil rights movement, U.S., 51, 57–58
"Clash of civilizations," 26, 123, 183
Cleaver, Eldridge, 39
Clinton, Bill, 149
Colonialism, education and, 2–3, 30
"Colonization in Reverse," 3–4, 13, 14–18, 22
Color bar, 34, 37
Coltrane, John, 49
Columbus, Christopher, 67
Comintern, 56, 89
Commission on Racial Equality (CRE), 145
Commodities, 4
Commonwealth Immigrants Act (1962), 12, 29, 69
Commonwealth system, 10
Congress on the Dialectics of Liberation, 49, 53, 55
Congress Party, 5, 132
Contact zone, 20
Contradictory Omens, 61–64
Cosmopolitanism, 25, 30, 63
Counter Intelligence Program (COIN-TELPRO), 21, 59
Count Suckle, 28, 85
Coward, Noel, 175
Creole: Caribbean nationalism and, 2–3, 18, 30, 33, 54; continuum, 54, 61–64, 66. See also Nation language
Crick, Francis, 149–50

Darwin, Charles, 151
Decentering, 17
Deejays, 86
Defoe, Daniel, 6

Degeneration, 5, 16
Dependency: emotional, 30, 98–106; economic, 107–19
Descartes, Rene, 151
Diaspora: anticolonialism and, 7; mutation and, 127–28; national identity and, 7; unity, 19, 34, 50–51, 122
Dole, 107–19
Domestic violence, 44
Dub music, 21, 74, 86. See also Reggae
Duke Vine, 85

Egbuna, Obi, 72
Emecheta, Buchi, 22–23, 97–119
Empire Strikes Back, The, 19
Empire Windrush, 1–2, 4, 9, 10, 12, 15, 41
Ethnic absolutism, 127, 162. See also Racism
Ethnography, and literature, 61
Eugenics, 5–6, 13, 16, 18, 22, 25, 154–57, 160–61, 171–73. See also Racism: sexuality and
European Union, 186

Family, oppression and, 23, 95–120
Fanon, Frantz, 30, 40, 43, 63, 186
Fascism: National Labour Party, 28; racial supremacy and, 9, 16; Union Movement, 28, 78. See also National Front
Fatwa, 145
Feminism: black, 23, 80, 95–119; imperial, 100; middle-class, 108
Fiorenza, Elizabeth Schustler, 146
Forces of Victory, 74, 83, 93
Frankfurt School, 49
Fukuyama, Francis, 165
Fun-Da-Mental, 181–88
Fundamentalism, 24, 122–48; Hindu fundamentalism, 146; textual politics and, 133–40

Gandhi, Rajiv, 132
Garvey, Amy, 79
Garveyite movement, 57
Gender, community identity and, 23
Genetic determinism, 149–52
Geneva Convention, 177

Ghettos, as internal colonies, 55, 57–59, 68, 83
Gikandi, Simon, 61
Gilroy, Paul, 24, 86, 153, 162
Globalization, 14, 127
Gobineau, Arthur de, 156
Great Chain of Being, 5
Greater London Council (GLC), 60, 143

Haitian Revolution, 89
Hall, Stuart, 6, 22, 59, 80, 88, 96, 179
Hamilton, Charles, 67
Harlem Renaissance, 66
Harvey, David, 180
Hebdige, Dick, 86
Hegemony, crisis of, 80–81
Heritage, national, 77
Herskovitz, Melville, 61
Hi-Life Music, 31
Hip hop, 175–88
History Workshop, 107
Hodge, Merle, 36
Holocaust, 155, 159, 161
Hosein festival, 63
Hughes, Langston, 66
Human Genome Project, 149–50, 172
Humanitarian intervention, 25, 185
Huntington, Samuel, 123
Hussain, Hasib, 179
Hussein, Saddam, 180, 184
Hybridity, 10, 25, 26, 128–29, 144, 160–66

Ijtihad, 125
Immigration: class conflict and, 103; gender and, 13, 27–48, 95–120, 126–27; labor market and, 10–11, 66; legislation, 7–8, 11–13, 29, 51, 78; as mode of resistance, 2–3, 17; poverty and, 4–5, 66
Imperialism: apartheid and, 10; arrogance and, 5–6; blowback and, 177–88; imperial preference sphere, 5–6, 9; U.S., 70
Indentured labor, 76
Independence, national, 5
India, 125; communal conflict in, 131–33
Indian Workers' Association, 90
Indirect rule, 58
In the Ditch, 107–16

Industrial reserve army, 56
Inglan Is a Bitch, 80
Interculturation, 54, 61–64
Internationalism, 7, 20, 54, 71–72, 73
International Monetary Fund, structural adjustment policies and, 81
Intifada, 180, 184
Iran, 146, 180
Iraq, invasion of, 26, 176
Islam, 24, 53; Islamophobia, 145, 177–78, 181; Personal Laws, 132, 146; political, 167, 170, 182–84; Rushdie affair and, 121–25
Izzat, 124

Jahilia, 136
Jamaica, 4, 55, 85
Jamal, Abdullah, 178
James, C. L. R., 33, 42, 47, 57, 89, 91
Jerry, Bongo, 66, 74
Jessop, Bob, 14
Johnson, Linton Kwesi (LKJ), 21, 66, 73–75, 80–93
Jones, Claudia, 47, 69–72, 79

Kaiso, 32
Kalindas, 32
Kennedy, Bobby, 183
Kenyatta, Jomo, 42
Khama, Seretse, 42–43
Khama, Tshekedi, 42–43
Khan, Mohammad Sidique, 178
Khomeini, Ayatollah, 145
King, Dr. Martin Luther, Jr., 52, 70–71, 182
King, Rodney, 182
King Tubby, 86
Kipling, Rudyard, 53, 159
Kittay, Eve, 106
Knox, John, 5
Koran, 124, 135

Labor unions, racism of, 37, 58
Labour Party, 12
Laing, R. D., 49
Lamming, George, 18, 46, 61
Lamont, Norman, 178

Law and order, ideology of, 6
Lawrence, Stephen, murder of, 7
Lenin, V. I., 57
Lewontin, Richard, 156
Lion Youth mas' band, 87–88
Lipsitz, George, 181
London, Louise, 126
"London Is the Place for Me," 1–2
Lonely Londoners, The, 30–48
Look Back in Anger, 41
Lord Beginner, 2, 41–43
Lord Kitchener, 1–2, 41, 79
Los Angeles Uprising, 182
L'Ouverture, Toussaint, 89
Luxemburg, Rosa, 108
Lynching, 69
Lysenkoism, 163

MacInnes, Colin, 45–46
Macmillan, Harold, 12
MacPherson Report, 6, 22
Making of the English Working Class, The,
    107
Malcolm X, 51–52, 182
Mama, Amina, 118
Mandela, Nelson, 70
Manichaeanism, 136, 143, 176–77
Manley, Norman, 55
Manufacturing, 4
Marcuse, Herbert, 49
Marriage, 101–2
Mas' band, 32, 77
Masculinity: black, 29–48; crisis of, 159
McCarran Act (1948), 69–70
McCarthy era, 56, 70
McNee, Sir David, 92
Mendel, Gregor, 156
Mendes, Alfred, 33
Mercer, Kobena, 76
Mernissi, Fatima, 146
Middle Passage, 21, 32, 61, 64
Minorities, ethnic, 8
Miscegenation, fear of, 28
Misogyny, 35–48, 142
"Mix Up Matrimony," 41–43
Monbiot, George, 187
Mongrelism, 6, 28

Moral panic, 179
Morrison, Majbritt, 27
Morrison, Raymond, 27
Mosley, Oswald, 28, 78
Muhammad, 124, 135
Multiculturalism, 178, 186

Naipaul, V. S., 18, 61–62
Nairn, Tom, 77
National Front, 13, 52, 80, 92
Nation of Islam, 182
Nationalism: cultural difference and, 6;
    exclusion and, 6–7, 176–88; place and,
    77–78; politics of reproduction and, 16,
    122–48
Nationality Act (1948), 10, 12
Nationality Act (1981), 13, 126–27
Nation language, 20, 54, 65–66
Nawaz, Aki, 181
Nazism, 2, 155–57, 160. *See also* World
    War II
Negritude, 100
Neoliberalism, 14, 60, 118, 180, 187. *See
    also* Post-Fordism
"New Ethnicities," 88, 96
New Labor, 7, 178
New Left, 49, 107
New Negro, 66
Ngcobo, Lauretta, 116–17
Nigeria, 22–23, 38, 98–99
Nkrumah, Kwame, 42
Notes on Dialectics, 89

Organization of Petroleum Exporting
    Countries (OPEC), oil embargo, 81
Organization of Women of Asian and
    African Descent (OWAAD), 22, 95–96
Orientalism, 143, 145, 161, 177, 183
Osborne, John, 41
Othello, 65

Padmore, George, 47, 57, 89
Palmer, Leslie, 79
Pan-Africanism, 50, 54–55
Pande, Mangal, 158
Pankhurst, Sylvia, 108
Pape, Robert, 183

Patriarchy, 23, 95–96; African, 99–107
Patterson, Orlando, 60–62
Pax Americana, 180
Peach, Blair, 92
Peoples' War Sound System, 88
Perry, Lee "Scratch," 86
Picong, 32
Piven, Frances Fox, 185
Policing, repressive, 7, 21, 80–82, 92–93, 161
Policing the Crisis, 80, 179
Polycultural coalitions, 90–91
Popular authoritarianism, 6–7, 26, 59, 80–82, 176, 179, 187. *See also* Policing, repressive
Post-Fordism, 14, 118, 140, 152
Poulantzas, Nicos, 80
Powell, Enoch, 12, 81, 92
Price-Mars, Jean, 61
Prison-industrial complex, 60
Public Enemy, 181

Race, as social construction, 151–54
Race and Class, 74
Race Relations Act, 6
Race Today Collective, 20, 21, 74, 83, 88–89
Race Today Renegades mas' band, 84, 87
Racial Adjustment Action Society (RAAS), 52, 72
Racism: capitalism and, 8–14, 57–58; cultural, 29, 123, 176; derogatory labeling and, 19; popular, 8; resistance to, 7; scientific, 5, 156; sexuality and, 5–6, 13, 16, 18, 22, 25, 27–48; state and, 7, 12, 26, 29, 98; violence and, 52. *See also* Eugenics; Social Darwinism
Rastafarianism, 66–67, 86
Reggae, 21, 66–67
Religion: African culture and, 62, 68, 101. *See also* Fundamentalism; Islam
Renan, Ernst, 77
Resistance, modes of, 17–18
Rifkin, Jeremy, 169
Rights of Passage, 20, 54, 64–68
Riley, Joan, 101
Riots: British urban, 89; Notting Hill,

7–8, 11–12, 19, 27–29, 45–48; U.S. urban race, 58
Rock Against Racism, 93
Rose, Tricia, 181
Roy, M. N., 57
Royal Commission on Population, Report of, 10, 16
Rubin, Gayle, 99
Rushdie, Salman, 24–25, 121–48

Saghal, Gita, 143
Said, Edward, 164, 183
Samantrai, Ranu, 13
Sankofa media collective, 22, 88
Satanic Verses, 24–25
Saturday Night and Sunday Morning, 41
Saudi Arabia, 133, 146
Scapegoating, 6, 13, 179
Scott, James, 18
Second Class Citizen, 98–107
Sedgwick, Eve, 143
Selvon, Sam, 18–19, 33–48
Senghor, Léopold Sédar, 100
Sepoy Mutiny, 158
September 11, 176
Sexuality: cultural nationalism and, 23; female, 16; male, 18; regulation of, 24–25, 97–98, 107–19, 142–47
Shiva, Vandana, 168
Sillitoe, Alan, 41
Sivanandan, A., 91, 178
Slavery, 4, 31, 76
Smith, Neil, 84
Smith, Zadie, 25
Social Darwinism, 5, 156–57, 159
Sound systems, 84–87
South Africa, 28, 42, 70
Southall Black Sisters (SBS), 96
Southall Youth Movement (SYM), 90, 93
Soviet Union, 89, 163
Spatial scale, 84
State power: racism and, 5, 8–9
Steel, John, 28
Steel pan band music, 79, 85
Stoler, Ann, 156
Stolzhoff, Norman, 85

Student Nonviolent Coordinating Committee (SNCC), 20, 49
Subaltern studies, 107
Subculture, 165
Subjecthood, British, 4, 8, 10
Suez Crisis, 46
Superfly, 65
Surplus humanity, 60
"Sus" laws, 81
Swamping, fear of, 92, 161
Swaraj, 5

Tanweer, Shehzad, 178
Teddy boys, 78
Terrorism, 175–88
Thatcher, Margaret, 13, 60, 91, 95–96, 161, 178
Third World, 59
Thompson, E. P., 107
Trickster figure, 38
Trinidad and Tobago, 21, 31, 55, 76

Umma, 180, 185
Uncle Tom, 65
UNESCO, 155
Uneven development, 5
United Nations, 69
United Nations' Convention Against Torture, 186

United States, 21, 28, 46, 51, 53, 69

Venter, Dr. J. Craig, 172
Vernacular aesthetic, 74, 76. *See also* Creole; Nation language
Vietnam war, 49–50, 53, 84

War on terror, 7, 25, 187
Warner, Marina, 124
Watson, James, 149
Watts, Dave, 181
Weismann, August, 156
Welfare state, 15, 23, 37, 60, 80, 97–98, 107–19
West Indian Federation, 55
West Indian Gazette, 47, 55, 70–72
"White Man's Burden, The," 53
White Teeth, 25, 152–73
"White Woman Listen!", 96
Williams, Ruth, 42
Women Against Fundamentalism (WAF), 25, 121–25, 137, 146
World War II, 2
Woolf, Virginia, 108
Working class, British, imperial entitlements of, 16, 58, 71

Young, Robert, 166
Yuval-Davis, Nira, 126, 143

Printed and bound by CPI Group (UK) Ltd, Croydon, CR0 4YY

09/06/2025

14686123-0002